Russell Crowe
THE UNAUTHORIZED BIOGRAPHY

Russell Crowe

THE UNAUTHORIZED BIOGRAPHY

James L. Dickerson

SCHIRMER
TRADE
BOOKS

NEW YORK/LONDON/PARIS/SYDNEY/TOKYO/BERLIN/COPENHAGEN/MADRID

Front Cover photos: © Derek Henderson/Headpress/Retna Ltd.

This edition published 2003 by Schirmer Trade Books,
an imprint of the Music Sales Publishing Group

Order No. SCH 10121
International Standard Book Number: 0.8256.7283.X

Exclusive Distributors:
Music Sales Corporation
257 Park Avenue South, New York, NY 10010 USA
Music Sales Limited
8/9 Frith Street, London W1D 3JB England
Music Sales Pty. Limited
120 Rothschild Street, Rosebery, Sydney, NSW 2018, Australia

Printed in the United States of America
by Vicks Lithograph and Printing Corporation

CONTENTS

ONE

NEW ZEALAND—THE CLOCK BEGINS

In the 1840s, when the first white settlers started arriving in New Zealand, there were an estimated 400,000 Maoris living on the islands. The brown-skinned natives were related to the Hawaiian and Tahitian tribes that inhabited other western Pacific islands. By 1890, the number of Maoris on the islands had fallen to only 40,000, due to combat with European explorers and the diseases that accompanied white settlers.

Today, out of a total population of 3.8 million, there are more than 350,000 Maoris living in New Zealand. They are prominent in all walks of life, but for more than a century and a half they were subjected to all the weapons of institutionalized racism—military domination, social isolation, economic deprivation, and religious persecution. For many years, they were second-class citizens who were looked down upon by the white population and segregated as much as possible from the island's mainstream social and economic activities.

It was into that world that Russell Ira Crowe was born on April 7, 1964, in Strathmore Park, a suburb of Wellington, New Zealand, to Alex and Jocelyn Crowe, bearers of the Maori bloodline. In the eyes of some New Zealanders, Russell was born a half-breed. His maternal great-grandmother was Maori, and in a country that prides itself on racial purity, it was a distinction that was not without importance; it affected him profoundly for years to come, both as a man and as an actor.

Alex and Jocelyn were working as movie caterers when Russell was born. There was not a huge movie industry in New Zealand, but there was enough work to keep the Crowe family gainfully employed. They had good connections within the industry because Jocelyn's father, Stan Wemyss, was a noted cinematographer. On those occasions when there was no movie related work to be found, Alex sometimes worked as a pub manager to support the family.

Russell spent the first seven years of his life in Wellington, growing up in the shadow of his older brother, Terry. Although Wellington is the capital of New Zealand and offers the largest port facilities, it is not a large city by American or European standards and only had a population of around 150,000 in the early 1960s, approximately ten thousand of whom were Maoris.

To be born of mixed blood in New Zealand in the latter half of the 1900s was tantamount to being born of mixed African-European blood in the American South. There was a social stigma attached to people of mixed blood, however subtle and unobtrusive. For many years, New Zealand limited immigration opportunities for non-Europeans, especially Asians and those of African descent. Today there are fewer than twenty thousand Asians living in New Zealand and, statistically speaking, there are *no* Africans. Racially, it is one of the whitest countries on the planet.

Despite conflicts over the years between the white settlers and the Maoris, New Zealand shaped up into one of the most progressive counties in the world. It was the first country to allow women the right to vote, the first to provide social security pensions to all residents, and the first to require management and labor to submit their disputes to arbitration. It was that clash between a liberal social outlook and conservative racial beliefs that created a unique awareness of self in Russell. By the time he came of school age, Russell was understandably ambivalent about his heritage.

As a youngster, two qualities most clearly defined Russell—he loved music (his parents bought him his first guitar at the age of six) and he loved to mimic those around him, especially if they had unusual accents or speech patterns. Alex and Jocelyn often had to apologize to guests who found themselves the target of Russell's mimicry.

In 1970, when Russell was six, the family moved twelve hundred miles away to Australia, where Alex and Jocelyn received an offer of employment from her godfather, the producer of a new television series called *Spyforce*.

As caterers, it was a big break for them, for unlike movies, which usually wrapped in four to twelve weeks, television shows offered open-ended employment. If they were lucky, the television show could run for years.

Spyforce starred thirty-year-old actor Jack Thompson, who would go on to star in more than fifty movies and television series, including *Star Wars: Episode II* and *Midnight in the Garden of Good and Evil*. In 1970, when he signed on to do *Spyforce*, he was considered one of Australia's most dynamic up-and-coming stars.

By that point, Russell had become interested in acting. When Joycelyn learned that the casting director was looking for a child to play a recurring role in *Spyforce*, Jocelyn used her influence with her godfather to arrange an audition for Russell. He didn't get the role, but he was hired to play one of several orphans who were rescued from certain death by the character played by Thompson.

Russell had only one line of dialogue, but it was enough to hook him on acting. Movies and television shows were a constant topic of conversation in the household. Joycelyn's father, Stan Wemyss, was considered a pioneer in the New Zealand television and movie industry. He first made a name for himself as a World War II cinematographer, filming Allied troops in Japan and Papua, New Guinea, then went on to establish a film studio in association with his wife, Joy.

In many ways, Stan Wemyss was a greater influence on Russell than his own father. Stan was a rugged individual, a man's man who had risked his life during the war, although he never talked about it and acknowledged it only by putting on his uniform to march in annual veterans' day parades, especially on Anzac Day, held each April 25 to honor returned servicemen and women. Russell looked up to him and wanted to please him. It was only natural that he measured his life goals against those of his grandfather, clearly the most successful member of the family.

Despite the help of his mother's godfather and the encouragement of Stan and Joy Wemyss, Russell was unable to land another television role. He continued to try for several years, but those ambitions faded quickly after his tenth birthday, when he lost his front tooth playing rugby. There just wasn't much demand for gap-toothed child actors.

At that point, Russell turned his attention toward music, which in the early 1970s was more of a cultural force than motion pictures or television. Australia was in the throes of the same cultural revolution that was taking place in the United States, primarily because of the Vietnam War. In 1970, when Russell arrived in Australia, antiwar protests were rocking both Australia and New Zealand.

At issue was the draft. With 6,800 troops in Vietnam—all of them supplied by conscription—the Australian government came under intense pressure to terminate its involvement in the war. Public opinion polls showed that about two-thirds of those asked were opposed to drafting young men to send to the war. The New Zealand government was in much the same position, though with only 470 soldiers in Vietnam, government leaders did not feel the same degree of pressure to make a hasty exit.

In 1971, Australia elected a new prime minister, William McMahon, who promptly announced the withdrawal of one thousand troops from Vietnam. The following year, he withdrew all remaining combat troops and abolished the draft.

The antiwar protests and the clashes between the Vietnam War generation and the World War II generation dominated the music of the early to middle 1970s. When Russell started teaching himself to play the guitar, the music that he heard on the radio was the same music that was being listened to in the United States and England. The Beatles were on the charts with "Let It Be," Simon and Garfunkel with "Bridge Over Troubled Water," and Edwin Starr with "War." The local music scenes in Australia and New Zealand reflected much the same international themes.

Accompanying the turmoil in the streets was a corresponding restlessness within Russell's family. When *Spyforce* ceased production, Alex and Joycelyn resumed catering for movie production companies, but that meant frequent relocations and school changes for Russell and Terry, events that affected their sense of family.

Eventually, Alex gave up the catering business entirely and started working as a hotel manager. To Russell, the two professions—film caterer and hotel manager—were closely related. "Because of our association with hotels and film, we've always been associated to a certain degree with performers," he told the *New York Times*. "A hotel is like working behind the scenes as a caterer: you get to see the best and the worst of people. In the morning all the glamour is gone, and it just smells of stale beer."

In 1981, at the age of fourteen, Russell returned to New Zealand with his parents and his brother, Terry. After a ten-year absence, during which time the family had lived in ten different places in Australia, the movie catering business in New Zealand had dried up. Alex and Joycelyn had never meant for the Australian experience to be permanent; they had simply followed their dream of becoming players, however small, in the entertainment business.

Back in New Zealand, they settled in Auckland, a city of about 150,000 inhabitants on the North Island. Situated on the northeastern shore of the island, it lies on the hills of a six-mile-wide isthmus. Often referred to as the largest city in New Zealand, it is larger than Wellington by a slight margin; over the years the two cities have developed a friendly competition for attention from the outside world.

Alex and Jocelyn chose Auckland over Wellington because it had a better reputation as a resort area and offered more opportunities for employment in the hotel industry. They were hired to run the pub at the Albion, a popular hotel that offered amenities to its guests such as refrigerators, balconies, and daily maid service. New Zealand hotels are different from American hotels in that their pubs are major drawing cards for local residents seeking entertainment and a place to socialize.

Visiting his parents at the pub was an eye-opening experience for Russell. "When people drink, they go to a lot of weird places emotionally," he told the *New York Times*. "I've been in a room where fifty people are punching each other because they're drunk. I was basically a kid faced with adult fury. This is tattooed in my brain."

Alex and Joy felt comfortable moving to Auckland because they had family members who already lived there. Russell was enrolled in Auckland Grammar School, where his cousin Martin was a year ahead of him. If there is such a thing as an alpha-kid, Martin fit that description, for he was a bit of a local hero to his classmates, Russell included. Martin was handsome and popular with the girls, and he ruled the schoolyard by virtue of his outgoing personality. Russell had a second cousin, Jeff, who was several years older, but despite the age differences, the three of them often got together to pursue mischief of one type or another, and they remained close well into adulthood.

Russell didn't do terribly well in school, academically or socially. For the most part, he hung out with his older cousins and brother, playing the role of the ruffian at every opportunity. After a year at Auckland Grammar, he and Terry were transferred to Mt. Roskill Grammar, where it was hoped they would find more academic stimulation.

Warren Seastrand, former head of English at Mt. Roskill, told the *New Zealand Listener* that Russell got out of Auckland Grammar before he was asked to leave. "He was unhappy at Auckland Grammar, but he wasn't expelled," Seastrand explained. "He would do enough to get by, usually at the C-plus, B-minus level. He was capable of much more."

At the age of fifteen, Russell's life was about to change radically. What he seemed to want most was an image, something to identify him and set him apart from his peers. He was not handsome in the traditional sense, not in the way his cousins were. He was slender and gangly, and unlike his cousins, he had inherited some of the physical characteristics of the Maoris: his shoulders were rounded, not squared in the macho European tradition, his eyes were hooded and deeply set, he had a high, sloping forehead, and the back of his head was slightly flattened.

Perhaps because of that, Russell underwent an identity crisis shortly after they returned to New Zealand. He expressed displeasure to his parents over his Maori heritage. They tried to reason with him, arguing that it was something he should be proud of, but he would have none of that. Finally, Jocelyn sought help from Russell's great-uncle Huturangi Wemyss, who sat him down for a man-to-man talk. After that, Russell was all right with his heritage, or at least his parents got that impression.

Like most teenage boys, Russell desperately wanted to find something he could excel at. He never once saw himself as a follower. To his way of thinking, he was a leader in waiting: all he needed were the tools to lead with.

When they lived in Australia, his parents had insisted that he take dance lessons to further his anticipated career as an actor. As a teenager, he used those skills to his advantage, for it gave him a sense of control whenever he was in a crowd.

Later in life, he bragged that his dance skills enabled him to get the measure of the actresses he played opposite. Early in the production process, he found an excuse to dance with them so that he could get a sense, from their dance movements, of whether they liked him, trusted him, or had the capacity to improvise on short notice.

Once, when he traveled to Wellington to visit his grandparents Stan and Joy Wemyss, his grandmother took him out to a tennis court to teach him a thing or two about the game. "He was determined to beat me, but I'd been playing a lot and soon had him running all over the place," she later recalled to the *Daily Mirror.* "He got really angry, threw a temper tantrum and chucked his racquet down the length of the court. Eventually he calmed down and shook my hand, but he didn't like going home and telling his parents that grannie had beaten him."

By fifteen, he knew already that he would never develop a persona as a scholar or athlete: he simply wasn't gifted in those ways. He desperately wanted to hone an image for himself, but he foundered on a direction.

One day he dropped by his father's pub to visit while Tom Sharplin, one of New Zealand's most durable rock 'n' rollers, was performing. Russell was star struck by the entertainer and his band, the Cadillacs. Sharplin had recorded five singles in the 1970s, including "Love Is a River"/"I'll Get Along" and "Love Is a Beautiful Song"/"We've Got a Groovy Thing Going," which peaked at No. 12 on the New Zealand national charts. He was an old-time rocker who preferred the music of the founding fathers of rock 'n' roll to the overproduced music of leading early-1980s pop groups such as REO Speedwagon, Styx, and Air Supply.

After the show that day, Russell stopped by the dressing room and introduced himself to the band. They were nice to him, especially Sharplin, who detected a kindred spirit in Russell. He bombarded them with questions about music, forming a band, and how it felt to play rock 'n' roll.

When he left the dressing room that day, Russell knew what he wanted to do with the rest of his life: he wanted to be like Elvis Presley and his early bandmates Scotty Moore and Bill Black (one of Russell's earliest memories is of an Elvis Presley record that his mother owned, titled *Elvis Sings Golden Hits*). Sharplin was a gritty, rough-about-the-edges version of that image, but it was close enough to inspire Russell to put together his first rock band, a group he named the Profile.

It was the custom then for students who were in bands to perform in the school's assembly hall. One day, Russell and one of his bandmates went to assembly to listen to a competing band. When the band began playing, they demonstrated their displeasure by turning around in their seats with their backs to the stage. Their antics so incensed the other students that when the time came for Russell to perform with Profile, the entire class, which was seated in the first three rows, turned their backs on the band. Russell was unfazed by the incident, finding the negative attention just as sweet as praise.

Later that year, Russell enlisted the help of Sharplin in putting together a new band to make a record (most of the players came from Sharplin's own band). At Sharplin's suggestion, Russell gave himself the stage name Russ le Roq. At last, Russell had the persona he had been searching for. Despite being only fifteen-going-on-sixteen, Russ le Roq was a suave, semi-sophisticated rocker who radiated the dark, down-and-dirty, leather-jacketed side of rock 'n' roll.

Sharplin arranged for Russell to record his first album at Gulf Studios in Pakuranga. The Crowe-penned A-side of the first single, titled "I Just Wanna Be Like Marlon Brando," was apparently written as a tribute to Sharplin and his band, who were then hot because of a new album that produced the Top 40 single "Pretty Blue Eyes"/"I Knew the Bride."

"I Wanna Be Like Marlon Brando," featuring Russell on guitar and vocals, was released by Ode Records and sold only five hundred copies. The flip side was another song written by Russell, titled "It Hurts So Bad."

Russell was stunned by the record's failure, but he did not give up on Russ le Roq, for that was who he was now. However, he did give up on school. To his parents' displeasure, he dropped out at the age of sixteen to work for an insurance company.

After five months of selling insurance, he persuaded Sharplin to hire him as a DJ for a new nightclub he had opened named King Creole's. Meanwhile, he continued to nurture his persona as Russ le Roq. In early 1983, Ode Records released a second single from Russell's album. It was titled "Pier 13." The flip side was "So You Made It Now."

When the time came to shoot a photograph for the dust jacket, Russell insisted that it be done in one of the best hotels in the city. "He waited inside this plush hotel until the bellboy had a huge trolley of luggage," Sharplin told the *Daily Mirror*. "As this guy wheeled it out, Russell stood in front of him smoking a fag and yelling at the photographer to start shooting. He wanted to look cool and successful."

To promote the new single, he put together a new four-piece group. They called themselves Russ le Roq and the Romantics. Inspired by Sharplin, who was very much an old-style showman, he designed a 1950s-style uniform for the group. Each band member's name was emblazoned on his jacket. To promote the band, he created a newsletter for an imaginary fan club.

The early 1980s were an exciting time for music in New Zealand. In addition to Sharplin and the Cadillacs, other groups such as the Radars ("That Lucky Old Sun"/"Tahiti Nui") and the Crocodiles ("Tears") enjoyed success. All around him, Russell saw musicians finding success either as recording acts or in well-paying performance venues—and he saw no reason why he could not join them.

Unfortunately, his single "Pier 13" received no airplay and sank like a rock. Undeterred by the failure of his first two singles, his record company released a third single, "Never Let Ya Slide." The dust jacket was done in bright pink and contained a warning that the contents of the record were "Roq & Roll." The liner notes proclaimed, "This is 'Roq & Roll' music. It is not a rock 'n' roll revival disc. Anyone caught saying it is will be murdered by death, or shot, by hanging or…forced to play session on my next record." The liner notes were signed "Moi."

In Russell's eyes, he was bigger than rock 'n' roll. He was arrogant and impatient, a caricature of the leather-jacketed rebels-without-a-cause who populated movie screens in the 1950s and 1960s. Yet, unlike his American and British counterparts, who in moments of candor always admitted that they got into music to get girls, Russell never showed much interest in the opposite sex during his teenage years.

With his swagger and tough-guy attitude, he was much more interested in impressing his male contemporaries than in wooing young ladies. Whether he underwent gender confusion during those years is perhaps known only to him, but certainly the girls his age were attracted to him, for they showed up at his performances in impressive numbers, at least by local standards. More often than not, he waved them away.

"The Russell that I remember was extremely arrogant, very driven," musician Mark Rimington recalled to the *New Zealand Listener.* "Whatever he was focused on, it was at the expense of anything else. The women fell by the wayside pretty quickly. If people had a use, he would certainly find it. I wouldn't describe him as the most caring person in the world."

Of course, it was much tougher to live the life of a rock 'n' roller than it was to simply be a rock 'n' roller. Russell's music brought him nothing even close to a living wage, so he went through a series of day jobs to support himself. He once worked as a bingo caller on the small resort island of Pakatoa, where he got into trouble for making irreverent calls such as "Number one—up your bum."

In 1983, Russ le Roq released two new singles. The first was a song he wrote titled "St. Kilda." On the flip side he covered Bruce Springsteen's song "Fire." The second release was a song he cowrote with Graham Silcock titled "Shattered Glass (You Broke My Heart)." It was a love song—sort of—about broken bottles and broken hearts, a plea to a lover who was looking elsewhere for love. Both singles quickly ended up in the discount bins of local record stores.

In early 1984, he raised enough money to open his own nightclub, called the Venue. It was an unlicensed club, which meant that he could not sell alcohol, but he was optimistic that the young people of Auckland would support the club because of the music. Russell saw himself as a player in the music industry, a mover and shaker. Without diluting his "roq & roll" image, he expanded his recording interests by producing a compilation album of unknown groups titled *All Dressed Up and No Place to Play*. It bombed, as did all his earlier solo efforts.

Nine months after it opened, the Venue closed its doors. Russell's belief in music had been too altruistic. He booked some of the best groups in the city—the Mockers, the Dance Exponents, and the Katango—but there was simply not enough interest among Auckland's young people to support an unlicensed club.

If his father explained the economics of running a nightclub to him—music brings customers into the club, but it is alcohol that makes a profit—he ignored him. It also worked to his disadvantage that the Venue was on a rough side of town, not a location that inspired confidence among parents who feared for their children's safety.

The Venue did bring him good fortune in the sense that it introduced him to a wide variety of musicians, many of whom had similar ambitions to make it big— somewhere, somehow. One of them was a guitarist named Dean Cochran. Born in Invercargill, affectionately called the "ass end" of New Zealand, Dean was a year younger than Russell and fancied himself a songwriter.

Dean's tastes in music were more hard-edged than Russell's (he was a fan of the heavy-metal band AC/DC), but when Russell heard him play and saw his impressive Ibanez Firebird guitar, he talked Dean into joining forces with him. They saw themselves as the Lennon-McCartney of New Zealand's music scene.

Russell dropped his music affiliations, and Dean pulled out of his group, Third Wave, and together they put together a new band they named Roman Antix. They added a third guitarist, Mark Rosieur, and assembled a rhythm section. They were not the best band in Auckland, but they were one of the most persistent.

After a year of playing local clubs and writing original songs, Roman Antix released its first album, *What's the Difference?* The title was entirely appropriate, for record buyers greeted it with overwhelming indifference. But that didn't matter to Russell and Dean, for they were both driven to succeed, and they saw failure as little more than an obnoxious bump in the road. They were not on a mission from God, but the ambitions they shared were intense enough to provide them with missionary zeal.

Roman Antix added a new drummer in 1985, a fellow named Don Brown, but the acquisition did nothing to increase the band's popularity. Russell endured another year of rejection and indifference. By the age of eighteen, Russell was getting too old to successfully maintain his teen-ruffian image. He needed a new direction, a new identity.

In 1986, auditions were announced for a New Zealand production of *The Rocky*

Horror Show, a stage musical that first surfaced in England in the early 1970s, then went on to become a hugely successful movie in 1975, starring Tim Curry, Barry Boswick, and Susan Sarandon. The movie version also featured a newcomer named Meat Loaf, who went on to have a tempestuous career as a rock star in the late 1970s and early 1980s.

The Australian and New Zealand rights to the stage production were purchased in 1980 by two theater novices, Peter Davis and Wilton Morley, the son of the famous British actor Robert Morley. Using Morley's connections, they put together a production company that consisted mostly of British actors for the leads. The other parts they filled with locals. When the first show was presented in the resort area of Queensland, Australia, it did not do well, so Morley and Davis decided to take the show to New Zealand, where they thought it would find more sympathetic audiences.

The Rocky Horror Show is about a young married couple, Brad and Janet, who get lost in the rain and come upon a castle inhabited by Dr. Frank-N-Furter, a transvestite who just happens to be hosting a convention of visitors from the planet Transsexual. When Dr. Frank-N-Furter unveils his laboratory creation, a young man named Rocky Horror, all hell breaks loose at the convention and the doctor announces that he intends to return to the galaxy Transylvania. Shocked by what they see as the corruption of traditional morals, Brad and Janet try to come to terms with their new environment.

Russell auditioned for the show and was hired to play the part of Dr. Everett von Scott, an elderly man in a wheelchair, and the part of Eddie, portrayed in the movie by Meat Loaf. The two characters were never on stage at the same time (Eddie comes out, sings a song, and gets killed right away), but the timing was such that Russell had to rush backstage to change costumes at a dead run so that he could return as Dr. Scott.

One scene called for Dr. Scott to wheel himself out on stage, come to a sudden stop in front of Brad (who at that point is standing in his underwear), and hurl himself into Brad's arms. Sometimes things did not go as planned, such as the time Russell threw himself into Brad's arms, causing him to fall back on his backside. He landed with such a jolt that he farted, a sound that was picked up by one of the stage microphones and broadcast loudly throughout the two-thousand-seat auditorium.

Russell's next line was supposed to be, "Brad, what the hell are you doing here?" Instead, using a Southern accent, he drawled, "Brad, what the hell have you been eatin', boy?" The audience was much too polite to laugh, but the amplified fart was a topic of conversation for weeks.

At last, Russell had found his true calling. He was a rock 'n' roller deep down at the core of his soul—no guitarist ever had more grit inside him—but he also liked the idea of getting in touch with his feminine side by dressing up in garish clothes and wearing stage makeup.

The Rocky Horror Show was immensely successful in New Zealand, often playing to sellout houses, and it provided Russell, who was still going by the name of Russ

le Roq, with his first real taste of success.

When the play's five-month run ended, Russell went out on the road with Roman Antix on a month-long tour, but without much success. Whatever the reason—whether the music was not up to par or Russell himself was not convincing as a lead singer—the band simply did not catch on. The worse the attendance at their concerts was, the more irritable Russell became. He soon developed a major attitude.

"He wasn't scared of talking to someone in charge of something we were doing, and telling them they were a fuckin' wanker, at any time—within earshot or to their face," bandmate Brad Rimington told the *New Zealand Listener*. Rimington, who also worked with Russell in *The Rocky Horror Show*, said, "He rubbed people up the wrong way often. He rubbed me the wrong way and I nearly snotted him once, told him to pull his head in. We got on really well, because I understood where he was coming from. I knew he was an arrogant prick and told him so."

After the ill-fated Roman Antix tour, nineteen-year-old Russell indulged in some serious soul searching. When he learned that the *Rocky Horror Show* producers planned to take the show to Australia, he re-joined the company, this time with the expectation of playing the lead character, Dr. Frank-N-Furter.

In 1987, at the age of twenty, Russell left his homeland for the second time to make a new life for himself in Australia. He carried some serious emotional baggage with him. He was a high school dropout whose arrogance masked an inferiority complex that simmered inside him with increasing heat. He was a mixed-blood New Zealander who was ambivalent about his Maori ancestry. He loved his Maori heritage, to the point that when he turned twenty, he registered to vote in Maori electoral districts, but he also understood the hatred that others felt toward those of mixed blood, and he obsessed about it in ways that sometimes made him angry about his heritage. Was it possible to love yourself and hate yourself in the same instant?

Then there is the matter of his sexuality. There is absolutely no indication that he ever considered himself homosexual, but there are indications, expressed by his preference for male companionship and his penchant for foppish clothing, that he was troubled by traditional concepts of sexuality and by his social skills with the opposite sex.

Brad Rimington, who performed with Russell in Roman Antix and *The Rocky Horror Show* once told reporters that he had never seen Russell with a girlfriend. He just didn't seem all that interested in girls. One exception was a girl named Shona, who sang backup on one of his albums. Russell dated her for almost a year, but cynics said it was because she owned a car and could drive him places.

At the age of twenty, the two things that interested Russell the most were rock 'n' roll and acting. If one led to the other, fine, but he would settle for either, and at any cost. Clearly, he did not have a strong concept of self at that point in his life. By his actions, he defined self as something that existed outside of himself, something that would have to be acquired and slipped into for a proper fitting.

When he left New Zealand, he had it in mind to enroll in Australia's National Institute of Dramatic Art, but that goal was sidetracked when he was hired to perform in the Australian version of *The Rocky Horror Show.*

This time around he played the lead role of Dr. Frank-N-Furter, a part that required him to wear stiletto heels and fishnet stockings. He relished the role because there was something inside him that was fascinated by the various manifestations of perverse sexuality depicted in the production.

Even so, wearing high heels and fishnet stockings often left him vulnerable to various levels of audience participation. One night, a man in the audience complimented Russell on his legs as he walked out on stage. Russell shouted back to the man that he would never make it as a transvestite because there wasn't enough lipstick in the world to cover his big mouth.

On another occasion, at a less-than-exclusive venue in Sydney, he was on stage when he felt a spot of wetness on his costume. "This person in the front row kept squirting me…with a water pistol," he related years later to Diane Sawyer on *Primetime.* "Every time I would turn upstage, you're only wearing black pants and fishnets, you know, I kept getting squirted and at one point I turned around and I said, 'If you squirt me one more time with your water pistol I shall come off the stage and I shall jam my stiletto in the crack of your [deleted by television editor].' So it stopped."

It was a typical response from Russell, who was still struggling with his concept of masculinity. He already had determined that a "real" man could dress up like a woman without losing the essential element of his manhood, but other than that he was not entirely certain where to draw the line.

Was a real man gentle with women or always tough? Was a real man always striving to physically dominate his male friends, or was there a margin for polite coexistence among peers? Would his grandfather, Stan Wemyss, the true hero in his life, ever have worn high heels and fishnet stockings? Hell no, but neither would he have been afraid to do so if the situation warranted it. At the age of twenty, those were the issues that troubled Russell the most—that and the matter of his identity as a rock 'n' roller.

Moving with him to Australia was his bandmate and friend, Dean Cochran. They continued to write and perform together, usually on street corners—where they earned as much as possible before the police arrived to chase them away— or in small clubs, where Russell could earn enough to pay his $3.50-a-day living expenses.

When *The Rocky Horror Show* was not up and running, Russell continued to seek work as an actor. He did television commercials, played the lead in a Seventh Day Adventist film, and for a very short time was hired for a children's pantomime. Always, he considered acting to be his day job. In his heart, he was a rock 'n' roll musician, and fulfilling that destiny was all that really mattered.

Those were heady times for musicians in Sydney. A duo named Air Supply had opened the door to international success in the early 1980s with a No. 1 pop hit titled "The One That You Love." Their success story was well known to Russell

and all other aspiring hit-makers in Sydney.

Air Supply's Graham Russell and Russell Hitchcock had begun their illustrious careers by starring in the Australian production of *Jesus Christ Superstar*. From that launching pad, they released a single, "Love and Other Bruises," that made the top three in Australia. They parlayed that success into a gig as opening act for Rod Stewart when he undertook his Australian and American tour.

If Air Supply could jump from *Jesus Christ Superstar* to international fame as recording artists, Russell reasoned that he could do the same thing by using *The Rocky Horror Show* as a launching pad for his musical ambitions.

Air Supply was by no means the only Australian pop-music success story. Sydney-born Rick Springfield had used a career as an actor on ABC-TV's daytime drama *General Hospital* to attract attention to his work as a recording artist. His No. 1 hit, "Jessie's Girl," shot up the charts in 1981, just as MTV went into operation. With his good looks and actor's presence, Springfield was a perfect artist for the new television network to exploit. The enormous amount of publicity generated by the hit record and his success with MTV programmers hammered home the importance of acting ability in achieving international stardom as a rock 'n' roller.

Other 1980s Australian recording acts such as Men at Work, who had a No. 1 hit with "Who Can It Be Now?" and the Little River Band, who scored big with a string of hits including "Lonesome Loser" and "The Other Guy," raised expectations among Australian musicians that international stardom was attainable.

Coupled with that was the emergence of Australian-born actors such as Mel Gibson, who had used his role in the Australian-made film *The Road Warrior* to become one of Hollywood's most sought-after leading men, and Paul Hogan, whose starring role in 1986's *Crocodile Dundee* had made him an overnight star.

Russell looked at Mel Gibson and Paul Hogan as role models for his own eventual success, and he viewed Air Supply and Rick Springfield as symbols of the culmination of that success. Actors had a power that musicians did not have, unless, of course, they were Elvis Presley or Mick Jagger or one of the Beatles. Russell once told a friend that the best way he knew of to get a standing ovation as an actor was to take his shirt off on stage. It took more than that to get a standing ovation as a musician, and that fact made the music profession more respectable than acting in Russell's eyes.

In 1987, Russell and Dean met a bass player named Garth Adam, and the three of them started working together, performing informally and recording the occasional demo. At this point in their careers, Russell and Dean saw themselves as working songwriters who needed a hit song in order to put together the type of rocking band they really wanted. They often performed as a duo in clubs like King's Cross, the Quay, and Martin Place, and they sometimes went out on the road with established bands like Amnesia, Beyond Recall, and Happy Cardboard.

Meanwhile, Russell continued performing with *The Rocky Horror Show* throughout 1987 and 1988, tallying up 415 performances when the New Zealand shows were added to the total. Occasionally, he ventured into the service industry when

he needed fast money.

Once he was working as a waiter in a restaurant when an American customer ordered a decaf coffee. That request was a bit much for Russell, who was used to instant coffee in Auckland. The concept of different types of coffee—long black, short black, cappuccino, café latte, etc.—was more than he could appreciate. Not sure what decaf coffee was, but certain it was something he did not know how to prepare, he fetched a cup of boiling water and plopped it down in front of the customer.

"This is boiling water," the woman said, confused.

"Lady, when we de-caffeine something in Australia, we don't fuck around," he answered.

Of course, Russell was fired on the spot. Luckily for him, he had other employment options. In 1987, he landed a brief role on the popular television series *Neighbors*, which chronicled the lives of residents on a single street in a fictional Australian suburb. The story revolved around three families—the Robinsons, the Clarkes, and the Ramsays—who went through a continuing series of ups and downs. Begun in 1985, it went on to become the longest-running drama series in Australian history. Russell only appeared in four episodes, during which he threw his first make-believe punch, but he earned enough money to keep his songwriting habit going for months.

Russell was still not interested in pursuing a steady relationship with a woman during this time, but he did manage to experience the occasional one-night stand, typically after meeting women at the clubs where he and Dean performed for tips.

When he was with women, he simply didn't have all that much to talk about, so he had a difficult time envisioning women as life partners. One morning, a woman he had bedded awoke to find Russell gone and an autographed copy of one of his albums on the pillow next to her. She never saw him again, but she was impressed with the gift.

In 1988, shortly after *The Rocky Horror Show* closed, Russell landed a role in the musical *Blood Brothers*, a Liverpool drama about twin brothers who were separated at birth and meet later in life with dramatic consequences. It is probably best known for the songs "Tell Me It's Not True" and "Easy Terms."

Russell played one of the brothers, working opposite actor Peter Cousens, who played the other brother. Unlike Russell, who was self-taught in everything he did, Cousens was drama-school graduate with ten years of professional experience. He and Russell seemed to dislike each other from the day rehearsals began.

One of the dramatic moments of the play occurs when Russell's character aims a gun at his brother, after which a loud roar echoes throughout the theater. It is at that point that Cousens's character falls to the floor as the gun is tossed across the stage. Unfortunately, when Russell tossed the gun, he did so directly at Cousens, so that it sometimes struck him with a painful thud.

"One night when the gun landed on me yet again, I blew my top, marched into his dressing room and called him an arrogant amateur," Cousens told *New Idea*, an Australian weekly. "He tried to punch me, but the guys in the dressing room held him back. He was hurling abuse and finally broke free and head-butted me in the face. Blood poured out—the bastard had broken my nose."

The play had only been running for a month when the incident occurred, so director Danny Hiller took swift action to restore a semblance of order on the set. He demanded that each actor write a letter of apology to the other. Cousens, who had to attend his daughter's christening with a busted nose, wrote out an apology to Russell, but the hot-tempered New Zealander refused to reciprocate and was promptly fired.

In 1989, two years after Russell arrived in Australia, he experienced the first real tragedy of his young life. He was in the kitchen of his apartment when a seventeen-inch kookaburra, a bird known for its loud braying sound, flew in through the window and looked him squarely in the eyes. Shivers went up his spine, for the kookaburra is well known in Australia as a messenger of death. He rushed to a telephone and called his mother, who informed him that his grandfather, Stan Wemyss, had just passed away.

A very modest man, Stan never told his family that he had won a Member British Empire (MBE) medal for his service in World War II. Late in his life, his wife discovered the prestigious medal one day while dusting. "I asked him what it was," she told the *Sun Herald*. "Only then did I realize what a hero he'd been."

Only after his death did she share that information with other family members. The fact that he never missed an Anzac Day parade with his fellow veterans, yet refused to wear the medal so that his friends would not think he was bragging, made an lasting impression on Russell, who was both devastated and inspired by his passing.

Russell had attended many Anzac Day celebrations with his grandfather in Wellington. Typically, the day began with a dawn commemoration at a local war memorial, at which veterans and active military personnel gathered to pay tribute to their fallen comrades. There was a short service, followed by prayer and the singing of religious hymns and the national anthem.

Later that morning, the veterans—dressed in their well-worn and ill-fitting uniforms, complete with medals—participated in a parade amid colorful banners and company standards, marching up and down the streets to the cheers of enthusiastic onlookers. When the parade ended, everyone usually gathered in a hotel pub to reminisce about past glories and lost friends, their memories stimulated by ample amounts of rum and beer. At sunset, they enacted a final ceremony, a dignified retreat, then returned home to resume their ordinary lives.

As a spectator, Russell always found the ceremonies exciting, all the more so because his grandfather was a proud participant. Later in life, the ceremonies took on even more meaning for Russell, especially when he thought about the splendid medal his grandfather could have worn as he paraded up and down the streets of Wellington.

TWO

ROMPER STOMPER
LOVE SONG

Primarily because of his lack of education and his Maori blood—two factors that he felt set him apart from his Australian contemporaries—Russell never felt much at home in the Sydney arts community. Almost everyone else, including superstar Mel Gibson, had channeled their career through the National Institute for Dramatic Arts, but every time Russell came close to taking that step, he pulled back.

"The amount of bodies on the roadside from going to NIDA is a hell of a lot more than the stars," he explained to *Detour* magazine. "A lot of people's dreams and ambitions have been destroyed by going there. I probably would have been one of those people. I'm not a student for anybody else's agenda. I go out and find the answers to the questions that become apparent to me in life, not from somebody's else's list."

Fear of failure, fear of ridicule, fear of being miscast as the figment of someone else's creative imagination—all conspired to keep him an outsider in the Sydney arts community. It turned out to be a good decision for him in the long run, but at the time it was professionally risky, because a great deal of the moviemaking that took place in Australia at that time was subsidized by the national government, and the NIDA was considered an important gatekeeper for the talent rising up through the ranks.

Also contributing to his decision to spurn the NIDA was his belief that he was not so much an actor as he was a musician who used acting to pay the bills. If he paid too much reverence to the institution, would it not devalue his music? He already felt that he was prostituting himself to take acting roles anyway. Throwing his lot in with the NIDA would have been a little bit like a whore joining a hookers' association—it would have branded him with the union label.

Two years into their move to Australia, Russell and Dean were still nowhere near having their dreams of musical stardom realized. In late 1989 and early 1990, the top international music acts were slick pop recording artists such as New Kids on the Block, Phil Collins, and Milli Vanilli (slicker than anyone realized because they turned out to be a studio fabrication).

The music that Russell and Dean pursued was a throwback to the raw sounds of early Elvis Presley, Carl Perkins, and Jerry Lee Lewis. By 1900, American CD buyers were calling that type of sound "roots music," a tribute to the music's origins in the American South. That created a problem for Russell and Dean, because New Zealand had no rock music that was not derivative of the American South.

They attempted to write and perform music of a type that was not on the charts but sounded like the music of previous generations. What they needed was music with a New Zealand or Australian edge to it, something that would give them a marketable identity. But try as they might, they could not find it.

As they drifted musically, Russell pressed forward with his acting career. Because of his work on stage and television, he was able to land a starring role on a feature film titled *The Crossing*, which was to be directed by George Ogilvie, who had directed the 1985 hit *Mad Max Beyond Thunderdome*.

Before production began, however, Russell was contacted by Steve Wallace, a film student of Ogilvie's, who was about to begin production on a film of his own titled *Blood Oath*. He wanted to "borrow" Russell for a small role in his own film, a project that would end well before production began on *The Crossing*. Still recovering from the shock of his grandfather's death, Russell readily agreed, perhaps feeling that it would be viewed as a tribute to his grandfather's wartime service.

Blood Oath (a.k.a. *Prisoners of the Sun*) was a serious film about World War II atrocities. The idea came to screenwriter Brian A. Williams after he discovered a shoebox while rummaging through his father's garage. In the box, along with photographs of human skulls and graves, were transcripts from a controversial trial held in 1946 on the island of Ambon; it was one of the largest war crime trials ever conducted and proved to be a real test of the Australian justice system and the Japanese code of honor.

Based on those transcripts, *Blood Oath* tells the story of the prosecution of ninety-one Japanese officers and men who controlled the prison camp on Ambon Island, where captured Australian soldiers were brutalized and murdered in a manner similar to that of Jews in the Nazi death camps in Poland and Germany. Williams's father was one of the lawyers assigned to prosecute the case. To give the story even greater authenticity, Williams interviewed former Ambon prisoners of war before writing the screenplay.

In 1989, when filming began, Bryan Brown was one of the top actors in Australia. He was asked to play Captain Cooper, the tough prosecutor who made it his life's calling to bring the Japanese responsible for the atrocities to trial. Russell played Lieutenant Corbett, Cooper's assistant. It was a small role—basically he was Cooper's shadow, ever ready to assist him in the court proceedings—but it did catapult him into the big leagues, at least by Australian standards.

Before signing on to do *Blood Oath*, Brown had made a name for himself in *F/X* (1986) and in two 1988 films, *Gorillas in the Mist* and *Cocktail*, in which he played Tom Cruise's suicidal mentor. He was exactly the type of establishment actor that young Australians looked to for leadership. Russell took advantage of the situation and peppered him with questions about the script. Not unhappy with his role as a mentor to younger actors, Brown was patient with Russell and generous with the time he gave him.

Russell only had a few lines in *Blood Oath*, so the best part about it was traveling north to Queensland, where the film was shot. Favored by tourists because of the splendid beaches surrounding the Great Barrier Reef, Queensland is also famous for its outback cattle ranches and the cowboy culture it has nurtured over the years.

After spending nearly three months in Queensland, Russell returned to Sydney and resumed his life as a musician. He and Dean picked up where they left off, but Russell was a changed man in many respects. For the first time, he had enjoyed a fleeting glimpse of the artistic possibilities in filmmaking. Performing in stage musicals was not all that far removed from playing in a rock 'n' roll band, but making a feature film, with its many stops and starts, and—most notably—its lack of instant applause, was another world entirely. For the first time, Russell saw a future for himself as an actor.

When *Blood Oath* was released in 1990, it was well received in Australia but got little attention in the United States, where it garnered only a handful of reviews. Writing in the *Washington Post*, movie critic Hal Hinson never noticed Russell's contribution to the film, but he did note Bryan Brown's effort: "Cooper is an uncompromising as a pit bull, and Brown brings his usual virile competence to the part. It's an adequate piece of acting, maybe even more. He makes Cooper's hard-headed relentlessness seem like an aspect of machismo."

Three months before production began on *The Crossing*, director George Ogilvie introduced Russell to his two costars, Robert Mammone and Danielle Spencer It was Mammone's first feature film, although he had appeared in a made-for-television movie, *The Hijacking of the Achille Lauro*, and a couple of television miniseries. Twenty-year-old Danielle Spencer was even greener than that, having appeared only in a television series titled *Home and Away*.

Ogilvie hoped that Russell's two costars would have a better reaction to the actor than he had when he met him for the first time at a casting session. "He had a very, 'I'm Russell Crowe, who are you?' attitude," Ogilvie told *Elle* magazine. "He was very polite, very gracious, but he made no effort to please me at all." If Russell's costars had the same reaction, Ogilvie knew the film project could be headed for major problems.

Fortunately, both Robert and Danielle had a different impression. During the three months prior to production, Russell, Danielle, and Robert formed a close friendship that continues to this day. They went to the gym together and planned outings, primarily at Russell's insistence, since he was eager for them to get to know one another well before filming began. Despite the time they spent together and the closeness of their association, Danielle had a boyfriend at the time and considered Russell simply a friend with whom she was developing a professional relationship.

The younger of two children, Danielle spent the first ten years of her life in Great Britain, living first in Yorkshire, then in Cambridgeshire, where her father, Don Spencer, worked in television, primarily as the host of a children's program called *Play School*. He also achieved a measure of pop stardom by touring as an opening act for the Rolling Stones, the Hollies, and the Four Seasons.

Danielle's mother, Julie, was a former dancer, and she encouraged her daughter's interest in show business at an early age. Danielle and her older brother, Dean, often performed with their father. When Danielle was ten, the family moved to Australia, where Don worked in children's theater for several years, after which he formed a film catering enterprise with Julie. Danielle grew up in Turramurra, a northern suburb of Sydney, where she expanded her interests in show business, especially singing and dancing. While in high school, she appeared in student productions of *Fame* and *Cats*.

Early on, she displayed a flair for the dramatic. One day she persuaded her friends to dress up in outrageous costumes—Danielle wore fishnet stockings and high heels—so that they could travel to the city for the sole purpose of shocking strangers. They paraded in and out of fast-food restaurants all across town, flaunting their jailbait sexuality until they received the hoped-for stares and catcalls.

In 1987, after graduating from high school, Danielle landed a part in the chorus of the stage musical *Rasputin*, which starred Angry Anderson, Terry Serio, and Jon English, whom she dated for a time. She followed that up with a role in the television series *Home and Away*. She was like Russell in that she had enjoyed just enough success on the lower rungs of show business to appreciate a costarring role in *The Crossing*.

Petite and blonde, with a striking face and slender figure, Danielle caught Russell's eye the moment he met her, but while her attraction to him was obvious to everyone who worked with them, she kept her emotions on a slow fuse. She was already in a relationship and saw no reason to end it. Besides, her interest in Russell seemed to be based on something deeper than physical attraction. The more she talked to him, the more she realized that they had the same dreams—indeed, many of the same experiences.

Like Russell, Danielle had a lifelong interest in music. Throughout her teen years, she performed—often with her brother—in numerous pop and rock bands, including Baby Loves to Cha Cha and the Heavy Petals. Her repertory consisted largely of Michael Jackson and MC Hammer covers.

In Russell she saw a kindred spirit, someone who believed that he could satisfy the deep yearnings of his soul with music and acting. The fact that both their parents had worked as film caterers—and had encouraged their children to seek out their unfulfilled dreams—seemed to provide them with yet another bond. Emotionally and spiritually, they could have been fraternal twins.

The Crossing begins with a remembrance of fallen soldiers (shades of Russell's memories of his grandfather's participation in Anzac Day), then moves to an intimate scene between Johnny (Russell Crowe) and Meg (Danielle Spencer). As their family members attend the sacred ceremonies, the teens lie in bed making love. That tender scene is broken abruptly when Meg's father comes home from the ceremony and throws open the door, catching them in a compromising position.

Later, Meg's father chides her for allowing another boyfriend, Sam (Robert Mammone), to get away, and he lets her know in no uncertain terms that she and Johnny will have to get married as a result of their intimacy. As Meg sorts through those feelings, Sam returns to the small rural community. He had left town without her to pursue his dream, and now he wants her back.

Johnny and Sam also have a history as best friends. When Sam returns, Johnny does not have the heart to tell him that he is dating his old girlfriend. He tries to be enthusiastic about his friend's return, but he is fearful that he might lose Meg, and muted antagonism is the most generous response he can muster.

Later that day, Meg encounters Sam for the first time at the veterans' day parade. "What'd you come back for?" she asks, puzzled that he is in town.

"For you," he says.

With that, she turns and runs into Johnny's arms. Not until that moment did Sam realize that the two people closest to him had become lovers. Meg's most overpowering emotion is guilt, for although she has betrayed Sam by sleeping with Johnny, he had betrayed her by leaving town without her.

As Meg ponders what she should do about that uncomfortable triangle, Johnny's friends ask him if he has talked to Sam about his relationship with Meg.

"I didn't get a chance, did I? He just moved in on her."

"I though he was your mate," said the friend.

"He was the one that left."

Later, Johnny builds up the courage to talk to Sam and tells him that he has asked Meg to marry him. Says Johnny: "I know Meg. I know what she wants, what she needs—more than you ever did."

Sam goes to Meg's house to plead his case.

"Why did you leave?" she asks.

"I couldn't stay," he says. "It was like drowning—dad and me, this town."

Sam tells Meg that he has missed her and wants her back. Clearly, she still has feelings for him, but she is torn between those old feelings and the new feelings that she has for Johnny, who represents what she perceives to be lifelong security.

There is a dramatic, heroic ending to the story that changes all their lives.

Russell did an excellent job portraying an awkward farm boy in *The Crossing*. He comes across as raw and uncomplicated, a country bumpkin who has a difficult time understanding his own emotions. Danielle's task was just the opposite—to weave the relatively simple emotions of love and guilt into a complicated tapestry. She gave a touching performance as the thoughtful farm girl who dreams of life in the big city. Her character was pretty in a fresh, natural way that gave credibility to the story.

The most difficult scene they had to do was the nude scene that appeared early in the movie. Neither of them had ever done anything remotely like that. Danielle had to expose her breasts to the camera, and Russell had to kiss her and make love to her. It proved to be an interesting challenge to their blossoming off-camera friendship.

Not only did that scene capture their first kiss on film, it gave them their first taste of cinematic nudity, not an easy task for actors who had no previous experiences as photographic models. Danielle later described the scene as very confronting.

"I was so young and it was summer and very, very hot," she told *Hello* magazine. "I had a boyfriend back in Sydney and when you have a crew around it's very difficult to get involved in the sexual aspect of the scene because it's sort of embarrassing. It was a closed set, but it was still very nerve-wracking. We were both very nervous and self-conscious. Russell is obviously an attractive guy, but I just wasn't thinking along those lines at that point because it was a big movie for both of us and we were very focused on that."

After production on *The Crossing* wrapped, they went their separate ways—Russell to work on a film titled *Proof* and Danielle to work on a film titled *What the Moon Saw*—but they stayed in touch through telephone calls and letters, and whenever the two of them were in Sydney at the same time, they made an effort to get together.

What impressed Russell the most about working on *The Crossing* was not the nude scene with Danielle but George Ogilvie's unorthodox directing style. At one point, Ogilvie found himself at a loss for words to describe how he wanted Russell to handle a particular scene. He pulled Russell aside and confessed that he had been thinking about the scene and simply didn't know how to explain it to him.

At first, Russell was perplexed. "I really didn't know his history, and then I find out later he was this fabulous actor and when he became a director he decided he was going to make a nine hundred percent switch," Russell explained to Molly Meldrum in an interview that aired on Australian Network 10. "So he goes, 'I can't explain it to you, so I'm just going to do it.' So we're standing in this car park, right, and he just went on a dime—bang! The most radiant, deep, emotional serious information just came out of his eyes. And because I knew what moment he was talking about in the script, I could see all of that information coming out at me, and that was an incredible, incredible lesson."

Equally impressed with Russell was the Australian Film Institute, which nominated him for a coveted best-acting award for his performance. He didn't win that year, but *The Crossing*'s cinematographer, Jeff Darling, did take home an award, and that was important kudos for the film in which Russell had his first starring role.

As it turned out, Russell ended up owing Ogilvie for much more than a great breakthrough movie role. Before production began, the director took Russell out for a cup of coffee so that they could talk in an informal setting. He was troubled that one of Russell's front teeth was broken.

When Ogilvie asked Russell about the tooth, he said that he had never seen any need to get it fixed. He had appeared in a feature film, done television commercials, and performed in two major stage productions, all with his snaggletoothed smile on prominent display. Why mess with a good thing, he argued?

Ogilvie persisted, saying that for the life of him he couldn't think of a reason for his character in *The Crossing* to have a broken tooth. He said he thought it would be distracting to the audience and diminish the impact of the character. Russell tried to talk his way out of getting his tooth fixed, but Ogilvie was so gentle in his approach that the only excuse Russell could think of for not doing it was a lack of money. Ogilvie shot that argument down by giving him the money to get a new tooth.

In 1986, would-be director Jocelyn Moorhouse heard a story about a blind photographer that grabbed her interest. That a blind person could find substance in a visual medium fascinated her, and she began working on a movie script to flesh out the idea. Typically, the first thing that an Australian screenwriter does when he or she has an idea is to approach the Australian Film Commission, or some other government entity that provides subsidies for motion picture projects, to request funding for the project.

Moorhouse didn't want to do that because she had never written a script for a feature film, at least not one that had ever been produced, and she wanted it to be perfect before anyone read it. All of her work to date as a writer and director had been on shorts, features that took less than fifteen minutes of film time.

It took three years for Moorhouse to get the script the way she wanted it, but when she finished it, she started showing *Proof* around to various funding organizations and received support from both the Australian Film Commission and Film Victoria.

It was while the project was being scheduled for budgeting that producer Lynda House heard about it (her boyfriend was in charge of the paperwork, and when he raved about the script, she asked to read it). By page three, House was hooked on the story and asked to produce it.

Together, House and Moorhouse assembled the cast for the film. They were given a small budget ($1.1 million or about $600,000 in U.S. dollars), but since the story didn't require expensive sets or special effects, it was adequate for their needs.

For the role of Martin, a blind man in his early thirties who viewed life through what others told him about the photographs he took, they chose Hugo Weaving, a thirty-year-old Nigerian-born actor who had moved to Australia at the age of sixteen. He was a graduate of the Australian Film Institute and had ten feature films and television series to his credit, including *Almost* and the popular miniseries *Bangkok Hilton*, which featured newcomer Nicole Kidman.

For the role of Celia, Martin's obsessive housekeeper, they signed thirty-four-year-old Geneviève Picot, a veteran of seven feature films and television series, including *Undercover*, *To Market to Market*, and *The Four Minute Mile*.

Russell Crowe, who was by then twenty-three, was hired to play the role of Andy, a young restaurant worker who befriends Martin and takes it upon himself to interpret his photographs. Russell was excited about doing the project because of Moorhouse, who "knew every inch" of the script. He also seemed to be attracted to the prospect of working on a female-dominated film, but whether that was because of his enlightened feminist sensibilities or because he felt a female director and producer would be easier for him to manipulate has never been adequately explained.

Proof begins with Martin (Weaving) making his way along the street with the help of his walking cane. As he does that, Andy (Crowe) is taking trash out the back door of a restaurant to place in a back alley, where a cat is eagerly awaiting the arrival of fresh garbage. By the time Martin turns up the alley, Andy has taken a seat on the back steps to have a smoke. He watches as Martin stumbles over some bottles and causes a trash pile to fall on the cat, presumably killing it. He says nothing and watches Martin amble away.

When Martin arrives home, his housekeeper, Celia (Picot), is waiting for him. She offers to cook him dinner, but he says he plans to eat out, so she leaves. It is apparent from her demeanor that she is more than a housekeeper, at least in her own eyes.

Later, Martin has dinner in Andy's restaurant. He has a difficult time getting attention from the waitress, so he upturns a wine bottle and allows the red wine to pour onto the white tablecloth, a calculation that quickly gets the waitress's attention.

As he leaves the restaurant, Russell tells him that he's killed the cat. Not believing that, Martin checks the cat's pulse and determines that it is still alive. With Andy accompanying him, he takes the cat to a vet for treatment. While they are waiting, Martin takes Andy's picture with the cat, the first clue Andy has that Martin is a photographer.

After bonding over the cat incident, Martin and Andy become good friends. Andy agrees to look at the photos that Martin takes and to describe what he sees so that Martin can put descriptive Braille strips on the backs of the photos.

As the story evolves, it is apparent that Celia is romantically interested in Martin. One day, while looking over Martin's photos, Andy comes across an image of Celia. Martin asks him to describe her. Andy says that she is somewhat plain, with blues eyes and brown hair, then adds, "Is she your sweetheart?"

"Hell no—sweetheart? Celia has no heart. Celia's my housekeeper—a vile woman. I hate her."

"If you hate her so much, why do you keep her on?"

"She wants me. I know that if I continue to deny her what she wants, she can never feel pity for me. Instead, I can pity her."

Clearly, Martin has deep psychological issues dealing with his blindness, troublesome issues that have colored the way he perceives the world in general.

One of the most entertaining scenes in the film occurs when Andy takes Martin to a drive-in movie theater and gives him a scene-by-scene description of what is happening on the screen. When Andy goes to get refreshments, a carload of bullies (yes, Australia has its own brand of redneck) gets irritated with Martin when he looks in their direction and holds up a package of condoms he has found in the car.

Thinking it is a homosexual gesture, the thugs attack the car as Martin locks himself inside. Andy returns with an armload of snacks and sees what is happening to his car. After a brief fight, Andy jumps into the car and, with Martin still behind the wheel, starts the engine and orders Martin to hit the accelerator. They speed out of the theater lot and onto the street—and ultimately into the rear of a police car, with Martin still behind the wheel.

As their friendship deepens, Martin confides to Andy that his mother was always ashamed of him because of his blindness. He never quite trusted her because of his fear that she did not really want him around. Growing up, one of the things he wondered about was what lay beyond the back windows of their flat.

When he asked his mother to describe what she saw, she told him about a beautiful garden. As the seasons changed, so did the descriptions of the foliage. Doubtful that she was telling him the truth, he took a picture from the window with the intention of getting someone to describe it to him. His mother died before that could happen and he held onto the photo, hoping that he would someday meet someone he trusted enough to describe the image and thereby solve the mystery of his mother's trustworthiness.

Annoyed by Martin's continuing cool reaction to her, Celia boldly puts his hand on her breast, thinking that would be enough to get his hormones soaring. Instead, he rejects her. Frustrated, she then seduces Andy in Martin's house, an occasion that provides Russell with the second nude scene of his young career.

Eventually, Martin comes home and catches them in the act. He feels betrayed by Andy, who tells him that he and Celia are in love. Martin angrily tells them both to leave his house, after which Celia takes Andy to her own home. Andy is astonished to discover that her walls are covered with photographs of Martin. She is just as obsessed with Martin as he is with avoiding close human contact. She coldly tells Andy, "He won't forgive you—not now." In the end, Martin must come to terms with his lifelong distrust of people by choosing between Andy and Celia.

When the film wrapped, everyone felt they had a winner. It was a "small" film, but it had enormous heart. "I think I achieved what I wanted with it," Moorhouse said in an interview published by the Australian website Urban Cinefile. "And I feel the happiest I have felt about any of my work. With most of my shorts, I was less confident as a director than as writer, but this time I'm very happy."

Prior to release, the film was submitted to the prestigious Cannes Film Festival for consideration. To Moorhouse's surprise, it was shown at the festival, where it won the director the Golden Camera award. Russell accompanied Moorhouse and the other actors to the south of France for the festival and sent a postcard to Danielle Spencer in the hopes of suitably impressing her with his good fortune.

When *Proof* was released in 1991, critics were generally enthusiastic. *Chicago Sun-Times* critic Roger Ebert didn't have anything to say about Russell's performance, but he was impressed by Moorhouse's abilities as a director. "[Moorhouse] has the gift of creating characters who are interesting just because of who they are," he wrote. "The movie doesn't depend on a contrived plot or any manufactured surprises. It simply introduces us to Martin, Celia and Andy, and the situation Martin has carefully made for himself, and as they develop their games of power and control, we become completely absorbed."

Seattle Times film critic Michael Upchurch liked the film, but he was especially impressed with Russell's performance: "It's Crowe who holds *Proof* together....His Andy is the kind of 'ordinary' character you don't often see in the movies: easy-going but impressionable, decent but directionless…Crowe plays him with uncanny subtlety and charm, making him the prism through which the film's thoughts and tensions are reflected. He's so natural on the screen that it's easy to forget he's giving a performance."

Writing in the *Washington Post*, Rita Kempley described the film as "hypnotic" and compared it to Michelangelo Antonioni's *Blow-Up*. About Russell she wrote: "It's the hubris that first attracts Crowe's Everyman Andy. Like the other actors, Crowe is indigenous to the project, a Down Underling whose sunny ordinariness helps liberate Martin, the architect of his own Gothicism."

Also impressed with the film was the Australian Film Institute, which gave Russell an award—his first—as the best actor in a supporting role. In addition to Russell, Moorhouse won for best director and Weaving won for best actor in a lead role.

The AFI award wasn't the only thing Russell got for making the film. He also took home a reputation as an unusually vocal ladies' man, after an extra he bedded in his trailer kissed and told about it later. The astonished woman revealed to friends that at the height of his thrusting passion, Russell began chanting "Go, Russ, go! Go, Russ, go!"

Back in Sydney, after finishing work on *Proof*, Russell got in touch with Danielle and they went out to dinner. They had lots to talk about. She had finished work on *What the Moon Saw* and was about to start work on a television movie, *Mission: Top Secret*. He was about to start work on *Spotswood*, starring the legendary Anthony Hopkins, surely a sign that his career was about to soar to new heights, and he was still overflowing with observations about the Cannes festival.

Success, even at the modest level at which he was finding it, gave Russell confidence in his conversations with women. He opened up to Danielle in ways he had never done with other women. For the first time, he began to understand the concept of partnership. She made him feel good about himself and encouraged his ambitions, especially in music, since that was a passion that she shared with him.

When they strolled past a store window that displayed miniature doll furniture, she told him how much she liked that sort of thing, and when she told him about her early love of the piano (she had started lessons at the age of five), he made a mental note to revisit that thought. But of all the conversations they had that night, none caught Russell's attention quite so much as the one in which she told him that she had broken up with her boyfriend. She was now free to pursue other relationships.

After dinner that night, they went to Russell's apartment and experienced their first non-movie kiss. They went out often in the days and weeks that followed, establishing what quickly became Russell's first serious relationship. He wrote love songs about Danielle and played his guitar for her, often singing to her during their quieter moments. The attraction was mutual, but for Danielle it occurred at a somewhat different level. "I knew him so well before it got romantic that the things I like about him were things other than his good looks or sex appeal," she once confided to *Hello* magazine. "I'd gone beyond that stage."

When Russell went to Melbourne to work on *Spotswood*, they spoke often on the telephone, and he sent her a constant stream of gifts. Recalling her comments about doll furniture, he sent her a miniature grand piano and other pieces of doll furniture, then followed those items up with toys and novelty gifts such as a sponge that inflated into an animal when tossed into bath water. Day to day, she never knew what to expect. One day, something would arrive that would made her laugh, and the following day something would arrive that would make her cry, such as a dozen red roses.

While he was away, Danielle stayed at his apartment. When he returned, they spent every moment together, with Russell often doing the cooking. His best dish was barbecue, but he sometimes came home with an armload of seafood, which he cooked for dinner. He pampered her with relentless devotion, often treating her as if she were royalty. He didn't take it upon himself to do all the housework, but he did his share.

For the first time in his life, Russell found himself trying to please a woman. It was an important moment in his life. From his teen years onward, he had experienced a certain amount of confusion, not sure exactly where to draw the line. He liked to wear stage makeup and dress in outlandish clothes, but he enjoyed playing rugby and roughhousing with his male friends. He enjoyed sex with women, but he also enjoyed trading stories with his buddies. Cooking was something he took pleasure in, but he couldn't help but think it was wrong for a man to roll his sleeves up in the kitchen. At least that had been his impression growing up in New Zealand.

What he found in Danielle was a woman who made all the gender issues of the past seem insignificant. He wanted to experience *everything* there was in life with her. When it came to romancing a woman—as compared to simply banging her—he discovered that gender issues no longer existed; everything under the sun was fair game.

Russian-born director Mark Joffe had only made one feature film since 1986's *Watch the Shadows Dance*, an ill-fated Nicole Kidman movie that got poor reviews, so he and the producers wanted to give *Spotswood* their best shot.

They began by hiring Anthony Hopkins to play the role of Errol Wallace, a strait-laced efficiency expert who makes a living telling companies how to increase their profits, and by injecting Australia's fastest rising star, Russell Crowe, into the mix with a subordinate role as Kim Barry, a factory worker who wants nothing quite so much in life as to get ahead—at any cost.

Spotswood (subsequently retitled *The Efficiency Expert*) begins with a business meeting at which Errol Wallace and his partner attempt to sell a new business plan to an auto manufacturer. It is evident that Wallace and his partner have different ethical standards. The next day, Wallace is sent to the small town of Spotswood to evaluate a moccasin factory named Ball's. For the past several years, the owner, Mr. Ball, has been selling off assets to keep the factory going,

After evaluating the various departments, Wallace suggests that Mr. Ball lay off half his work force, a recommendation that is greeted with surprise and anger. However, after getting to know the workers better, Wallace has second thoughts and goes to Mr. Ball to offer him a plan for keeping full employment at the factory.

Wallace's motivation for helping the factory is unclear even to him. When his wife asks him about his new assignment, he responds: "Oh, it's strange. It's like visiting my grandfather's house and it's full of people." Wallace and his wife are emotionally estranged. She looks bored and discontented every time she looks at him. When he makes a comment that could lead to a wider discussion, she fails to follow up on it, typically walking out of the room to occupy herself with something else.

Kim Barry is an officious young man, a bully who wants to have his own way, regardless of whom it hurts. One day he sidles up to Wallace and asks, "What do you make of this operation? Bit of a dog, eh?"

"Huh," answers Wallace.

"Most of the blokes here are a shrimp short of a barbecue."

Barry asks him if they can do lunch, but Wallace ignores him and walks away. Later, Barry steals financial ledgers to show to Wallace. He wants to help Wallace so that the older man will find him a better job.

A subplot deals with Carey, a young stock clerk, a second-generation worker who can't choose between the boss's sexy daughter, who doesn't especially like him, and another, dowdier girl who really cares about him. Carey receives the scorn of other workers when Wallace picks him to be his assistant. He takes the rich girl to the movies, but when he leaves his seat to get ice cream, Barry plops down next to his date. When Carey asks for his seat back, Barry backhands him to the floor.

Spotswood was billed as a comedy, but it has few truly funny scenes. One that stands out occurs when Carey sees Wendy (the dowdy girl) out on the lawn picking up snails. A gentleman, or so he fancies himself, he stops to help her with the snails. No sooner does he stop than her father steps out onto the porch and shouts, "What are you doing out there...Is that a man?"

"No, it's just me, Mr. Robinson—Carey!"

"Carey, oh, that's all right," the father responds. "I thought it was a man."

"No, it's just me."

Anthony Hopkins was his usual competent self in the movie, but for some reason the story never seemed to take off. Russell was little more than a diversion, a role he played with obvious enthusiasm, even though it did not really warrant it.

When *Spotswood* was released, the reviews were mixed. Rita Kempley, writing in the *Washington Post*, described it as "an innocuous homage to old-fashioned paternalism....[It] is basically hokum, but without the heart it claims to cherish."

The *Chicago Sun-Times*'s Roger Ebert had a more positive view, writing that "Hopkins [who made this movie soon after winning the Oscar for *Silence of the Lambs*] has a light in his eye that nudges the story to another level. It is about eccentricity, yes, and paternalism and romance and goofy supporting characters, but it's also about forgetting your stopwatch and pausing to hear the music."

Word of the film spread like wildfire on the streets of Sydney. Someone was going to expose Australia's dirty little secret, the unacknowledged fact that racism was a ticking time bomb on the streets of cities such as Melbourne and Sydney, where small bands of skinheads roamed the streets at night, attacking nonwhite elements of the population, especially Asians.

When Russell heard that a movie titled *Romper Stomper* was going to be made about the skinheads, he put out word that he was interested, long before there was a script to read. That's because it went to the heart of an issue that had plagued him since his teenage years—his Maori bloodline. He understood the fear and hatred that the skinheads felt toward Asians because he had once felt that way about his own mixed blood heritage. Doing the movie would be one way to confront his simmering self-doubts and fears.

When Russell contacted the director, Geoffrey Wright, about being in the movie, he was told that another actor, Ben Mendelsohn, was under consideration for the main role of Hando, the leader of a particularly nasty group of skinheads. Undeterred, Russell argued his case, making clear his passion for the role. Wright stood firm. Russell could be in the film, he explained, but he would have to play a supporting role.

That was the way it played out, right up until a week before rehearsals began. It was at that time that Wright asked the actors to shave their heads so that he could see how they would look in the film. To his surprise, Mendlesohn's shaved head sloped up into a point, giving him sort of a conehead appearance, so that whatever else it was, it was not a menacing look. By contrast, Russell's head was smooth and round, perfectly fitting the stereotypical image of a skinhead.

"I didn't know anything about Russell at the time," Wright told the *New York Times*." But I thought he was the most menacing dishwasher I'd ever seen [a reference to his role in *Proof*]. There's always something threatening about him on screen. Right after I'd seen *Proof*, I called my producers and said, 'We may have our boy.'"

Much to his pleasure, Russell was given the role of Hando. It frightened him and excited him at the same time. Before it was over, he would have to reach deep within himself to explore the dark corners of his own still-evolving belief system. Part of him was afraid to make that journey, while another part of him thought that the film could end up becoming an important social document.

Romper Stomper begins at a Melbourne train station, where a gang of skinheads accosts two Vietnamese on a skateboard. Hando tells one of the skateboard riders, a young girl, "This is not your country," and gives her a vicious beating. He is a menacing figure, heavily tattooed, with a large swastika on his back.

Hando soon crosses paths with Gabe, a runaway rich girl who is the victim of incest with her film producer father. Gabe asks him why he has so much Nazi material in the abandoned building where he lives with other gang members.

"Because I don't want to become a white coolie in my own country," he tells her with bitterness. "'Cause it's not our country anymore. Because rich people bring in boatloads of human trash....I want people to know that I'm proud of my white history, my white blood. One day I might be all I have."

Hando shows her a map of Melbourne, with dwindling white areas marked, and extols Hitler's *Mein Kampf*. "If you don't know who the enemy is, you can't win the war," he philosophizes.

When the owner of Hando's favorite bar is sold to a family of Vietnamese, an irate Hando and a couple of his pals confront the Vietnamese, then beat them up, warning them that "it's our place." The Vietnamese follow them back to their hideout and set fire to their belongings.

As the drama with the Vietnamese unfolds, Gabe sets her father up for an attack by the skinheads. Warns one of the men, "We came to wreck everything and ruin your life." They trash the house and escape into the night.

Later, Gabe tells police where the gang is hiding out. When the police arrive, Hando escapes and teams up with Gabe and another man. Together they embark on a crime spree that has a predictable ending.

Russell faced many challenges making the film, not the least of which was an explicit sex scene with Jacqueline McKenzie, who played Gabe. She was nude several times in the film, but one scene required her and Russell to have sex in a standing position. It was a scene that left Russell greatly annoyed.

"I really resent the fact that when you're doing a scene like that the director will always take the female to one side and talk to her and look after her, whereas, if you're the bloke, you're left totally alone to cope with the situation," he explained to *Vogue Men*. "I also resent the notion that because you're a male you're trying to cop a free feel during a sex scene."

When the film was released, Australian film critics reacted with a mixture of outrage and admiration. One critic suggested that the film negative should be burned. Another critic proclaimed the movie a masterpiece. Australia's prime minister, Paul Keating, condemned it as morally bankrupt.

American reviewers were equally divided over the film's worth. *Washington Post* critic Richard Harrington wrote: "Despite its reputation as one of the most violent films in Australian history, *Romper Stomper* is not particularly gruesome in its effects. Its rage boils inside the actors, inside the story. But it's so misdirected that Wright could just as easily have titled his film *Rebel without a Clue*."

Under the headline "Plotless Romper Stomper a Study of Real-Life Monsters," *Miami Herald* writer Rene Rodriguez compared the film to Stanley Kubrick's *A Clockwork Orange*. "It's impossible to work up a whit of sympathy for any of these people, and when the drama requires you to take sides, it falls flat," he wrote. "For a good while, though, *Romper Stomper* works as a horrifying quasi-documentary on the neo-Nazi movement."

Seattle Times critic Jeff Shannon wrote: "Wright's brutally stark portrait of the last days of a Melbourne neo-Nazi skinhead gang won't easily be shaken, and it can't be thoughtlessly dismissed as an unnecessary reflection of an unpleasant problem...it demands to be responded to, for the simple reason that, if this film were to be viewed by a superior alien race, they would instantly deem humans primitive and unworthy of survival."

For his performance in *Romper Stomper*, Russell won best-actor awards from the Australian Film Institute, the Film Critics Circle of Australia, and the Seattle International Film Festival, thus establishing him as Australia's top actor. But he also received a great deal of criticism because of the violent nature of the film and because there was some confusion about whether Russell himself was a skinhead.

The perception that he looked favorably upon the skinheads came about because Russell and other cast members stayed in character and in costume throughout the filming and once visited a Melbourne housing project where a number of Asian families resided. Someone called the police, and Russell and the other cast members were arrested. Russell never adequately explained what their purpose was in visiting the housing project, but it would appear that they did it simply to see how people would react.

In interviews Russell made it clear that he was not a skinhead. *"Romper Stomper* doesn't glorify any ideology and it certainly doesn't glorify the results of racial hatred," he told *Preview* magazine. "Therefore, it's not a film that people jump up at the end and say: Right, I'm going out to hit somebody. By the end of the film you're generally a little too drained to even contemplate anything like that. This is not a film about heroes or skinhead role models."

THREE

TOFOG FINDS
LOVE IN LIMBO

Within days of finishing work on *Romper Stomper*, Russell was sleeping in a car parked outside a stable, becoming, in his own inimitable fashion, the character of East Driscoll, a horse trainer in an Australian drama titled *Hammers over the Anvil*. For Russell, that meant two weeks of eating with the horses, sleeping near them, and riding them hour after hour until he felt totally at ease on horseback.

Hammers over the Anvil is based on a collection of short stories written by Australian author Alan Marshall, best known for his semi-autobiographical novel *I Can Jump Puddles*. Generations of schoolchildren in Australia have studied the novel with adoration, prompting a television series in Australia and a feature film in Europe. However, no one in Australia had yet attempted a feature film.

"As a property, *Hammers over the Anvil* had been in development for some years with an actor/producer named Peter Harvey-Wright," explains Gus Howard, who was then supervising producer at the South Australian Film Corporation, the same studio that made two of Australia's most enduring films, *Sunday Too Far Away* and *Breaker Morant*. "He had not had much success financing the project, because it was going to be expensive to produce and was pitched at a young audience, quite reasonably, due to the success of Marshall's most famous work, *I Can Jump Puddles*.

"The property came our way, and we [Howard, along with fellow producers Peter Gawler and Janet Worth] realized that trying to make the material work for a children's or family audience was not the way to do justice to these dark and fragile characters. Peter Harvey-Wright agreed, and we developed a feature film script which headed in the direction of the film as it now stands—an adult film about childhood."

Hammers over the Anvil is loosely based on Marshall's life. Set in the period between the end of the nineteenth century and World War II, it views life through the eyes of a polio victim who must learn to cope in a world where physical strength is the measure of manhood.

"All the stories [in the book] are told from the perspective of Alan as a boy or Alan as an adult, and there are some recurring characters—many of whom found their way into the screenplay—who are often quite tragic, but they are presented in a quietly empathetic way," says Howard. "In Australia, despite our apparent hedonism, we are—through our cultural, military, and class history—very aware of the tragic nature of existence."

Howard and the other producers considered several directors for the film but decided to offer the job to Ann Turner, based on the success of her first feature film, *Celia*, a story about growing up in the 1950s. They thought that since she had done so well with a story about a girl coming of age, she would be perfect for a story about a boy coming of age.

"As I recall, she fairly readily agreed to take on the project, and although we did several more drafts of the script for her, the film was financed and made reasonably quickly," Howard says. "I don't think it took much more than a year from the time we took up the project to getting it financed."

British actress Charlotte Rampling was cast as Grace McAlister, the female lead. She portrays a woman who is married to an older man, the wealthiest landowner in the region. During the 1970s, Rampling, who began her career as a model, was one of the world's reigning sex queens. Typically, her films dealt with the kinkier aspects of human experience. In *Man, My Love* (1986) she took a chimpanzee for a lover, and in *Angel Heart* she played an occult expert who was found dead, minus her heart.

Rampling was not the first choice to play Grace McAlister. Turner had an Australian actress in mind for the part, but when the director started meeting with the producers and the discussion moved to "who would you really like to work with?"—Rampling's name arose. As a result, Turner went to Europe to meet with the actress.

By the time she was asked to be in *Hammers over the Anvil*, Rampling was forty-six years old, still very attractive but no longer the smoldering beauty she was in the 1970s and 1980s, when she played opposite high-profile actors such as Paul Newman, Mickey Rourke, Robert Mitchum, and Sean Connery. Even so, she was the perfect actress to portray a middle-aged woman who struggled with the lure of respectability and the burning passion of illicit romance.

When the time came to cast the role of East Driscoll, the lowly horse handler who develops a lusty passion for the highly placed Grace McAlister, Ann Turner suggested Russell Crowe. "Ann had close connections with the makers of one of his previous films, *Proof*," says Howard. "Even if we had not known him before our film, he would have been the standout in any screen test for the role of East. There was never much debate about it. In Australia at the time, Russell was not only respected as a talent, he was in the next-big-thing category."

Russell accepted the role, partly because he wanted to work with Charlotte Rampling and Ann Turner but also because he wanted to cleanse his artistic palate of the emotional aftertaste that had accompanied *Romper Stomper*. He didn't want to be known for the rest of his life as Hando the Barbarian.

Film production commenced in the summer of 1991 in locations near Adelaide and continued on into the fall. A few days before production began, Russell went north to the outback to spend a few days with his horse and the wranglers who would help out on the film. One of them, a veteran wrangler named Bill Willoughby, ended up doubling for Russell in some of the more ambitious action scenes. Even though Russell had not had much experience with horses, Howard thought that he was pretty good at what he did and seemed to enjoy that part of the work.

The area around Adelaide is a favorite with filmmakers because of the landscape, which can vary from green and lush to stark and rugged, and because of the varied light possibilities. "There were no studio sets built, although the designer, Ross Major, adapted many existing locations and built some sets on location," says Howard. "The cast were accommodated in the usual kind of comfortable apartments when working out of the city, and the company spent a few nights in a wine-growing district near the country location which served as Alan and East's hometown. We were certainly not in the outback or under any great duress, but there were some pretty long days."

Hammers over the Anvil begins with Russell's character, East Driscoll, bathing in a river with his horses. At one point, he hoists himself up on the horse, naked, and rides in and out of the river, watched all the time by an eleven-year-old crippled boy named Alan Marshall, played by Alexander Outhred.

Later, Driscoll breaks a wild horse, while Marshall and others look on with admiration. Driscoll, a horse trainer who lives alone with his animals, is widely admired in the small, rural community for his prowess with horses. It was a time in Australia when physicality was a necessary ingredient for hometown celebrity.

Everyone has a special place in the community, but it is Mr. McAlister, the most prominent landowner in the area, who sets the pace for daily living, along with his newly arrived wife, Grace, played by Charlotte Rampling. Grace, much younger than her husband, is eager to make new friends and explore the countryside.

To impress his new wife, McAlister has a trainload of ostriches shipped to their community, a gesture that goes awry when they escape and run through the streets and into the country, creating quite a stir among local residents.

Watching everything that takes place in the community is Marshall, who quickly develops a crush on Grace, a woman of uncommon elegance and poise. This is essentially a coming-of-age story in which Marshall learns about manhood, women, and his neighbors' sense of fairness, or lack thereof.

Early in the story, Russell plays guitar and sings a love ballad. It was one of the reasons why he wanted to be in the film. To him, it had the ring of Elvis Presley's musical musings in *Love Me Tender*. He hoped it would invigorate his music career and lead to bigger and better things for himself and his songwriting partner, Dean Cochrun.

One night, the ever-present Alan Marshall sees Grace arrive at Driscoll's cabin. He muses, "When you meet a man in the dark, you know he's going to the pub or something. But women are always coming home from someplace or going somewhere they shouldn't."

Marshall watches Driscoll and Grace having sex. When they become aware of his presence, they quickly dress and confront him. "What in the hell are you doing here?" Driscoll demands angrily. "Listen—open your mouth, I'll ring your neck!"

Sensing that a more delicate approach is needed, Grace intervenes. "Alan won't tell anyone, will you?"

"Of course not," he replies.

"And a friend can always be relied upon to keep a secret," Grace adds.

Marshall nods yes and Driscoll apologizes for losing his temper. Grace kisses Marshall on the mouth to seal the bargain.

As the affair continues, Driscoll falls in love with Grace and asks her to leave her wealthy husband. She refuses, of course, since true love was never on the list of things she wanted from Driscoll. When he starts obsessing over her, Marshall tells his friend that he should write Grace a letter to express his feelings. Driscoll loves the idea but confesses that he never learned how to write. Marshall volunteers to write the words as Driscoll dictates them.

When the letter fails to bring the desired results, Driscoll goes to a barn dance that he knows the McAlisters are attending. He sends Marshall inside to plead with Grace to come outside and talk to him. She declines and Driscoll snaps. He goes inside and boldly asks her to dance with him. Afterward, he asks her to go outside to ride horses with him. She refuses, and he starts a fight and is dragged outside by the other men. Humiliated, he angrily rides away on his horse.

The next day, Marshall finds Driscoll in bad shape, apparently thrown and dragged by his own horse. Marshall manages to climb up on Driscoll's horse, something he had never before been able to accomplish, and he rides off to get help. Unfortunately, he, too, falls from the horse and is dragged into town.

Both Marshall and Driscoll end up in the hospital, where Driscoll is found to be seriously injured. Soon it becomes apparent to Grace that she must make a life-altering choice between her husband and Driscoll.

Hammers over the Anvil made a respectable showing in Australia, but it was not released in the United States except in video format. That is a shame, since it is an excellent film. Two years after the film's release, Russell won the best-actor award from the Seattle International Film Festival.

One of the few surviving reviews was written by Fincina Hopgood in a book titled *Australian Film 1978–1994*: "The film's strength lies in the rapport director Ann Turner encourages between the inexperienced Outhred and the expert ensemble cast....As with her feature debut *Celia* (1989), Turner presents us with a child's view of adult behavior which is historically specific in its detail and yet timeless in its observations of human nature."

Producer Gus Howard said that they encountered no backlash from Russell's opening nude scene with the horses. "We don't worry that much what people think here," he says. "The horse scene, also observed by Alan, set precisely the sort of tone we wanted. This was an adult film about childhood. Just maybe, if we'd played it down we could have had the film placed commercially in the same space as something like *Stand by Me*, but we all felt those elements of the film were done well and were a necessary part of the presentation of young Alan's journey into adulthood."

On the screen, *Hammers over the Anvil* flows with calm, artistic inevitability, creating a seamless view of life in another era. Making it look that way took a lot of hard work. Especially difficult to shoot were the scenes at the ball and at the hospital. "The shooting went on longer than scheduled for those," says Howard. "The ball required a lot of setups and a lot of hours. Many other scenes took longer than scheduled, but the director and crew had to be allowed the time to finish. *Hammers over the Anvil* would be remembered by many of the crew as a pretty tough shoot, but the crew was first class and never gave in.

"The love scene in the barn was naturally a bit fraught. Ann did a lot of setups for that, and watching the rushes for what we knew was finally going to have to be a strong and erotic scene was pretty hard going. Ann was rightly determined not to let that scene get misty and soft-edged. It was a basic, animal sex scene, shocking but fascinating for a kid like Alan to stumble across."

One of the big unknowns was how Russell would interact with Rampling. In some ways, it was like trying to mix oil and water. "I don't think I know what Russell really thought of Charlotte Rampling, but he had had strong and experienced women cast against him in some of his earlier films," says Howard. "You don't put a shrinking violet against the Russell Crowe screen persona. I also think Russell expected good things to come his way even then. So why not work with Charlotte Rampling? They clicked. I found [her] to be extremely professional and self-contained. There was never a moment when I felt we were going to be overwhelmed by her. She did not come with an entourage, and she fitted into the low-key ambiance of an Australian set well. A review of her career shows her to be unafraid of risk."

There were several reasons why Russell wanted to be in the film, but one of the most publicly repeated reasons was to work with director Ann Turner. What he hoped to gain from that experience, however, is unclear, since he sometimes seemed to go out of his way to make life difficult for her. There was a part of him that wanted to dominate the women he worked with and another part that wanted to solicit their approval. He had struggled with the gender issue since his early teens, and it was nowhere near resolution.

"I never felt the need to vet Russell before he came onto the show," says Howard. "He had a reputation for young male actorly behavior, but when we met, and always after that, he was pleasant and cordial to me. Having said that, his on-set process—at the time anyway—was to dismantle the director's plan for a scene and work it from the ground, on the spot. He had a way of working things out in front of the camera, which may be all right on his present projects, but for us it was a strain, despite the results.

"This is very hard for any director and was hard for Ann Turner. It meant we were going to have schedule problems from one end of the shoot to the other. The production team moved mountains to keep pace, and there were all the usual other difficulties, but once we knew the score, we made our own adjustments. Ann was conscientious about shooting the whole script, which made Russell's work method an ever bigger strain for her and [producer] Ben Gannon."

When Howard thinks of the film today, he envisions the faces of the characters in the sun or in darkly toned close-ups. The film has a dreamlike quality to it. He is happy with it but not sure he would ever make a film quite like that again. Today he seems almost amused that Russell is the ingredient in the film's composition that has evolved over the years with the most clarity.

"Russell was good," Howard says. "We never had the chance to get particularly close, as can often happen in this business, but he worked very hard on the film....Naturally, I have watched his career develop with great interest. He doesn't mention *Hammers over the Anvil* much in interviews, and I note it is not always on his biography. The film did not get a great run commercially. I came to feel that we could have recut the last couple of scenes to a slightly different effect, but there was no support from the investors or distributors for that, and I certainly never got to discuss it with Ann Turner. It is now behind us all."

Among those impressed by Russell's performances in *Proof* and *Romper Stomper* was David Elfick, who had just signed on to produce and direct a comedy titled *Love in Limbo*. The forty-eight-year-old, Sydney-born filmmaker had a long string of feature films to his credit, including *Starstruck, Undercover,* and *Around the World in Eighty Ways*.

The idea for *Love in Limbo* came to him one day while he was out on a boat with a successful businessman who entertained his guests with stories about growing up in Perth. "When he was a young man, he was a salesman for a ladies' underwear company, and he was a very funny guy," recalls Elfick. "He told us all these stories, and I thought this would be a good basis for a movie. So I hired a local scriptwriter, a South African guy called John Cundill, who is now a resident of Australia, and I suggested he hang out with this guy and just get down all these stories and see if he could fashion it into some kind of 1950s, coming-of-age movie. We worked on the screenplay for six or seven months, then a government financing corporation put up a decent amount of money and the film got made."

Elfick and casting director Christine King had already signed two of the three main actors needed for the film, Craig Adams and Aden Young, when King brought up Russell's name for the third part.

"She said, 'Why don't you see if he would do something in which he would play against the type he has done in the past and play comedy?'—and clearly when you look at *Proof* and *Romper Stomper*, he is a versatile actor," says Elfick. "I offered him the part and said, 'Look, you can do any English accent you want to, but basically I want you to be a twenty-one-year-old, anal-retentive English virgin.' And, of course, he smiled at that, because he thought that would be a challenge."

"OK," responded Russell, "if I can do any accent that I want to."

Armed with that delectable guarantee, Russell decided that he wanted to do a Welsh accent in the film. During the making of *Spotswood*, he had been greatly impressed by Anthony Hopkins's vocal presence, a result of his Welsh birthright.

At his own expense, Russell went to Wales and spent a couple of weeks living in a small town so that he could absorb the rhythm and tonal subtleties of the Welsh accent. It was an expensive trip and took a nice chunk out of his paycheck, but he considered it a challenge, and he felt that the end result would justify the out-of-pocket expense.

Love in Limbo is a coming-of-age story, Australian style, about three friends who go on a trip to the mining town of Kalgoorlie to lose their virginity in a brothel. Russell played the part of Arthur Baskin, a nerdish young man who is determined to experience the secret pleasures that only women can dispense. Along with him on that journey was Barry McJannet, played by twenty-year-old Aden Young, who had three feature films to his credit, and the main character, Ken Riddle, played by Craig Adams.

"We had great trouble casting the lead, because Russell was the major supporting actor and the other supporting actor was Aden Young, who had just done *Black Robe* not long before that," says Elfick. "Both of those guys were leading men, feature-film actors, and yet we couldn't find someone right for the lead and we ended up getting Craig, who was very inexperienced."

Once the three roles were cast, Elfick told the men that it was important for them to display a believable sense of camaraderie on the screen. "Russell was great, because every Friday night he would go out with Craig and Aden and they'd hang around in the bars of Perth and play pool and do things like that, forming this mateship," says Elfick. "On the set, Russell was particularly generous in being very giving as an actor to Craig. When you see the film, you don't see the leading man out of his depth, because the other two really helped him."

Elfick said that Russell was a very professional actor to work with, one who underwent "fantastic" preparation for his role. That attention to small detail has been known to drive directors crazy, but it didn't bother Elfick. His only disagreement with Russell occurred over a wardrobe item.

"I wanted him to wear a woolen tie with a kind of plaid design on it, and he didn't want to wear it—he wanted to wear a bow tie," Elfick explains. "We were having a bit of an altercation over it, and I said, 'Russell, I have English parents, and I believe that a young Welshman in the 1950s, when the film is set, wouldn't wear a bow tie. American people wore bow ties. English people wore neckties.' I said, 'If you can get me a photo of a Welshman in a bow tie, I'll let you wear it, but if you can't, you'll have to do what I say.' He said, 'Fair enough,' and that was it.

"I had been reasonable about it and he couldn't come up with the goods, so he had to go along with what I said. I found that's the way Russell is. He'll question something if he doesn't understand it or doesn't believe it, but if you can say, 'Well, this is what it is'—and give him some evidence of it—he says 'fair enough' and gets on with it."

Most of the film was shot in Perth, where the actors were given comfortable apartments to live in, but some scenes were shot in the remote town of Kalgoorlie, where the cast and crew were put up in motel-style accommodations.

Russell didn't seem to mind the less comfortable accommodations at Kalgoorlie, primarily because of the town's woolly history as a gold-rush destination. It was best known in the late 1800s and early 1900s for its hotels (it had more than ninety), its gaming establishments, and its toleration of prostitution (it is still said to be the best place in Australia to find dedicated hookers).

Since the two things that Russell appreciates most in a shooting location—a sense of history and a rugged landscape—are both amply present in Kalgoorlie, he had no occasion to complain, except perhaps for the fact that he would be away from Danielle for two months. It was the first real relationship of his life, and he reveled in the sense of security and excitement that it afforded him.

One of the things that set Russell apart from other cast members was his dogged determination to get inside the head of his character. He became so focused on his character, Arthur, that the wardrobe girl once complained to Elfick about what she perceived to be strange behavior on Russell's part. "When he isn't working, he comes in and puts on all his wardrobe, gets his hair done, and just sits in front of the mirror and looks at himself," she told the director. "Then he starts walking around in front of the mirror, looking at himself. Does he have a bit of an ego?"

"Don't be silly," Elfick told her. "He's trying to understand what he looks like as that character. All his movements—his hand movements, his head movements, the way he walks, the way he sits down—all are going to be developed in light of what he looks like. That's just an actor really preparing for his part."

Production proceeded without any serious difficulties, although the cast and crew did run into problems one day while shooting in the desert near Kalgoorlie. It rained so much that they had to truck in tons of red dirt to cover up the sandy mush beneath their feet. That worked for a while, but then the red dirt turned into clay that stuck to their shoes as they walked along the streets, slowing production and irritating everyone involved.

On another occasion, they were hit by a cold wave while filming in Perth. "We had to do a sequence where they were getting drunk in the sand hills for the first time, and even though Perth has quite a temperate climate in the middle of winter, we were shooting at night and it was fuckin' freezing, and we were sitting in the car, just freezing," recalls Elfick. "Russell and Craig and I were sitting in the car, going over lines and things, when Russell says, 'Why don't we go into the pub and get a hip flask of rum, since we're supposed to be drunk? It will warm us up a bit.' So we get the hip flask of rum and Russell and Craig and I took a swig of it, and then we just went out and did a stream-of-consciousness scene. It was good. The rum got them warm and they were a bit pissed, so they just let the scene flow."

Looking back on the experience ten years later, Elfick says he never had any arguments with Russell and considered the project one of his happiest experiences as a filmmaker. Asked what advice he would give directors working with Russell for the first time, he says: "Russell doesn't have much time for fools. If you believe in something, you've just got to show him what you're saying is the truth. He has a low tolerance for bullshit, I think. But he's an incredibly talented actor and I found him to be a real team player. He really helped me out with that young lead.

"The best thing you can say to any director who has Russell in their movie is how lucky they are, because he's one of the great actors, and it will be a challenging situation for any director and actor because he really puts a lot of his heart and soul into it. It sounds like I'm doing a complete whitewash on a guy who has a reputation for playing up, but I never experienced that—he just has no truck for fools."

When *Love in Limbo* was released, it got poor distribution in Australia and did not do well at the box office. As a result, it never made it to the United States and was never offered for videocassette distribution. Today it is next to impossible for anyone outside Australia to view the film. Nonetheless, for years it remained one of Russell's favorites, and he was never hesitant to give a copy of it to casting directors as an example of his acting range.

"He showed it to people because he thought he did a good job in it," says Elfick. "He said people would say, 'This is a good little film, why haven't we seen it?' But that's one of the unfortunate things about filmmaking. Films sometimes don't get the breaks they need to make them more successful than they were."

Perhaps spurred by his singing performance in *Hammers over the Anvil*, Russell felt musically invigorated. In 1992, he and Dean Cochran formed a new band they ultimately called Thirty Odd Foot of Grunts. The name is taken from a movie script notation in which a specified number of seconds (measured in feet of film) was requested for a fight scene. Instead of saying, "Give me thirty seconds of crowd noise," the screenwriter called for "thirty odd foot of grunts."

That phrase stuck with Russell, so when the time came for him and Dean to have an official name for their band, Thirty Odd Foot of Grunts rose from the ashes of cinematic shorthand to become a battlefield banner for Crowe & Company.

Music was a huge part of Russell's concept of self. He was not, frankly, a great guitarist, but he was good enough to express what he was feeling, and that, not public adulation, was what it was all about for him. Guitarists are born, not made, and Russell was born with a guitarist's personality. The core emotion in any great guitarist's background is rage, an emotion that has dictated many of Russell's life choices.

After doing a series of stressful motion pictures, Russell felt the need to get in touch with those feelings of anger and discontent that he had been able to express in music from a very early age. "I was feeling the pressure, the weight of the films I was doing in Australia," Russell once told the *Austin Chronicle*, when asked why the band got together. "I really wanted to get back into what I used to do, with the music, so we started doing it again regularly."

The new lineup consisted of Russell on vocals and guitar, Dean on guitar, Garth Adam on bass, Don Brown on drums, and Mark Rosieur on guitar. The demand for Thirty Odd Foot of Grunts (or TOFOG, as the band came to be known) was not great, so putting together a tour was out of the question. Instead, Russell and his bandmates rehearsed a lot, wrote new songs, and played pub bookings (pubs are called beer barns in Australia) when they could get them.

For Russell, playing in a band was not a distraction from his movie career, it was an extension of it, making it difficult at times to know where one began and the other ended. "It is a great way to learn how to maneuver an audience," Russell told *Elle* magazine. "You get out in the country somewhere, and there hasn't been a band there for about a month. There's four hundred expectant faces. At the beginning of the night they're all looking at you sideways from the back of the room, then they come down closer to the stage. I used to get really silly and walk on the stage and put a dramatic light up and say, 'come to me children'—and they would."

When Russell first read the script for *The Silver Brumby* (a.k.a. *The Silver Stallion*), his first thought was that it would be a perfect movie for his brother's daughter, Chelsea. None of his movies to date had been for children, and he felt bad that he was unable to share his growing fame with his niece. He also liked the fact that, like *Hammers over the Anvil*, the story involved a rugged landscape and lots of contact with horses.

Directed by John Tatoulis, *The Silver Brumby* was an adaptation of Elyne Mitchell's novel of the same title. It was filmed in the mountains of Victoria, in and around Mount Hotham and Dinner Plain, in the spring and early summer of 1992. In contrast to *Hammers over the Anvil*, in which a wrangler did most of Russell's stunts, Russell decided to do his own stunts this time around.

"I spent three or four months in the mountains in Victoria riding a horse, rounding up cattle, and cooking steaks at five o'clock in the morning in this little hut I was living in," he later told actress Kim Basinger, who spoke to him for *Interview* magazine. "I had maybe half a dozen lines of dialogue. It wasn't like making a film—it was like experiencing a totally different lifestyle."

Costarring with him in the film was British actress Caroline Goodall, best known at that time for her work in *Every Time We Say Goodbye* and *Hook*. She played the role of Elyne Mitchell, the mother of Indi (played by Amiel Daemion).

The Silver Brumby begins with horseback riders thundering through a rainstorm at night to tell Mrs. Mitchell that they repaired a stretch of fence on her property that had fallen down. Surreptitiously watching the conversation from the bushes is Wild Brumby, a stallion that was named for the wild wind that blew in the day he was born.

Later that night, Mrs. Mitchell tells her daughter about the Silver Brumby, a magnificent stallion with a cream-colored coat and a silver tail. It is a tale that she is in the process of weaving for a children's book.

Unaware of what is taking place on Mrs. Mitchell's ranch is Russell's character, referred to throughout the movie simply as "The Man," a literary device meant to give early warning that it is, after all, a story about horses and not humans. We first meet The Man as he comes upon a calf mired in the mud. He rescues it and turns it loose, then takes a nap. Later, he is awakened by the Silver Brumby, still a young colt. The Man tries to capture him, but the colt's mother arrives and drives The Man away.

One day Mrs. Mitchell takes Indi into the bush to teach her things about life. She tells her, "Do you know how you can read a book and not understand it? It's the same with the bush." Before the day is over, they find an injured kangaroo and take it home to nurse it back to health.

Meanwhile, The Man comes across a herd of horses. He looks for the Silver Brumby but can't find him. He and a fellow wrangler round up about twenty horses, after which he spots the Silver Brumby and his mother. He chases after them, but they are too fast and clever, and they again escape into the bush.

The story jumps ahead two years, by which time the Silver Brumby is fully grown. The Man is still determined to catch him, but the wily horse always manages to stay a step ahead. One day the Silver Brumby watches as his father loses a fight with another male horse and then dies, allowing the new male to inherit his father's herd of mares and colts. He realizes on that day that his life will never again be the same.

Obsessed with the Silver Brumby, The Man buys a palomino mare at auction and trains her at his cabin. If it was his plan to use the mare to attract the Silver Brumby, it worked long before he was able to put it into place, for watching The Man lead the mare back to the cabin was the Silver Brumby. Clearly, he wanted the mare for himself.

In the spring, when she is with foal, The Man helps her deliver as the Silver Brumby watches from a hilltop. It is a female, clearly the Silver Brumby's offspring. Says The Man to his horse, "Do you ever get the feeling you're being watched?"

The Man chases after the Silver Brumby, but the horse gives him the slip once more and circles back to get his mare and daughter.

Eventually, Indi learns that her mother's story is true and that the Silver Brumby really does exist, a discovery that upsets her because she knows that The Man is seeking to capture the horse. In the end, the horse leaps off a cliff rather than be caught, and we are left to wonder whether he escaped or died. For years to come, local residents tell stories of the ghost horse appearing and then vanishing with a wild cry that could only belong to the Silver Brumby.

The Silver Brumby did well in Australia, but producers were unable to land a distributor in the United States. More than a year after its release in Australia, the film was shown at the Seattle International Film Festival in the hopes of attracting a theatrical release in the States, but that didn't happen, and it went straight into videocassette distribution.

Even so, the film attracted positive attention from film critics at the festival. Wrote John Hartl of the *Seattle Times*: "This sad and lonely Aussie film stars Russell Crowe as a cowboy who tries to capture a wild stallion in the mountains of Victoria....The finale is a spellbinding tearjerker in the tradition of Albert Lamorisse's *White Mane*."

Even though Russell had very few lines to deliver in *The Silver Brumby*, it remained one of his favorite films. It was one of the few movies in which he was not asked to do a love scene. That is not to say he did not fall in love while making the movie, for he did—with a dog named Coolie!

When Russell was first introduced to the dog intended to be his sidekick and constant companion in the film, he asked if he could take him home so that they could develop a sense of mutual trust. The trainer refused and told him that he could only communicate with the dog on the set during working hours. Once shooting for the day wrapped, the trainer explained, Coolie would have to go home with her.

Unhappy with that arrangement, Russell persisted until the trainer relented and allowed Coolie to go home with him. As a result, Russell got very attached to the dog, a decision he probably regretted when production wrapped and man and dog had to go their separate ways. For months afterward, all that Russell could talk about was his admiration for the dog, especially the way he tried to keep up with him on horseback. No one could recall him ever talking about a human in such glowing terms.

After completing *The Silver Brumby*, Russell signed on for a role in a stage production titled *The Official Tribute to the Blues Brothers*, a musical that was scheduled for Sydney's Metro Theater. It had been a while since he had appeared on stage, and he relished the opportunity to focus attention on his musical talents, something that was very much on his mind at the time.

In June 1993, before starting rehearsals for the Blues Brothers tribute, Russell went to America for five weeks to read scripts and to audition for Hollywood movie roles. One of the films he auditioned for was *The Shawshank Redemption*, starring Tim Robbins and Morgan Freeman. It was a small role, but he thought the script was terrific. At a meeting with the casting director and one of the producers, he told them what he thought about the script and why he thought he should have the role.

After he left the meeting, one of the producers followed him out into the hallway to give him some friendly advice. The producer told him not to be so honest the next time he did a reading, because no one really gave a damn. Then she gave him an unsolicited pointer that made his skin crawl. Next time, she said, try to talk like an American.

To his surprise, Russell found himself the subject of media scrutiny during his American visit, primarily because of his role as Hando in *Romper Stomper*. A favorite question was whether he saw himself as another Mel Gibson, to which he always responded no—not in the least—adding tongue-in-cheek that he most often compared himself to his fellow Aussie Judy Davis.

He ended up doing a fair amount of traveling outside the confines of Hollywood. Interviewing him for *USA Today*, Karen Thomas asked what he thought about America. "When I'm somewhere rural, or in a city the size of Seattle, I really enjoy it," he answered. "But L.A. has a sort of air about it, an air of violence about it, that I don't really enjoy. The line between the haves and the have-nots is written right down the middle of the city. You see it on the pavement. It's bothersome."

Russell returned to Sydney empty-handed but determined to do better next time. So what if America did not yet recognize his talent? There would be other opportunities, he was certain of that. Meanwhile, his Blues Brother role seemed perfect for his needs at the moment. Making movies was a grand adventure, but it kept him away from his friends and bandmates, not to mention Danielle, whom he often described during that time as "long-suffering," primarily because of her acceptance of his relationship-straining travel and work schedule. Doing the Blues Brothers tribute would allow him to come in off the road for a couple of months and spend time with Danielle and his friends. Unfortunately, things didn't work out that way.

The stage show opened as planned, with Russell playing the John Belushi character, Jake Blues, but after only one performance he was forced to drop out when he developed throat problems. His doctor said that his voice would return to normal within a week, but the show's promoter decided to replace Russell, a decision that made it appear that the actor's voice might not have been up to the challenge.

Once he recovered from the Blues Brothers fiasco, Russell went back to the United States to look for feature film opportunities. He didn't land a new film role—at least not right away—but he did sign with a prestigious management firm, International Creative Management. ICM agents represented some of the top actors in the United States, stars such as Tommy Lee Jones, Charlton Heston, Paul Newman, Meg Ryan, and Mel Gibson.

ICM hosted a party for Russell, at which he was expected to mingle with the guests and make a good impression, but unfortunately all his old insecurities about his Maori heritage and lack of education surfaced, sending him packing out the back door. Nonetheless, after getting off to a rocky start, his agent, George Freeman, was able to land him a starring role in a low-budget, Canadian film titled *For the Moment*.

Canadian filmmakers are similar to their counterparts in Australia in that they receive government subsidies and enjoy hiring actors from abroad to give a more international flavor to their projects. *For the Moment*'s producers were interested in Russell because the film was about young men who traveled to Canada from the United States, Great Britain, and Australia during World War II to receive pilot training. Who better to play an Aussie would-be pilot than Russell Crowe?

Even though he had a deathly fear of heights and flying, Russell leaped at the chance to play the role of Lachlan, a full-of-himself Aussie who is determined to become a pilot so that he can fight the Germans.

At that point, Russell had become discouraged about his career, especially after running into so much passive-aggressive opposition in Hollywood. More often than not, his telephone calls back home to Danielle were punctuated with tears and self-pity. However, by the time he left for Manitoba, Canada, to start filming *For the Moment*, he was again at the top of his game, optimistic and fearless about the future.

Directed, produced, and written by Aaron Kim Johnston, a Manitoba-born director who had only two films to his credit (*Heartland* and *The Last Winter*), the film was meant to capture the lives and times of the young men who volunteered for what was virtually a suicide mission as World War II fighter pilots. Equally important to Johnston were the local women who loved the men and the influence of the rural, somewhat eccentric farm community that supported the air base.

Russell's love interest in the movie was Christianne Hirt, chosen to play the role of Lill, a young married woman whose husband had already gone off to war. At the time, Hirt was a veteran of twenty-two feature films and television series. In 1992, a year before production began on *For the Moment*, she had attracted good reviews for her touching, sometimes riveting portrayal of Hannah Peale Call in the television series *Lonesome Dove*.

For the Moment begins with a biplane soaring over the clouds. Lachlan and his fellow pilot Johnny (played by Peter Outerbridge) land the plane in a field, where Lill is driving a tractor. They are not there to visit Lill, however, but to see Johnny's fiancée, Kate (played by Sara McMillan), who just happens to be Lill's sister.

From the outset, it is apparent that Lachlan is attracted to Lill. She is headstrong and independent, as evidenced by her wearing men's work clothing and driving a cranky tractor, but she is also bright-eyed and, by local standards, cute as a button. She pokes fun at Lachlan, a sure sign that she is attracted to him, even if she is not willing to admit it to herself.

After the visit, Lachlan and Johnny return to the base, where they resume their combat training. Meanwhile, the other important characters in the story are introduced. There is Betsy (played by Wanda Cannon), an attractive farmer's wife who sells alcohol and sexual favors to the soldiers while her husband is overseas fighting the Germans, so that she can keep the farm going and give her two children the things that they need. There is also a flight instructor named Zeek (played by Scott Kraft) and Lill's brother, Dennis (played by Kelly Proctor).

One night Lachlan and Johnny take Lill and Kate to a barn dance. Again, Lachlan and Lill are cool to one another, but there is a mutual attraction that shows signs of growing into something that could pose a threat to Lill's marriage. Soon after the dance, Lill's brother Dennis leaves to go overseas. Now Lill has two loved ones overseas.

Lachlan is the first to acknowledge an emotional connection. He rides a motorcycle out to the farm to see Lill. To impress her, he gives her a bouquet of flowers. Says Lachlan, upon presenting the flowers, "I had to travel halfway around the world to bring those to you." She appreciates the gesture, but she knows full well that they were picked in an adjacent field. She is decidedly unimpressed, so he takes her for a ride on his motorcycle. They go to a hilltop, where he recites poetry to her. To his surprise, she admits that poetry is her biggest weakness.

Lachlan picks up on that at once, saying: "Three years of university, sign up, spend two months bobbing across the Pacific in a rusty bucket, through the Panama Canal, being bounced up the Atlantic, buffed down the St. Lawrence, banged on the train. Meet you, find out you have a soft spot for poetry, and I only bloody well know one. It's criminal."

With that, they kiss on the hilltop. He falls in love with her, but she falls more slowly, and more meetings occur before she agrees to go to bed with him. During one of their secret rendezvous, Lachlan says, "I just realized we're running out of time." To which she responds, "Well, we never really had any."

The worst sight that any mother, sister, wife, or girlfriend can see during wartime is a military car making its way up the driveway. It's never good news. When Lill sees the military car on its way to the farmhouse, she instantly knows that someone had died. What she doesn't know is whether it is her brother, Dennis, or her husband, Frank.

Later, she explains her emotions to Lachlan: "And then I realized that deep inside of me I was starting to make a choice. If only one could be alive, which one did I want it to be?…and by the time he reached me I found myself hoping it would have Frank's name on it. That way, my brother would be alive…and I'd still have you.…O God, help me!"

As it turns out, it is Dennis who died. He had only lasted a week overseas before being killed on his second mission. After the funeral, Lachlan and Lill are caught in an embrace. Lill later tells her sister and her father everything about her affair with Lachlan. Her horrified sister wants her to repent, but she can only offer the observation that Lachlan "made me feel alive." She's not sorry that she did it, but she is sorry if it caused pain for others.

In one of the more dramatic scenes in the film, Zeek crashes his plane while instructing a young pilot. Since the crash happens within sight of the air base, a number of trainees, including Lachlan, run in the direction of the smoke to help rescue the two men. But when they arrive, they see that the situation is hopeless. The trainee is dead, and Zeek is trapped inside the mangled wreckage, with fuel pouring out of the fuselage.

Zeek spots Lachlan in the crowd and asks him to please shoot him if the fuel ignites, so that he will not burn alive. To his horror, Lachlan is forced to do exactly that, an act that sends him into Betsy's comforting arms for the night. While he is asleep in her bed, Lill walks into the barn where Betsy services her clients, and she says goodbye to Lachlan without him ever knowing she was there.

There is only one ending possible, with Lachlan and Johnny getting their wings and then heading off to an uncertain future. It is Lill who must reconcile the conflicting emotions felt not just by her but by all the women in the community.

When the film was released in April 1994, the reviews were mixed. Kim Williamson, writing for *Boxoffice* magazine, felt that the film was flawed, but she was impressed by Russell's performance. "As Lachlan, Crowe—who rocketed to prominence with dynamic performances in *Proof* and *Romper Stomper*—offers a finely understated turn (similar to that of Tom Hanks in an analogous role in the 1986 Israeli film *Every Time We Say Goodbye*)."

Los Angeles Times critic Kevin Thomas found the film attractive but thought that the pacing was too slow and affected by extraneous elements. "Crowe and Hirt, however, are highly appealing, and Lachlan and Lill emerge as individuals of substance," he wrote. *"For the Moment* has an authentic period look and feel that is one of its key pluses. It's a nice movie that you want to be better than it actually is."

After Russell finished the movie, his Hollywood agent found him a starring role in a film that looked very promising. *Red Rain* was a blood-guts-and-sex thriller that costarred Jennifer Beals, best known for her huge success in her first film, *Flashdance,* ten years earlier. In *Red Rain,* Russell would play an archaeology professor who is forced to dig deep within himself to discover the secrets of his own past.

Russell was excited about working with Beals and equally pleased to travel to Italy, where the Australian-financed film was scheduled to begin production in September 1993. Unfortunately, his excitement was short-lived.

Only one week into production, Russell and Beals received telephone calls instructing them to pack and leave the hotel as quickly as possible because the police were on their way. Stunned, Russell and Beals did as they were told, not finding out until later what had happened. "They hadn't been paying the bills, and there was no money," Russell told *Who* magazine. "It was cool: I got to meet Jen—she's a really nice girl—and I got to go to Italy."

Red Rain was canceled and everyone was sent home. The embarrassed producers explained to the news media that there was a funding problem with Australia's Film Finance Corporation. They said that Russell had been paid a "fair" percentage of his salary and would be paid in full if the production company was able to recover damages in a lawsuit filed against the finance corporation.

Russell returned to Los Angeles, wondering why his luck had abandoned him. He need not have worried. Within days he was on a plane back to Sydney, where he was scheduled to begin work in October on a new film that was certain to be the most controversial of his career.

When Russell first heard about a film titled *The Sum of Us,* the story of a heterosexual father and his gay son, both of whom are looking for Ms./Mr. Right, he wanted to do it before he even read the script. Sexual differences and preferences had perplexed him from an early age, and portraying a gay man in a film seemed like an excellent way to gain a deeper insight into the issue.

After reading the script, he felt even stronger about being in the film. "I wanted that part so much because the script, by David Stevens, was one of the best I've ever read, even though it would have meant I'd have to kiss a man," Russell told *Vogue Men.* "After I heard Gerard Depardieu say that it was the hardest thing he'd ever had to do in a film, I thought, 'If Gerard can do it, so can I.'"

Unfortunately, when Russell's agent pitched him for the part of the gay son, Jeff Mitchell, he learned from director/producer Kevin Dowling that although the story was set in Australia, he was talking to an American investor who wanted an American cast. So, initially, Russell was turned down for the part. Russell was livid. The idea of an American playing a gay Australian man seemed like a supreme injustice.

Actually, Dowling was not in the least anti-Australian: He was having a difficult time obtaining a financial backer for the film. He had directed *The Sum of Us* for four years off-Broadway, but he had never directed a motion picture, and there was a feeling in the investment community that he did not have the credentials.

"In Hollywood they think directing a movie is nuclear physics and it can never be mastered by a mere stage director," he told the *Philadelphia Inquirer*. "They wanted someone else to direct, and they wanted to shoot it in the United States. They didn't think it would make any money if it was set in Australia."

A few weeks after Dowling rejected Russell for the part, the primary American investor died unexpectedly. With that, Dowling decided to seek funding from Australian government sources. There was interest in the film, but not in him directing it. The Aussies expressed concern that the film did not have an Australian director.

Dowling, who is British, closed the deal by adding noted Australian cinematographer Geoff Burton as codirector. Once the film was funded, one of Dowling's first decisions was to offer Russell the role his agent had sought for him.

Friends advised Russell not to accept it. They argued that if he wanted to crack the action/adventure market in America, playing a gay man might make producers hesitant to consider him for those types of roles.

Russell understood that argument, but his passionate desire to be in the film, and his nagging lack of self-confidence about his ability to ever crack the American market in a big way, overrode those considerations. He also wanted to be in the film for sentimental reasons. Playing opposite him would be Jack Thompson, the former star of *Spyforce*, the television series in which Russell got his start as a child actor.

With three dozen feature film and television series credits, including classics such as *Breaker Morant* and *Sunday Too Far Away*, Thompson was one of the most respected actors in Australian cinema. If Thompson could stand the heat of playing a movie character who had a homosexual son, Russell reasoned, then he certainly could find the courage to be that son.

Chosen to play Russell's love interest was John Polson, who had costarred with him in *Blood Oath*. Polson was not as well known as Thompson or Russell, but he was viewed as an up-and-coming actor who was destined for stardom.

Heralded by Sydney's sizable gay community, production began in October 1993 amid great fanfare. The film was based on the play of the same name by David Stevens, who attributed much of the dialogue to situations taken from his own life. The story was well known to Australian gays, who were enthusiastic about seeing it transferred to film. That is not to say that the production did not run into difficulties because of the controversial subject matter. A beer company hired to cater the crew's alcoholic needs during production pulled out in a huff when it learned about the film's theme.

The Sum of Us begins with black-and-white home movies taken during Jeff Mitchell's childhood. Narrated by Jeff, they offer a glimpse into his childhood, especially as it involved his grandmother and her close female friend.

Then the film jumps to present time, this time in color, as Jeff is shown playing football as a young adult. Jeff lives with his father, Harry Mitchell, who looks into the camera and explains that his son is gay and that is all right with him, though he, of course, has never had a gay thought in his life.

Harry is saddened by the fact that neither he nor Jeff has a significant other, and at every opportunity he encourages his son to find a suitable mate, even if it is another man. During one of his dinner-table lectures, he says: "There's amazing things waiting for you just around the corner, wonderful things, like love—the greatest adventure of all. Your grandmother said it once. I'll never forget it. The greatest explorers, she said, are the explorers of the human heart."

To which Jeff snapped, "Is that why she became a dyke?"

"Your grandmother was not a dyke!" responds Harry. He then explains, not convincingly, that she was a lesbian, not a dyke. Jeff shakes his head, unable to see the difference.

Harry is supportive of his thirty-four-year-old son, asks him about his relationships, and feels bad when he falls in love and it doesn't work out. Harry understands loneliness because that is the way he has felt since Jeff's mother died. Without telling Jeff, he enrolls in a dating service in hopes of meeting someone with whom he can have an intimate relationship.

After dinner, during which they decide to set the lesbian issue aside, Jeff leaves to meet his date, Greg (played by John Polson), at a local bar. He's very nervous about the date, as is Greg, and their conversation is awkward and strained. When Greg tells him that he is a swimmer, Jeff makes the first pass by saying, "I wouldn't mind seeing you in your Speedo." Then they go for a walk so that they can talk in private.

When Jeff asks Greg if he would like to go home with him, Greg answers in the affirmative, but when they reach the house, Greg becomes concerned about Jeff's father. Jeff tells him not to worry about it, that his father knows that he is gay.

After chatting on the sofa for a time, Jeff leans over and kisses Greg on the mouth, a moment that is interrupted by Harry, who walks into the room and says, "Well, aren't you going to introduce me?" After shaking hands with Greg, he takes a seat on the sofa and encourages Greg to sit down beside him.

With Jeff seated on the sofa on the other side of Greg, Harry lifts his beer and offers a toast: 'Well, happy bum!" Greg almost chokes on his beer and Jeff cracks up with laughter. He explains that his dad was only making a joke.

When Jeff goes into the kitchen to pour a couple of scotch whiskeys, Harry invites Greg out into his garden, where he shows him his prize tomatoes. Greg pays proper tribute to the plants, admiring their shape and color; then the two men anoint the shared moment by pissing on the vines.

Finally, Harry goes to bed and leaves the two men alone. They kiss again and Jeff takes him into the bedroom and guides him down onto the bed. After a few moments of groping, during which Jeff starts to unfasten Greg's belt, Harry sticks his head in the bedroom door and asks Greg how he would like his tea in the morning. With that, Greg says he wants to go home.

"It's Dad, isn't it?" asks Jeff.

Greg says no, but leaves anyway.

Later, Harry tries to console his son with, "He seemed like such a nice lad."

"Yeah, didn't he?" says Jeff sarcastically.

"Seeing him again?"

Jeff doesn't answer.

"Plenty more fish in the sea, eh?" says Harry with his customary optimism.

The following day, Harry goes out on a date with Joyce, the woman he met through the dating service. He takes her to the races, then to dinner. After several more dates, Harry asks Joyce to marry him. She says no, that it's much too soon, so they agree to give their relationship another three months.

Everything is going well for Harry until Joyce discovers that Jeff is gay. She gets very upset because he didn't tell her. She tells Harry that he should be ashamed of his son and then she leaves the house, making it clear that the relationship is over.

Hit hard by the breakup and by Joyce's harsh criticisms of his son, Harry has a heart attack, followed by a stroke that leaves him mute. The event changes the dynamics of the household, for Harry has taken care of Jeff his entire life, and now it is Jeff's turn to take care of his father.

When *The Sum of Us* was released in 1994, it was greeted by a firestorm of publicity, partly because the Australian government had begun an anti-discrimination campaign against homophobia at the beginning of the year. Only a few weeks before the film was in the theaters, the national government vetoed anti-sodomy legislation passed in Tasmania, setting off a series of violent anti-gay protests. On top of all that, the gay men and lesbians of Sydney decided to stage their first-ever Gay and Lesbian Mardi Gras, an event that was covered by national television.

Perhaps because of the publicity, *The Sum of Us* was a big success in Australia. A year later, when it was released in the United States and Canada, box-office receipts were sufficient to earn the film a profit, something no one involved with it ever envisioned.

For the most part, American critics were enthusiastic about the film. Under the headline "All of Us Should See 'The Sum of Us,'" Barry Walters wrote in the *San Francisco Examiner* that the film was the equal of the best films made the previous year. "Particularly in its early scenes, *The Sum of Us* is extraordinarily funny," he added.

Rita Kempley, writing in the *Washington Post*, described the film as a "funny, facile Australian tearjerker, saved from banality by the good-heartedness of its filmmakers and its captivating costars, Jack Thompson and Russell Crowe."

Los Angeles Times critic Kevin Thomas thought the film had a "fresh spin" on the subject of family responsibility: "The film's setting, furthermore, gives it a pungent particularity. In the land of Crocodile Dundee, gay men are often as macho as straight guys, and there's an open bluntness about both homosexuality and homophobia."

Russell was shocked by reaction to the film in Sydney, for he was elevated to heroic status in the gay community, something he did not anticipate or particularly need at that juncture of his career. Several years later, in a revealing interview with Kim Basinger for *Interview* magazine, Russell was asked about the role. For the first time in his life, he spoke of the gender issues that had bothered him since his teen years.

"There are many questions I would ask a character—for instance, 'Do you believe in the death penalty?'—before I ever got round to, 'What's your sexuality?'" Russell said. "I think other factors are more important in terms of human relationships and the way society operates than what someone's sexuality is. Sexual orientation is not something that people necessarily choose; it's just who they are."

For months after the release of the film, a debate raged in Sydney over whether Russell himself was homosexual. Gay groups were quick to claim him as one of their own. One day, Russell's girlfriend, Danielle, went into a bar and got involved in a conversation about the film with a couple of men, neither of whom knew her identity. One of the men informed her that he knew the man that Russell dated when he was in town. Danielle left the bar shaken, but she later learned that the "date" in question was a man who had helped him research the gay lifestyle.

Debates over his sexuality never ceased to amuse Russell. He once told one of the film's directors, Geoff Burton, that if he were a homosexual, he would be a "screaming queen—that's where the fun is."

The best part of making the film, Russell later recalled, was working with Thompson and Polson. The older man constantly challenged Russell by surprising him with improvised dialogue. Russell's favorite improvisation occurred when Harry first met Greg and sat down beside him on the sofa and offered the toast, "Well, happy bum!" The comment caught Polson completely off guard, with the shock clearly evident on his face.

"We didn't discuss with him what we were going to do to him at all," Russell said to Molly Meldrum. "We just put the pressure on him, just a whole lot of pressure, and that thing just came out. I think that's the first take that's in the movie, first or second take, something like that."

Polson walked away from the movie with a new appreciation of Russell's talent, but he was quick to point out to interviewers that that appreciation did not extend to the kissing scenes he did with him. He described it as one of the "most unsexy" experiences of his life, not unlike kissing a woman with whom he was not in love. He compared it to kissing Nicole Kidman in the television miniseries *Vietnam*, a kiss that he said was only "marginally more enjoyable" than his kiss with Russell.

As time went by, however, he gained a new appreciation of the kiss, especially when he learned that women "want to kiss somebody who's kissed Russell." To that end, he concluded that the kiss had proved "quite helpful."

FOUR

HOLLYWOOD BECKONS
THE QUICK AND THE DEAD

By 1993, actress Sharon Stone was nowhere near where she wanted to be in her career. Best known for her sensual and emotionally charged role of Catherine Tramell in the 1992 erotic thriller *Basic Instinct*, she had appeared in two dozen feature films and television movies since 1980, none of which had done much for her career.

Catherine Tramell made her an overnight sensation, and all the actress had to do was remove her panties and uncross her legs in the glare of a bright light, strip naked whenever she was anywhere in the vicinity of costar Michael Douglas, dabble in lesbianism, and become reasonably proficient with an ice pick.

Not a bad tradeoff, considering the bitchy elusiveness of fame. Stone's sudden celebrity was so convincing that *Premiere* magazine proclaimed her "the first post-Madonna cinema sex goddess of the 1990s." It was a label that Stone, then thirty-five years old, did not relish.

"There were times when I thought that was a route to power or a route to happiness....I don't want to be like, 'Oh, I'm so big and fabulous,'" she told *Vanity Fair*. "Catherine Tramell was big and fabulous, and selling *Basic Instinct* was a big and fabulous adventure. But you want to know something? I ain't her. Smart people know I'm not her, but even smarter people know I can be her if I need to be."

In 1993, Stone followed the success of *Basic Instinct* with a second erotic thriller, *Sliver*, which did not do as well at the box office—or with the same critics that had praised Joe Eszterhas's script for *Basic Instinct* (he also wrote *Sliver*). It raised questions in the minds of many about Stone's range as an actress.

Making matters worse were serious thinkers such as essayist Camille Paglia, who defended *Basic Instinct* on the grounds that it revealed a postfeminist truth, namely, that women are inherently bitches who dominate men's sexuality for their own selfish purposes. Paglia thought Catherine Tramell was one of the greatest *femmes fatales* in cinematic history.

Even as the debate raged over the issues of sexuality raised in *Basic Instinct*, Stone started backpedaling on the film. If she didn't do something to stifle comparisons between her and the character—and quickly—she risked becoming another one of Catherine Tramell's victims. The fame associated with that character was so engulfing, so teasingly intense, it was as if an imaginary knife-wielding psychopath was pursuing Stone, with no one lifting a finger to help.

Stone's solution was to seek respectability as a producer. Even as she was making the rounds to promote *Sliver*, she was negotiating a deal to coproduce and star in a Western titled *The Quick and the Dead*, a film about a female gunslinger who comes to town to right a grievous injustice.

It was her job as coproducer to help hire the talent and supervise the overall mechanics of film production. She asked Sam Raimi, a veteran producer of action television programs such as *Xena: Warrior Princess* and *Hercules* and the director of movies such as *Army of Darkness* and *The Evil Dead*, to direct the film, even though he had no experience with Westerns. He knew how to capture violent action and make it seem contemporary, and that was what mattered most to her.

For the role of John Herod, the middle-aged outlaw who ruled the town with an iron fist, she chose box-office sure-thing Gene Hackman, who was identified by the public with films such as *Unforgiven* and *Geronimo: An American Legend*.

With Hackman as the film's anchor, Stone put together a strong cast of character actors, such as Lance Henriksen and Kevin Conway, then shopped around for new, breakout talent that she felt was destined for stardom. Her first choice was Leonardo DiCaprio, a nineteen-year-old actor who had enjoyed a two-year run on the popular television series *Growing Pains*. He had some movie success in *Poison Ivy* and *Critters 3*, but in 1993 he was not considered a major talent. Stone thought otherwise and signed him to play John Herod's rebellious son, known simply as "The Kid."

The role of Cort, a gunfighter-turned-man-of-the-cloth, went to Russell Crowe, who was largely unknown in the United States. Stone had been mesmerized by his performance in *Romper Stomper*, and she felt that he would be perfect for the part of a reformed gunfighter. She saw in him an old-fashioned manly quality that she felt was not present in many Hollywood actors. To her way of thinking, he was raw and unpolished but capable of emotional refinement.

Russell had just about given up hope of attracting attention in Hollywood when he received a call from his agent that Stone and Raimi were interested in him for a role in *The Quick and the Dead*. It seemed like a miracle to Russell, who had made more than a dozen trips to America in hopes of being discovered.

When he auditioned for the film, it was for a different, less important role than the one he ended up with. That's because at the audition Stone urged him to read for one of the three male leads. He did, and nailed it cold.

"When I saw *Romper Stomper*, I thought Russell was not only charismatic, attractive and talented, but also fearless," Stone told the *New York Times*. "And I find fearlessness very attractive. I was convinced I wouldn't scare him."

Stone was right about that. Russell later told friends that the actress, with all her trappings of success, did not intimidate him. He felt she understood that regardless of what happened on the set, he was going to do his job without thought to her status.

It was not until agent and director started talking specifics that it looked hopeless. They needed Russell in late October or early November, and he was deeply involved with the production of *The Sum of Us*. The studio advised Stone to choose someone else, but she was adamant that Russell was perfect for the part. She argued that Russell was so essential that it would be in the best interests of the film to delay production for a month or two so that he would be able to join the cast.

To her surprise, the studio agreed.

"I didn't think that I was ever going to go to America," Russell later recalled to *HQ* magazine. "I thought it was just a bit too big a thing for me to scale."

Russell saw the role as an investment, which is why he agreed to do it for minimum scale. He was touched by Stone's appreciation of his work and by the fact that she took a stand on his behalf, and so he viewed the role as an opportunity of a lifetime, not as just another paycheck.

When he arrived on the set in December, he discovered that no one there had ever heard of him or seen his movies, with the exception of Stone and DiCaprio, with whom he formed an easy, older-brother type of friendship. The others kept their distance from him, especially Hackman, who couldn't think of any reason to pal around with an actor whom he had never heard of before.

Russell's biggest challenge was not in playing against an icon like Hackman but in getting used to handling a handgun. Although he had never fired a gun in his life, he was expected to draw, twirl, and fire a pistol with the authority of a seasoned gunfighter. He viewed it as simply another physical task that he would have to master. He tackled it by going to a firing range in Tucson, Arizona (where the film was being shot), to practice with sheriff's deputies. By the time he left, he was a near marksman.

The hardest thing for him to master was a quick draw. Since his character had to go up against Hackman's character in the film, he wanted to be competitive with him, and it irritated him to no end that the older actor outdrew him every time. What Russell didn't realize was that Hackman has a reputation for having an extraordinarily quick draw. In the Old West the actor would have been a real contender as a gunslinger.

Hackman also has a reputation for improvising during a scene. During an early confrontation with Stone's character, he slapped her hard across the face with his gloves, an unscripted gesture that caught the actress completely off guard. The indignation and fury reflected in her face in response to being slapped was genuine.

Stone befriended Russell as soon as he arrived on location. She told him about her upcoming marriage and wondered aloud if she should have a prenuptial agreement drawn up, to which Russell responded, with his customary honesty, that any marriage built around a prenuptial agreement was not a marriage worth having.

Russell was grateful for Stone's support, but he also was a bit wary of her stardom. He had never been around anyone who possessed that level of celebrity, and it made him uncomfortable at times, mainly because he was uncertain how to relate to her. It was an old dilemma for him, this business of effectively communicating with women at a high social level, and Stone represented the ultimate challenge.

Russell had only been there a few weeks when production shut down for Christmas, a holiday he expected to spend alone. To his surprise, Stone called him early on Christmas morning and invited him to go with her to a local Salvation

Army mission to work in the food line. He jumped at the chance and rode with her to the mission, where he put on an apron and gave out coffee and orange juice and heaping portions of turkey.

"I'm like just full into it—and at one point in the day, I look over and Sharon's got her apron on, and it doesn't have any food marks on it," he told Molly Meldrum. "She is standing between two people getting her photograph taken for the local newspaper and the only time she picked the orange juice and coffee up was for that photograph."

Russell laughed about the incident, for it proved to him that stars like Sharon Stone lived in a different universe, one he had read about but never visited. He didn't feel critical of her for posing for the photograph, only amused by the fact that while they worked in a movie together, they really had very little in common.

Especially pleasant for Russell was working with director Sam Raimi. The director is a well-known fan of the Three Stooges, and Russell once compared working with him to hanging out with the fourth Stooge, a high compliment in both his and Raimi's eyes. He was also impressed by the director's willingness to experiment with various camera techniques, such as filming an actor acting backwards and then playing it back in reverse to determine the best angles for difficult shots.

Raimi was equally impressed with Russell. "[He's] bold and likes to challenge people," the director told the *New York Times*. "He reminds me of what we imagine the American cowboy to have been like....Russell's not dangerous physically. He's dangerous because he's always thinking."

When the script was first discussed, Stone vetoed doing any nude scenes. She knew that fans of *Basic Instinct* and *Sliver* would expect her to appear naked in a love scene, but she felt it would not add anything to the story; besides, she desperately wanted to get away from that image.

Midway through production, she changed her mind and requested, in her capacity as coproducer, that a nude scene be written for her and Russell. As a result, they spent two days in an old, abandoned whorehouse filming a steamy nude scene that called for her shirt to be ripped away and for Russell to kiss her with passion.

To no one's surprise, the scene was later pulled from the film, leading some observers to wonder why it was done in the first place. Why would anyone want to inject a nude scene into a film that had no love story? There were rumors that Stone was Russell's first American offscreen conquest, but both actors denied having a physical relationship, and fans of both actors were left to believe what they wanted to believe.

Filming ended without any major problems, but unanswered questions lingered long after everyone packed up and went home. *The Quick and the Dead* was meant to be a parody of the so-called spaghetti Westerns of the 1960s and 1970s. That Hackman was well aware of that shows clearly in his gestures and acting style, but Stone and the other two male leads, Russell and DiCaprio, seem not to have been made aware of the comedic nature of the film, for they played their roles with solemn seriousness.

In fairness to them, it must be said that it would be difficult to ascertain the true satirical nature of the film simply by reading the script. The humor did not derive from the terse dialogue but rather from the overview and the setups of individual scenes—all the responsibility of the director. If the joke was designed to obtain straight-ahead performances from the actors, then it will surely go down as one of the great directorial pranks in film history.

The Quick and the Dead begins with Sharon Stone's character, Ellen (a.k.a. "The Lady"), riding slowly across the plains, where she is ambushed by a man who takes a shot at her with a rifle. She pretends to be hit but then takes him prisoner when he approaches her to claim her belongings. After chaining him to his wagon, she rides into a dirty little town named Redemption, where a gunfighter contest, called the "Quick Draw Competition," is scheduled to take place.

Not long after her arrival in town, Russell's character, Cort, the gunfighter-turned-minister, is dragged into the bar and shackled so that he cannot escape. John Herod (played by Gene Hackman) goes through the motions of hanging him right there in the bar. At issue is whether the minister will participate in the shootout.

Herod tells him in no uncertain terms that he wants him in the contest. When Cort again says no, Herod has him hoisted onto a chair with a rope around his neck; then he shoots the chair legs out, one at a time. Before the chair can collapse, Ellen draws her gun and shoots the rope in half, saving Cort from certain death. Soon it becomes clear that Ellen is there on a mission of revenge and that John Herod is her target.

Cort's response to those who wanted to lynch him—and Russell's first line of dialogue in an American film—is "I'm faster than you." He speaks softly, giving credence to his reformation into a holy man, but his captors are unimpressed and they treat him with disdain. He is thrown out into the street, where children scorn him and beat him with firewood. Ellen asks him why he won't fight. "I'd like to kill them all for what they're doing," he answers. "But killing is wrong."

"Some people deserve to die," says Ellen.

Finally, Cort's captors unchain him and escort him into a gun store, where Herod suggests that Cort be given a pistol. Then he is taken back out into the street for a gunfight. He still insists he will not fight. At that point, Herod no longer cares whether he dies with a drawn gun or one still sheathed in its holster. There is a moment of drama when everyone wonders what he will do, but when the other man goes for his gun, so does Cort, only he is much faster and succeeds in killing his adversary.

Eventually, Cort befriends Ellen. He tells her he used to ride with Herod. One day, Herod ordered him to kill a priest. He refused, and Herod put a gun to his head. To his everlasting shame, he shot the priest rather than be shot by Herod.

When Cort is not participating in a face-off with another gunslinger, he is kept chained up like a dog. Unlike the other contenders, who have freedom to roam about the town and use whatever firepower they can muster, Cort is given only one bullet at a time.

By this point, the reasons for Ellen's hatred become apparent. Years ago, when she was a child, Herod and his men rode into town and strung up her father, who was the local sheriff. They gave Ellen an opportunity to save him by giving her a gun and telling her to shoot the rope in two, but she missed and shot her own father.

As the contest continues, Ellen becomes fearful that by the luck of the draw, she will not be able to face down Herod, so she challenges him to his face. "I'm going to kill you if I have to ride all the way to hell to do it," she tells him. He rejects her challenge and tells her, in effect, to take a number and sit down.

One by one, Cort, Ellen, and The Kid work their way through the gunslingers, until in the final two contests it is Herod versus his son and Ellen versus Cort. Herod is victorious in the fight with his son. As the young boy lies dying in the street, Herod mutters, "It was never proved that he was my son."

In the fight between Ellen and Cort, she appears to be the loser. She takes a hit to the chest and drops to the street, where she is pronounced dead. The last fight is between Cort and Herod. But before anyone draws his gun, explosions start going off in the town. From the smoke and confusion emerges Ellen, whose death turns out to have been faked; she then gets the face-off with Herod that she has dreamed about for most of her life.

When *The Quick and the Dead* was released in February 1995, the critics were brutal. Mick LaSalle, writing in the *San Francisco Chronicle*, praised Raimi's directing abilities but questioned whether anyone ever told Sharon Stone that the film was a comedy. "At the center of the film, its reason for being, is Stone, a very pretty actress making what appears to be a very silly career move: Sharon in leather pants. Sharon twirling a gun. At best she looks innocuous. But at worst she looks desperate, trying to be Clint Eastwood with all her might."

Chicago Sun-Times critic Roger Ebert had good things to say about Raimi, Gene Hackman, and cinematographer Dante Spinotti, but he had little good to say about Stone's performance: "As preposterous as the plot was, there was never a line of Hackman dialogue that didn't sound as if he believed it. The same can't be said, alas, for Sharon Stone, who apparently believed that if she played her character as silent, still, impassive and mysterious, we would find that interesting….Do you suppose she took the plot seriously?"

Steven Rea, writing in the *Philadelphia Inquirer*, called the film an overcooked melodrama. "[It's] a kind of *Mad* magazine version of a spaghetti western, a lost Sergio Leone epic with an impudent, cartoonish sensibility…the thing is more entertaining as an idea than it is as an actual movie. Caricature can only take you so far."

Stone was surprised, to say the least, at the panning that both she and the film received. All she wanted was respect for her acting abilities, with perhaps a nod to her fearlessness at being willing to take on a producer's role so soon after *Basic Instinct* and *Sliver*. But all she received was criticism from individuals who seemed to take Catherine Tramell more seriously than they did the actress herself.

Russell Crowe fared no better. It was meant to be his breakout role in America, yet few critics mentioned his name in their reviews. He did not walk away from the film as a household name, as he had hoped, but he did learn two valuable lessons: that glamorous actresses like Stone don't always get what they want, and that seasoned pros like Hackman usually do get what they want, even if they have to take it by working the trenches while no one is looking.

Overwhelmed by the experience of making a film with Sharon Stone and Gene Hackman, Russell passed over numerous offerings from major studios to take a starring role in a $1.3 million independent film titled *No Way Back*. By the time he left Australia, he was at the top of the A-list as an actor, but in Hollywood he was lucky to have his name included on the B-list.

The excitement of being in a film with the likes of Stone and Hackman dissipated fairly quickly after he saw the film. They had outshone him, out-acted him, and, in the case of Hackman, outsmarted him. He had played his role straight, just as the script had indicated; only later, when the special effects were added— bullet holes that you could look through, etc.—did he realize the film was meant to be a spoof.

Washington Post critic Desson Howe was one of the few reviewers to even mention Russell's name, but it did not come across as a compliment, at least not the kind that a New Zealander would want posted back home. Howe predicted that Russell's "pretty Australian face" would attract better scripts in the future.

As a result, Russell fell back on his own instincts and joined the cast of *No Way Back* because it was familiar territory to him—a low-budget film, with American-Japanese financing, that would enable him to be the unquestioned star.

Directed by Frank A. Cappello, who had directed only one other film, *American Yakuza*, it was about an FBI agent, Zack Grant (played by Russell), whose partner commits suicide during a botched undercover operation. The story revolves around his mission to bring those responsible for her death to justice.

Costarring in the film were Helen Slater, who played an overeager flight attendant, and Etsushi Toyokawa, who played an assassin. On paper that looked fine— Slater had appeared in twenty feature films and television series, including *City Slickers*, *Lassie*, *Ruthless People*, and *Supergirl*, in which she had the starring role—and Toyokawa had achieved superstar status in Japan, but the reality was much different.

No Way Back begins with a man on a bicycle towing a cardboard box in a toy wagon into a tunnel, where a homeless man is sleeping. The noise awakens the homeless man, who watches as the bicycle rider unhooks the wagon and rides away. Within seconds, a gang of skinheads storm into the tunnel with bats and clubs, which they use to pummel the box while a gang member spray paints a message on the tunnel wall: "Stay out of America." Their work done, the gang leaves the tunnel, at which point it becomes clear that the box contains the remains of a Japanese businessman.

Investigating the killing is FBI agent Zack Grant, who has devised a way to infiltrate the gang by sending rookie FBI agent Seiko Kobayashi into their inner sanctum, disguised as a hooker who has arrived to service the gang's leader. The plan is for her to drop a hidden microphone so that the FBI can listen in on the gang members' conversations. But something goes horribly awry, and Seiko flushes the microphone down the toilet and proceeds to gun down the gang members one by one.

When Zack suspects that something has gone wrong, he storms into the apartment and finds everyone dead except for Keiko, who levels her gun at Zack. Instead of firing, though, she lurches back through the window and falls to her death.

Zack is called on the carpet for the botched mission and for using an inexperienced agent. What happened is not his fault, of course: the agent was the daughter of the man who was beaten to death inside the box.

Baffled by Seiko's death, Zack sets out to solve the mystery. He learns that Seiko used a neighbor's telephone to talk to an Asian man named Yuji several times before going on the mission, and he goes in search of him.

Meanwhile, it comes to light that the skinheads' leader was the son of a Mafia crime boss, Frank Serlano (played by Michael Lerner), who is understandably upset over the death of his son. He kidnaps Zack's eight-year-old son and sends word that if Zack doesn't hand over the Asian man, he will kill the boy.

Zack captures Yuji after a spectacular shootout and decides to hand him over to the mobster. On the way to make the delivery, the airplane is hijacked by Yuji, who forces the pilots to land at small airport in Arizona. Mary, the flight attendant, enters the story when she is taken hostage by Yuji. Zack goes after them and, after a confrontation with trigger-happy mobsters, recaptures Yuji. Mary tags along because she has no place else to go.

In one of the worst-written and -acted scenes in the movie, Mary and Zack push the car while Yuji steers it. To Zack's annoyance, Mary begins singing, "She'll be comin' around the mountain when she comes."

"Shut up!" Zack snaps.

"I'm upset. I hum when I'm upset."

"Don't."

"Perhaps you should try it."

"Perhaps I don't want to try it."

"Music is a very powerful ally. It soothes the savage beast."

They get into a shouting match and don't notice that the car is pulling away from them, rolling downhill faster than they can run. It is a ludicrous scene, and Russell does some of the worst acting of his career, paired with an actress who is so over-the-top that it is painful to watch.

The ending is no more believable than any of the scenes that preceded it, and the viewer is left with one lingering question: Why is Russell Crowe in this movie? To this day, that question has gone unanswered, for Russell has never talked about the film. He liked the idea that he would get to play a dad for the first time, and he liked going up against skinheads, because of the flack he received for *Romper Stomper*, but other than that it is difficult to imagine what he was thinking.

Apparently, Russell and Slater had better chemistry offscreen, for when Russell learned that Slater was a songwriter and was working on new material in her off-hours, he volunteered his assistance. Rumors circulated about the two actors, but who knows? The fastest way to attract Russell's attention is not with a freshly baked pie or an invitation into the bedroom but rather with a few well chosen piano or guitar chords.

No Way Back premiered in Japan and was picked up by Columbia Tri-Star, which subsequently decided it was not strong enough for a theatrical release in the United States. Instead, it introduced the film to American audiences on the HBO cable network and then sent it directly into videocassette distribution. For that reason, movie critics passed on the film entirely, allowing it to slip into cinematic oblivion.

When a writer from *W* magazine went to Los Angeles in 1995 to interview Russell, along with a photographer and a crew of wardrobe and makeup people, there was no way of knowing that it would turn out to be the Interview from Down Under Hell.

Russell was pleasant enough during the interview portion, but he seemed to be distracted by an odd mixture of homesickness and false bravado. He couldn't understand why Americans hated the thirteen-hour flight to Sydney—he loved it! And he couldn't understand why Americans had such weird notions about alcohol and tobacco consumption—he loved to drink and smoke (he had been a smoker since the age of ten).

"I went to dinner with Bruce [Willis] and Demi [Moore]," he complained. "There was no alcohol, no cigarettes. It really is the most puritan of progressive societies. There's what's done—and what's said to be done. Even the Germans know how to have a good time, tell a few stories and have a few drinks."

Ever since his arrival in America, Russell had been undergoing successive waves of cultural shock. America was indeed the richest nation on earth, yet he saw pockets of poverty in Los Angeles that nearly brought him to tears.

In the movies he had seen about Americans, they were all hard-drinking, fist-happy rebels who didn't give a damn about the consequences of their actions. Yet what he found, particularly in Los Angeles, was a health-conscious nation that frowned upon fighting, drinking to excess, and smoking, even to the point of having a "smoke police" ready to escort violators from public places. And, while the greeting offered by the Statue of Liberty resonated deeply inside him, he discovered that many Americans were distrustful of foreigners, even Australians and New Zealanders who had fought beside them in World War II and Vietnam. Those discoveries led Russell to conclude that Americans were not nearly as special as they pretended to be.

When the time came for the *W* photographer to shoot the photos to accompany the article, Russell waved the stylist aside and insisted on picking out his own clothes, going for what the magazine writer called the "most garish" ensemble possible. As they went through the steps that led up to the actual photo session—clothes, hair, makeup, etc.—Russell refused to talk to the crew and made it a point to blow cigarette smoke into the hairdresser's face as she combed his hair.

Told by the photographer that he could do anything he wanted to do during the shoot, he responded that he wanted to go back to sleep. Later, when he started moving around the room beyond the range of the camera setup, he was told that the camera couldn't follow him. He shouted at the photographer and demanded to know when they were going to start doing what he wanted to do.

Inexplicably, Russell asked them to bind his wrists with masking tape, according to *W*, after which he hurled obscenities at the crew, tore the masking tape from his wrists in a rage, then demanded that his mouth be taped shut.

On top of all that, he called a crew member aside and displayed what he called "the hand of God." Wrote the *W* writer, "It turns out to be a small pistol with a cross embossed on it which he brandishes with bravado, ignoring the question of it being loaded. All in all, it's the scariest shoot anybody can remember."

When the article was published, the magazine wondered aloud whether Russell was schizophrenic or simply showing off for the crew. It was probably a little of both. Americans are such weaklings in his eyes, he seldom lets an opportunity pass to put the fear of God into them, New Zealand-style, so of course he derives gleeful enjoyment from "showing off" in their presence. As for the schizophrenic nature of his behavior, he was rattled that day with good reason. He was in the process of breaking up with his girlfriend of five years, Danielle Spencer, or rather she was in the process of breaking up with him.

Russell hinted at his distress during the interview when asked about the relationship. "It has to have a looseness to it now," he explained. "I railed against that for a while, but I was the one who was always leaving, getting on a plane. Now it's got that ring of the 'progressive relationship' to it, which I always thought was bullshit. But why should she quit doing things she's good at just to hang out with some dumb actor?"

Actually, Danielle was already gone, and the relationship was finished. He just didn't want to admit it. The problems began when she came to America to live with him, just as he began production on *The Quick and the Dead*. She gave up everything to be with him—her friends, her family, her career as a singer and actress.

Danielle loved him, but there was more to it than that. She felt responsible for him, something she had never experienced with anyone else. Whenever he called her from America, depressed at his inability to fit in socially with other actors and tearful from the painful loneliness he felt living alone in a country that he didn't quite understand, she felt compelled to comfort him. Essentially, that was why she came to America—to take care of Russell.

Danielle began her American adventure on the Arizona set of *The Quick and the Dead*. "People forget it can get lonely living on a set on your own for several months, even though it might look glamorous," she told *Hello* magazine. "I think it was really grounding and very comforting for Russell to have someone special there with him, someone to say, 'Hi, how are you?' after a busy day shooting."

Russell confided to friends that he wanted to marry Danielle. She was the only woman who had ever been able to put him totally at ease with the opposite sex—and with himself, which was no small accomplishment, since he still had moments of self-doubt despite his growing success.

When he broached the subject of marriage with her, she did not respond as he had hoped. Her life was in Australia, she explained, not America. He suggested that she audition for a few movie roles and give it a chance, but she was adamant that life as she knew it could only take place in Australia. Besides the family and friends issue, that was where her band was—and where she was scheduled to begin taping a new television show titled *Pacific Drive*.

When it got down to it, Danielle was not the type of woman who could live her life through the eyes of her significant other. She had her own dreams and ambitions, and they didn't include being a housewife to a Hollywood star. As a result, Danielle ended their five-year relationship, fittingly enough in Hollywood, a place that had come to symbolize the separateness of their dreams. "It was about life direction," she told *New Idea* magazine. "Things were starting to happen for him and I didn't want to be in L.A."

It was the first time Russell's heart had been broken, but it would not be the last. He was devastated by the breakup, even though they agreed to remain friends. On a subsequent trip back to Australia, he went with a friend to hear Danielle perform at a hotel and was in tears for most of the performance.

When Danielle began dating other people, she chose a popular Australian actor named Marcus Graham, best known for his work in films such as *Crimetime, Mad Bomber in Love*, and *Point of No Return*. Ironically, it was Graham who was dating Nicole Kidman when she moved to the United States and dumped him for Tom Cruise. Whatever else Danielle and Marcus had in common, they certainly could commiserate over the romance-busting siren call that radiated from the bright lights of Hollywood.

At the time, Danielle never looked back, but several years later she did seem to have second thoughts. "I sometimes regret [the breakup]," she told *Hello* magazine. "I possibly should have taken the opportunity to explore some career options over there and do some auditions. But I was working on things back in Australia and I had a band there, too, so it was difficult for me to make the break."

The most immediate effect on Russell was to make him more appreciative of his family. What he wanted most in the way of a relationship with a woman was the type of loving partnership that he had witnessed with his mother and father. In his mind, Danielle was the perfect partner for him. He compensated for that loss by refocusing attention on his parents, with whom he had had little contact over the previous two years.

Russell had given a lot of thought about where he wanted to put down roots. Although born a New Zealander, it was Australia that tugged at him the strongest. With that in mind, he purchased a five-hundred-acre ranch near Coffs Harbour, New South Wales, about three hundred miles north of Sydney. He moved his parents to the ranch so that they could be together when he visited, and he proceeded to transform the simple, weatherworn buildings on the property into a comfortable ranch house, gym, and stable for his horses. He also planted trees and filled the surrounding pastures with cattle. Now, instead of staying in Sydney when he returned to Australia, he stayed in relative isolation at the ranch, far away from the prying eyes of the media.

"I'm just a big softie when it comes to the farm," Russell told the *Mirror.* "The animals are my friends and I enjoy spending time with them because they open up my mind again when the small world of show business threatens to close it down."

The breakup with Danielle also affected the way he perceived his band, Thirty Odd Foot of Grunts. He had been neglecting them, just as he had neglected his parents. As he breathed new life into his relationship with his parents, so did he reestablish his connections to his bandmates. They started writing songs again and rehearsing whenever Russell returned to Australia.

In 1995 and 1996, despite long hours of working on movie sets, Russell proved himself to be a prolific songwriter. He also proved to be an aggressive promoter, so far as the band was concerned. When he went on location for his next movie, he did so with a promise from producers that the last song on the soundtrack, "The Photograph Kills," would feature Thirty Odd Foot of Grunts. As far as he was concerned, there was enough good fortune to spread around for everyone, especially his mates back home.

One of the benefits of making *The Quick and the Dead* was the buzz that it generated around Russell, a byproduct of which was an influx of scripts sent to his agent. One that caught his eye was *Virtuosity*, a science fiction thriller about a computer-generated killer named SID 6.7 that escapes into the real world.

Directed by Brett Leonard, whose four previous films included *The Lawnmower Man* (starring Pierce Brosnan), it had all the makings of a cutting-edge, virtual-reality classic. What interested Leonard most about the film was its use of high-tech devices to tell what is essentially a story about an ultra-violent robot. So it is surprising that Russell, who thus far in his career had been attracted to stories that explored the human condition, saw something in the script that grabbed his interest.

For the lead character, Lieutenant Parker Barnes, Leonard cast Denzel Washington, who had come off a series of big-budget movies, including *Philadelphia, Crimson Tide,* and *The Pelican Brief.* The then-forty-one-year-old actor was known for his versatility, meticulous character development, and onscreen sexuality—essentially the same qualities that Russell was seeking to project in his own career. Unlike Russell, however, Washington was married and had four children, living the offscreen life that Russell dreamed about.

For the female lead, Dr. Madison Carter, Leonard chose Kelly Lynch, a former Elite model. The thirty-six-year-old actress first attracted attention as Matt Dillon's drug-addict girlfriend in Gus Van Sant's *Drugstore Cowboy* in 1989, at which point there seemed to be a consensus that she was destined for superstardom. But the films that followed—*Curly Sue, Desperate Hours,* and *Warm Summer Rain*—did not live up to expectations, and by 1995 Lynch was viewed as more of a journeyman actress who would get the job done and look good doing it while not getting in the way of the male actors.

Leonard thought Russell would be perfect for the role of SID 6.7 after viewing *Romper Stomper*, in which the actor played the cold-hearted skinhead Hando. SID 6.7 was a computerized version of Hando—relentless, powerful, ruthless, and totally without redeeming social qualities. Leonard scheduled a meeting with Russell and, after talking to him, realized that they shared a common vision of SID 6.7.

Leonard ran into problems, however, when he submitted Russell's name to the studio, where executives expressed concern over Russell's low name recognition. They understood that he was well known in Australia, but they were investing millions in the film and wanted the closest thing they could get to a sure bet.

For seven months, Leonard argued his case with the studio. Finally, they allowed him to do a screen test with Russell and Washington. One of the shots involved Russell responding to a line delivered by Washington off-camera. There was actually a wire cage between the two men. The first time they did the scene, Russell played it pretty low-key, delivering the lines in a direct manner. The second time, he pumped up his delivery so that the lines would have a little juice in them.

Leonard shouted "action," and Russell reached down deep inside of himself and grabbed a dark, rumbling scream that he directed off-camera at Washington, the emotions cascading out of him like a bellicose Niagara Falls. Unfortunately, attached to the emotionalism of the scream was a big, fat glob of spit that navigated through the wire mesh and landed smack dab on Washington's mouth.

"Ninety-nine percent of actors would have just been like out of there, you know?" Russell related to television talk show host Conan O'Brien. "He just stayed there, because he knows it's like my screen test, the camera is on me. So he's like right there, does the line—absolutely cool. The director says 'cut' and he goes 'ahhhhhhhhhh' [Russell rubbed his mouth frantically with both hands]. And then he looks at me very seriously and says, 'You know, I love the taste of warm saliva in the morning.'"

Conan laughed and said, "And you knew then that you two had connected."

"Absolutely," said Russell. "That was there. We bonded."

Despite spitting on Denzel Washington, Russell got the part. It was unlike any other movie he had ever made because of the technical requirements. Much of his acting had to be done in front of a blue screen, a method that allows filmmakers to add computer-generated scenery and people at a later date. To be effective in that situation, an actor has to possess a vivid imagination and a fearless sense of self-confidence.

Months later, when Russell saw the finished product, he was amazed at the way the scenes had come alive, thanks to the magic of computers. The imaginary piano he had jumped on top of had become a real piano. The imaginary rose he had plucked from the air was now a real rose.

One night, after a day's shooting, Washington knocked on the door of Russell's trailer and handed him a big cigar and a bottle of cognac. They were sitting around talking about nothing in particular when Washington confessed that the character he really wanted to play was SID 6.7, primarily because Russell had made it look like so much fun. A role switch was not in the cards—for one thing, studio executives would have had a stroke—but that wasn't the real reason for the visit. It was simply Washington's way of welcoming Russell to the boys' club.

What Russell liked most about SID 6.7 was its psychological composition. The robot was programmed with the identities of nearly two hundred different well-known killers and deviant personalities, everyone from serial killer Ted Bundy to Charles Manson to Adolf Hitler.

To Leonard, Russell *was* SID 6.7. He told reporters that he considered the actor to be a new version of James Cagney, someone with a menacing level of intensity. Not only did he not have problems directing him, he considered working with Russell the best part of making the film.

Virtuosity begins with Denzel Washington's character, Lieutenant Parker Barnes, and another police officer searching for a suspected killer. They find him in a Japanese restaurant and open fire, even though there are diners in the restaurant.

The killer is SID 6.7, the computer villain played by Russell Crowe. There's no need to worry about the diners, though, because the entire scene is only a virtual-reality training exercise for police officers.

Later, inside the system, SID murders a fellow prisoner. "It was a real rush," the robot says, when confronted by its handler.

"O my God!" replies the handler.

"Which god would that be—the one who created you or the one who created me?" responds SID. "You see, in your world, the Lord giveth and the Lord taketh away, but in my world, the one who gave me life doesn't have any balls."

SID is clearly a nasty creature who has problems with authority figures.

Barnes was involved with the training film because he is serving a long sentence for killing a terrorist who murdered Barnes's wife and daughter. Known for his skills as an investigator, he was assigned to the training exercise for the purpose of going up against SID, the ultimate killing machine.

When SID escapes from the computer system and morphs into a human body, officials at the training center decide that Barnes is the only person who has a chance of stopping it. They promised him a pardon if he brings back SID. A psychologist, Dr. Madison Carter, played by Kelly Lynch, is sent with him, much to his displeasure.

As SID goes on a rampage, it assumes the separate identities of its many personalities. It severs its first victim's head and leaves "Death to Pigs" written on the wall, Charles Manson–style. It then terrorizes a disco, killing both humans and androids. Barnes catches up with SID at the disco and empties his gun into it, but it escapes in a police car.

From the disco, SID goes to an arena, where prizefights are taking place. When Barnes arrives, it again escapes and makes its way toward the subway. There it hides behind a female passenger and Barnes shoots her, apparently by mistake. Because of his error, Barnes is captured and ordered back to the prison.

By then, Barnes figures out that SID is rotating personalities. It has become the man who killed his wife and daughter, the better to taunt him. Realizing that, Barnes becomes concerned for the safety of his partner's young daughter. Rightfully so, as it turns out, because SID takes the girl hostage and challenges Barnes to come after him. The final slugfest occurs on a catwalk atop a high-rise building.

When *Virtuosity* was released in April 1996, the reviews were mixed, as is customary for big-budget Hollywood movies. Kevin Thomas, writing in the *Los Angeles Times*, praised the special effects but was taken aback by the violence. Even so, he found good things to say about Russell's performance: "Crowe's boyish looks set off SID's maniacal glee effectively in a portrayal radically different from the actor's recent role as a diffident gay in the Australian film, *The Sum of Us.* [This film] doesn't always compute, but like last summer's *Speed*, it is far more fully realized cinematically than many less commercial, more serious pictures."

The *Boston Globe's* Jay Carr found fault with Leonard's direction, but Russell's acting impressed him. "[The film] cries out for a clever director able to lean on its piquant subtext of violence…But it largely wastes the wit and mischief in Australian actor Russell Crowe's performance as the killer who escapes from the box and starts doing horrible things to people, but only gets a kick out if it if he has an audience to outrage."

Chicago Sun-Times critic Roger Ebert gave the film a three-star rating but found fault with the plot. "*Virtuosity* is an example of a struggle that goes on in Hollywood between formula and invention. The movie is filled with bright ideas and fresh thinking, but the underlying story is as old as the hills."

Russell returned to his Australian ranch shortly after making the film. Several months before its release, he gave an interview to Ruth Hessey of the *Sydney Morning Herald* in which he shared his ideas about the differences between American and Australian films.

Directors like Brett Leonard, he explained, are interested in the purely technical aspects of filmmaking, "and that's totally different to how we work here. In Australia, we tell stories." Russell said Australians should be proud of their home-grown films because they are so original. "You get an Australian script and it's a one-of," he said, demonstrating both pride in his adopted country and ambivalence toward the United States. "It's not copying any other movies.…If I ever achieve A-list status in America, it will be a byproduct, not because I care whether I ever make a film there again."

When French director Clare Peploe was working on the script for *Rough Magic*, a black comedy based on James Hadley Chase's novel *Miss Shumway Waves a Wand*, she found herself literally falling out of her chair with laughter.

Ordinarily that's a good thing. But in this instance, she decided the film version would be more effective with a little less humor and more depth of feeling. "When I was writing it, I changed it quite a lot—the tone," she told the *Daily Trojan*. "I was visiting Guatemala at the time....The Mexican magic [of the film] is actually experienced through Guatemala and became something deeper, more heartfelt, and less and less of something absurd. In the book it's all absurd."

Set in Mexico in 1949, the plot was complicated because it involved both a traditional story—the beautiful fiancée who flees America to escape both her impending marriage and a possible crime—and the hocus-pocus drama of black magic. Apparently, it was so complicated that it required the services of two additional screenwriters, Robert Mundi and William Brookfield, to get the script to pass muster for the studio.

At that point in her career, Peploe had had three of her screenplays produced, including the heralded *Zabriskie Point*, but she had only two credits as a director—the feature film *High Season* and a British television series, *Chillers*. Since she was a relative unknown in the United States, she had to cast well to get the $8 million budget she requested from the studio to make the film.

For the female lead, she needed someone with high name recognition but low salary expectations. Bridget Fonda, the granddaughter of movie legend Henry Fonda, daughter of Peter Fonda, and niece of Jane Fonda, had high name recognition with both the public and the film industry. She had come off a string of recent box-office duds, but her success in 1992 and 1993 with *Single White Female* and *Singles* more than made up for the stinkers that followed.

Fonda was eager to do the movie—what some would call an idiosyncratic flight of fancy—but that was nothing new for her: It was her habit to alternate roles, going from big-budget studio films to half-starved independents and back again.

With Fonda in the fold, Peploe's task was to find a male lead with similar name recognition. That proved to be more difficult than she had imagined. It is an odd little film, and A-list actors are usually reluctant to attach themselves to projects that won't have mass appeal. Plus, there was the matter of money: the director simply didn't have a checkbook large enough to attract an A-list actor.

It was at that point, while the film seemed to be adrift, that Fonda made a suggestion to Peploe: Why not talk to an up-and-coming Australian actor named Russell Crowe? The director reviewed his work and agreed with Fonda that he would be perfect for the role. He was not a household name, but the fact that he had costarred in *The Quick and the Dead* with Sharon Stone and Gene Hackman gave her selling points with which to convince the producers.

Russell was eager to work with Fonda, who that year had been selected by *Empire* magazine as one of the one hundred sexiest stars in film. And although he knew little about Peploe's work, he was enthusiastic about working with another female director. Women seemed to listen to his ideas with more rapt attention than men did, and he found them easier to move to his way of thinking.

Asked about the role by *W* magazine, he said, "On page it was lovely. I've done romantic leads at home. I mean, do I want to have the lead role in movies? Yeah!

So I like to keep the roles diverse. Repetition gets really bad for your head."

Once the cast was in place—veteran character actor Jim Broadbent was added to play Doc Ansell, and Kenneth Mars was chosen to play the magician—Peploe thought her problems were over. Actually, they were just beginning.

The film was scheduled to be shot in Guatemala, where arrangements were made for free hotels and other considerations, but political upheaval stifled those plans, and the shoot moved to Mexico, where new arrangements had to be hurriedly made. Once that was accomplished, the director was informed that she would be arriving during the rainy season, yet another setback that could eat into the budget.

What had begun with a hearty laugh for the director in the quiet privacy of her home had been transformed along the way into a nightmarish roller-coaster ride through the back roads of Mexico with a cast that was not entirely sure where the film was headed.

Rough Magic begins with Bridget Fonda's character, Myra, following a rabbit into an elevator, where she proceeds to pull live rabbits from the pockets of three men. She is wearing the costume of a magician's assistant. It's all a publicity ploy, of course, but it does set the tone for the story that follows.

Myra is thinking about leaving the magician to marry an aspiring politician named Cliff Wyatt. This wealthy Howard Hughes type is obviously not the right match for Myra, who is much too involved in the relationship to see its flaws. The needed clarity comes to her following a backstage altercation in which Cliff mistakenly shoots the magician, apparently killing him. Myra takes a photo of the shooting as it occurs, thinking it is a joke. When it becomes clear to her that it was not a joke, she flees the country, heading south to Mexico.

Meanwhile, Cliff loads the body into the trunk of his car so that he can dump it in the countryside, away from the city, but when he opens the trunk, the body has disappeared, a clear indication that there was more to the magician's death than met the eye. Once Cliff realizes that Myra, the only witness to the murder, has gone to Mexico, he solicits the help of a newspaper editor who arranges for his stringer in Mexico, Russell's character Alec Ross, to track her down.

When Alec locates Myra, they fall in love and decide to find a new life together, a decision that is complicated by their new association with Doc Ansell, a wily old character who wants them to help him get a secret elixir from a Mayan shaman. Doc Ansell would do it himself, but the shaman wants to turn him into a toad or worse because of his previous incursions into her secret world. Going after the elixir, he figures, is a job best left to novices.

Armed with little more than Doc Ansell's dream, Myra and Alec get a car and head south into rural Mexico in search of the magic elixir. Along the way they stop for gas and have an altercation with the gas station attendant, who insults Myra and tries to goad Alec into a fight (he refuses). Myra strikes a match and blows beer into the attendant's face, igniting the fumes with the match. As the attendant fights the blaze, they drive away without paying for the gas.

Later, Alec says, "For a sweet looking girl, you play pretty rough."

"I play smooth, too," she answers. "Depends on whose fingers are working the keys."

Alec and Myra link up with Doc Ansell and travel to the point where they enter Mayan territory, but Myra convinces them that she should go the rest of the way alone. When she meets the shaman, she drinks a potion that is offered to her and discovers that it has empowered her with her real magic. Meanwhile, as Myra is exploring her new world, Cliff flies to Mexico to kill her and get the incriminating photo.

When Myra does not return, Alex and Doc Ansell go after her. Finding her unconscious in a deserted camp, they revive her and take her to safety. On the way back to the city, the gas station attendant catches up with them and starts a fight with Alec. Angered, Myra calls the attendant a big fat sausage and watches in amazement as he turns into a sausage. The shaman was right—she can now perform magic.

When Cliff locates Myra and confronts her, she tells him to drop dead, thinking that her magic would work the same way it had with the sausage, but her magic mistakenly topples Alec, who was standing directly behind Cliff. Thinking that she has killed Alec, she leaves with Cliff to face whatever fate awaits her.

Later, while Doc Ansell examines Alec's body, a giant tarantula creeps out of Alec's mouth and scampers away, prompting Alec to come back to life. With that, Alec and Doc Ansell go in search of Myra. Along the way, they discover that the magician did not die after all, which means that Cliff is not guilty of murder and Myra has no reason to run, except for the fact that she does not want to spend the rest of her life with Cliff.

All in all, *Rough Magic* was a very difficult film to bring to life. Magic works best in the minds of those perceiving the sleight of hand, which is why translating the magic that occurs with the written word to a movie screen can be a formidable task for any director. Only Peploe knows if the finished product represents what she envisioned when she started out, but clearly studio executives had problems with it, for it was released in nearly every country in the world before it was made available to American audiences.

The film seemed to be jinxed. It was owned by Rysher Entertainment, which arranged for Savoy to release it, but that deal fell through when the company filed for bankruptcy. Rysher then gave the film to Orion for distribution, only it, too, went bankrupt. Next up was Goldwyn, which also filed for bankruptcy before the film could be distributed. It probably never would have been released if not for director Martin Scorsese, who saw the movie and successfully pushed for distribution in the United States by Columbia Tri-Star. It took nearly two years for the film to make it into American theaters.

When it was released in May 1997, critics were most unkind. Under the headline "'Magic' Is Rough on the Audience," *San Francisco Examiner* critic Barbara Shulgasser panned everyone associated with the film except for Russell Crowe, and she gave him only passing mention, which was probably fine with him. "Just as Fonda is technically beautiful, but generally a lifeless actress," she wrote, "Peploe is technically proficient but generally misses every opportunity for believable human interaction and the humor that often results."

Chicago Sun Times critic Roger Ebert thought the movie's greatest failure was in trying to blend two different genres—film noir and magic realism. "Nothing [Peploe] has done before is anything like *Rough Magic*, which seems to be a visitor from a parallel timeline: If film noir had developed in South America instead of California, maybe we would have seen more films like this." He found most of the actors engaging but quirky, and he thought Russell was "steady" in what he called the "Mitchum role," a reference to Robert Mitchum, the actor who set a new standard for tough-guy stoicism in the 1950s and 1960s.

John Anderson, writing for the *Los Angeles Times*, said the film was like a car constructed out of scavenged parts that "sputters, coughs, wheezes, lurches, spins out of control and runs smack into the springtime of our discontent." He found Russell to be "talented but consistently misused."

FIVE

L.A. Confidential Spawns
The Insider

Russell's first hint that that there was going to be a film titled *L.A. Confidential* came when he received the script from his agent George Freeman, along with a note that read simply, "What do you think of this?"

Russell read the script, which was based on James Ellroy's novel of the same name, and he was impressed. But because it was such a great script, he figured he didn't have a chance in hell of being a part of it. No one had a higher opinion of Russell's acting abilities than Russell himself, but he knew he was still at the bottom of the Hollywood pecking order as far as the top roles were concerned.

Even so, he gave director Curtis Hanson a call to see what he had in mind (it was Hanson who'd sent the script to his agent for consideration, Russell reasoned, so he must have an angle on *something*). Russell had never read the book, but he knew that James Ellroy had written *The Black Dahlia*, and that seemed a good omen for the project.

Hanson told him that he'd seen him in *Romper Stomper* and thought he would be perfect for the part of Officer Wendell "Bud" White in *L.A. Confidential*. The movie was about three cops in the Los Angeles Police Department who combine forces to search for truth in radically different ways in an atmosphere of corruption and violence.

The first cop, Ed Exley, was the son of a decorated police officer who wanted what his father had, so much so that he would do almost anything to get ahead. The second cop, Jack Vincennes, was not ambitious within the police department, but he desperately wanted fame and fortune and, like Exley, was willing to do whatever it took. The third cop, Bud White, was a simmering volcano who was ever ready to break the rules to obtain his version of justice; quick to throw a punch, he had a blind obsession for punishing men who abused women, which sometimes clouded his judgment.

Hanson told Russell that Bud White possessed the same inner rage that propelled his character Hando in *Romper Stomper*, the chief differences being that White was older and worked within the system to channel his violent impulses. That sounded great to Russell, who readily agreed to do the film. He asked who else was in it. "Just you," Hanson replied, indicating that he had just begun the casting process.

Hanson had directed seven previous feature films, including *Bad Influence, Losin' It* and *Karate Kids USA*, but he had never directed a film as ambitious as *L.A. Confidential*. He was not an A-list director, so he did not have easy access to A-list actors. What he hoped to do was cast B-plus actors with high name recognition—

stars who had reputations as A-list supporting actors—and by means of the excellent script he cowrote, catapult the project to some higher level.

With Russell signed on to play Bud White, Hanson finished casting the film. For the role of Jack Vincennes, he chose Kevin Spacey, a cerebral and sometimes enigmatic actor who has a reputation for injecting his characters with a dark sense of humor and a thoughtful approach to life. Those qualities were perfect for Vincennes, who was essentially a thinking man's cop.

Spacey was also a good counterpoint choice to rub against the visceral texture of Russell's character. Actually, despite the obvious differences between the two men, they had a great deal in common. Like Russell, Spacey was a self-made entertainer who began shaping his future career while still an adolescent. He cut class to attend film festivals, and he worked up a comedy-club act based on impersonations of celebrities such as Jimmy Stewart and Johnny Carson.

After graduation from high school, he attended a community college for a short time but then enrolled in the drama program at Juilliard. He left before completing the requirements for a diploma and auditioned for the New York Shakespeare Festival, where he landed a role as a messenger in the stage production of *Henry VI*. For the next five years, he worked on and off Broadway, with roles in Eugene O'Neill's *Long Day's Journey into Night* and in Henrik Ibsen's *Ghosts*. By the time he met with Hanson to discuss *L.A. Confidential*, he had appeared in a long string of successful movies, including *Consenting Adults, Swimming with Sharks,* and *A Time to Kill*.

To play the part of the third cop, Ed Exley, Hanson turned to Guy Pearce, another newcomer from Russell's backyard. Although born in England, Pearce moved to Australia with his family at the age of three. He became interested in acting at a very young age and appeared in amateur theater productions while in his teens.

Pearce's first professional break came in the late 1980s, when he appeared in the popular Australian daytime drama *Neighbors*. He was in several television series and in six feature films, including *Hunting, Dating the Enemy,* and *The Adventures of Priscilla, Queen of the Desert*, before he came to Hanson's attention. He seemed perfect for the role of Ed Exley, primarily because he can transform himself into the type of goody-goody overachiever that has haunted high schools since the advent of public education. Everyone knows an Ed Exley, and that is the type of stereotype that Hanson counted on to make the character convincing.

For the female lead, Hanson needed someone who was not only Hollywood glamorous but capable of projecting an aura of vulnerability, someone who could capture that "love goddess thing of past decades." Kim Basinger was the obvious choice to play Lynn Bracken, a high-class hooker with a heart of platinum. Even at the age of forty-four, she still had the type of good looks that could stop traffic.

Basinger began her movie career in 1982 with *Mother Lode*, but prior to that she had enjoyed nearly a decade of success as a highly paid model. That first movie role attracted little attention, but she followed it up with a role as a "Bond girl" in *Never Say Never Again* and quickly became a household name, especially after *Playboy* magazine did a splashy nude pictorial on her in 1983.

Her future as an actress was assured three years later with her sizzling role as Elizabeth in *9½ Weeks* and then as photojournalist Vicki Vale in the box-office smash *Batman*. By the time Hanson sent her a script for *L.A. Confidential*, she had appeared in nineteen movies, none of which really demonstrated her acting ability.

It was good timing for all involved. Distracted by her 1993 marriage to actor Alec Baldwin and the birth of their daughter, Ireland Eliesse, in 1995—and by a bad investment that left her near bankruptcy—Basinger had not made a movie in three years. Could she play a Hollywood hooker down on her luck and in need of a good man? There was no doubt in Hanson's mind.

"Once you're away from the screen, you get insecure and wonder if you can go back and click in—will you know how to do it?" she told the *Boston Globe*. "[Hanson] just had such a vote of confidence in me, he just said, 'You're doing it, and that's that.' He just saw me as her. That's a great director, someone who believes in who they cast."

Hanson rounded out the major characters in the film with a supporting actor who was money in the bank as far as supporting actors are concerned. Danny DeVito, best known to television audiences as Louie De Palma on *Taxi*, had made more than sixty films at that point, including classics such as *One Flew over the Cuckoo's Nest* and *Ruthless People*. He could always be counted on to give a stellar performance and, perhaps more importantly, to keep moviegoers in their seats. Hanson thought he would be perfect as Sid Hudgens, the unprincipled editor of a Hollywood scandal sheet.

"You look through that cast, there isn't a single person in that cast all the way down to the second bloke from the left that isn't magnificent in what they do," Russell told interviewer Molly Meldrum. "Curtis Hanson has a certain process, but he's a very deep thinker, so you'll always get answers to your questions."

That characteristic was important to Russell because he had just gone through a series of directors who he felt were making it up as they went along. He is the type of actor who likes to have scenes explained to him, and when a director fails to do that or seems rudderless while filming a scene, he reacts with anger. Russell likes to discuss scenes and offer ideas of his own, but if a director ever seems baffled and asks those around him what *they* think should happen next, it brings out the crazy inside him.

"One of the greatest things about Curtis Hanson as a filmmaker is that he just operates on a level of intelligence and sensitivity that the next man (or woman) doesn't possibly possess, or would care to possess," he told the *Austin Chronicle*. "Curtis was turned on to this whole idea by reading [James Ellroy's book], so it was still very important to Curtis that he preserve Ellroy's voice within the movie."

The more Russell looked into Ellroy's work—he read *L.A. Confidential*, *White Jazz*, and a book of short stories titled *Hollywood Nocturnes*—the more fascinated he became by the author, who showed up on the set during filming. Russell and Ellroy became friends, and during the downtimes on the set, the writer told him about a new book he was writing titled *My Dark Places*.

Russell found him to be a "goldmine" of information. It was the first time Russell had ever had the author of a story make himself or herself available to him. So that he would understand his character better, he asked Ellroy countless questions about what made Bud White tick. He wanted to know things that were not in the script or the book. He wanted to know what White would do in certain situations. He wanted to know more about Bud White's likes and dislikes than anyone else on the set.

L.A. Confidential begins with Sid Hudgens, a tabloid reporter for *Hush-Hush* magazine, typing out a salacious story. He's Hollywood's most successful merchant of sleaze reporting and he will do anything—or pay anything within his budget—to get what he needs. Not surprisingly, his most reliable sources are cops who aren't averse to making a little money on the side.

Bud White is not so much interested in making pocket money as he is in dispensing his own form of justice, usually on the spot. When he looks into a window and sees a man abusing his wife, he knocks on the door, drags the man out onto the front lawn, and gives him a good beating. Then he handcuffs him and issues a warning. If he ever touches his wife again, he warns, "I'll have you violated as a kiddy-raper beef. You know what they do to kiddy rapers in Quentin?"

Bud first meets Lynn Bracken in a liquor store, where she is stocking up on booze for her boss, who is waiting outside in a chauffeur-driven limousine. When he leaves the store, he looks into the limousine and sees a woman with what looks like a broken nose. Angered by what he thinks is abuse, he roughs up the limo driver. The situation is about to get out of control when Lynn approaches the car and tells Bud that the situation is not what it seems. He accepts that explanation without knowing the whole truth, and he allows them to drive away.

Back at the station, a group of Hispanic prisoners are brought in to be booked for beating up two cops. Outraged, the other cops in the police station, including Bud, start beating the prisoners. As a result, Bud is suspended from duty and ordered to turn in his gun and badge. Detective Lieutenant Ed Exley witnesses the beatings and tells the police commissioner that Bud and his partner Dick Stensland should be indicted. That doesn't happen, though, and Bud is soon reinstated by the captain, who promptly gives him an assignment that he thinks Bud "was born for."

Not so lucky is Stensland, who is suspended. That night, after turning in his gun and badge, he and several other people are killed gangland-style in a restaurant. Bud associates his partner's killing with the girl in the limousine, and he goes looking for Lynn in the hope of getting information that will lead him to the killers.

Meanwhile, Exley and Sergeant Jack Vincennes bring in three African-Americans and charge them with killing Stensland and the others in the restaurant. Vincennes is an arrogant, emotionally detached cop who sells his services to *Hush-Hush* on a regular basis. He's not beyond setting up celebrities for embarrassing busts so that the magazine can get a front-page story and he can pocket an extra fifty bucks.

Lynn is a hooker who works for a service that provides girls who look like movie stars. If the girls need a little help with their looks, the service pays for the needed plastic surgery so that they can earn top dollar.

Bud ends up falling in love with Lynn. They have an affair, during which he confesses to her his reason for hating wife beaters: his father tied him to a radiator and beat his mother to death with a tire iron while he watched. He also divulges that he thinks Exley and Vincennes arrested the wrong men in the restaurant massacre.

"That prick Exley shot the wrong guys…there's something wrong with the Night Owl [the name of the restaurant]. I just can't prove it, that's all. I'm not smart enough. I'm just the guy they bring in to scare the other guys shitless."

As the story behind the restaurant massacre unravels, it draws White, Exley, and Vincennes into an unlikely alliance to follow a conspiracy that leads them to the police captain and the district attorney. After Vincennes is killed, White and Exley work together to solve the mystery. The story ends on a note of cautious optimism, the kind that a forest ranger surrounded by a raging fire might experience upon discovering a canteen of water that he forgot he had packed.

In September 1996, three weeks after wrapping *L.A. Confidential,* Russell returned to Australia to work on a film titled *Heaven's Burning,* the brainchild of director Craig Lahiff and screenwriter Louis Nowra.

Lahiff and Nowra, who shared a love of the film noir genre and a respect for directors such as Don Siegel and John Frankenheimer, had talked about doing a project together for quite some time. One day Lahiff, who lives in South Australia, flew to Nowra's hometown of Sydney to meet with the screenwriter. Once they started talking, they realized they also shared a liking for black comedy.

"Louis showed me about three different one-page ideas, and the one that appealed most was "You Don't Know What Love Is," which was inspired by a real-life incident that occurred in Sydney a few years earlier," recalls Lahiff. "Sydney is a very popular location for Japanese honeymooners, and in one particular case the girl faked her own kidnapping to escape an unhappy marriage which had been arranged by her parents. Her disappearance sparked a nationwide hunt and a scandal in Japan that was in the headlines. Federal police eventually found her hiding in a seedy downtown motel."

It was that incident, plus the sub-theme of Australian racism, that provided the springboard for the plot of *Heaven's Burning.* "What appealed to me was a central character, a Japanese honeymooner—an outsider in a foreign country who speaks very little English and who undergoes a transformation from a meek and subservient girl into an assertive woman taking charge of her own fate," says Lahiff. "Both Louis and I wanted the film to be operatic, a roller coaster ride through different genres with action and black humor. Of course, black humor seemed the ideal way to treat the sub-theme of racism, although many Australians would not like to think of themselves as racist."

Using that real-life incident as a general outline, Nowra wrote a thriller about a Japanese woman named Midori who fakes her own kidnapping to escape from her new husband, Yukio. While in hiding, she becomes involved in a botched bank robbery and is taken hostage by Afghan mobsters. Her unlikely rescuer is an Australian flunky named Colin, who was hired by the Afghans to drive the get-away car.

Although the script was written in a thriller format, with lots of violent action, it was laced with large doses of black humor meant to make fun of everything taking place in the film, including the thrills and action.

With the script in hand, Lahiff secured financing—about $2.3 million (U.S.)—and began casting the film. For the role of Midori, he chose a Japanese actress, Youki Kudoh, who had received rave reviews for her portrayal of an Elvis-worshipping tourist in Jim Jarmusch's *Mystery Train*.

The actress accepted the role, despite her mother's frantic warning that Australian directors had a habit of killing actors, a fear apparently generated by the death of martial arts hero Brandon Lee while filming a movie directed by Alex Proyas. She was dead certain that if her daughter went to Australia, she would return home in a body bag.

For the role of Colin, Lahiff approached Russell Crowe. "[He] was always first choice to play the male lead, " says Lahiff. "He liked the script, and we arranged to meet first in a small coastal resort town—Victor Harbour, fifty miles south of Adelaide, where his band was playing at the local pub—then later in Sydney, where he invited me to spend the day watching a one-day international cricket match at the Sydney Cricket Ground. I remember Russell was particularly concerned at avoiding the crowd, who let out a rousing Russell chant at the end of the match."

Russell had an ulterior motive for inviting Lahiff to hear his band. Every movie he had ever been in had a soundtrack. Why, he wondered, couldn't his band, Thirty Odd Foot of Grunts, be the vehicle for some of that music? It became standard procedure for Russell, upon agreeing to be in a movie, to ask if the band could do a song or two for the soundtrack. Lahiff spent two hours listening to the band in a cramped hotel pub before deciding that it wasn't his kind of music and didn't have a place in the film.

Shortly after Russell committed to doing the film, he was offered the Bud White role in *L.A. Confidential*. Since he couldn't do two films at once, Lahiff agreed to postpone production on *Heaven's Burning* for several months so that Russell could do the Hollywood movie.

When Russell arrived in Adelaide to start work on Lahiff's film, he seemed like a different person. He was still in a Bud White mode, which is to say that he was intense, confrontational, and unable to disassociate himself from being the tough cop. He had been given nine weeks to get himself into character for *L.A. Confidential*, but because they already were running late on *Heaven's Burning*, the most that Lahiff could allocate for preproduction was five days.

Russell got along well with the crew, and he was always on time, but he seemed to be surrounded by a cloud of negative energy. It was as if someone had asked Bud White to play a role in the *Sound of Music*. Russell couldn't seem to get the tough Los Angeles cop out of his system.

"*Heaven's Burning* was a time for Russell when he had just made a big Hollywood picture, and I feel he didn't want to be doing a low-budget Australian movie," says Lahiff. [He] is extremely intense when he's working. He's always trying to give more than one hundred percent in his performance. It was a hard role to play, as his character of Colin was written as being largely passive, while the character of Midori was really the lead and the one who undergoes the transformation in the film's journey. I think Russell feels more at home playing angst-ridden roles as he does so well in *L.A. Confidential, The Insider*, and *Gladiator*."

Most of the film was shot near Adelaide, in and around small towns such as Port Wakefield, Balaklava, Murray Bridge, and Rapid Bay. That meant that the actors and crew had to commute from Adelaide to the countryside, about an hour's drive. Because of time constraints, it was a difficult shoot, with nearly a third of the day's ten-hour schedule devoted simply to getting from one place to another.

Perhaps because of the time limitations, Russell was not his customary playful self off the set. He got along well with the other actors and the crew while they were working, but once the last scene for the day was completed, he avoided contact, especially with Youki, who tried to make friends with him. According to Lahiff, Russell went out of his way to make it unpleasant for Youki, who Lahiff felt was trying very hard to get along with him.

"Youki found it difficult trying to communicate with Russell and, halfway through the shoot, wanted to go back to Japan," Lahiff recalls. "This was her first English language film, and it was a big strain struggling to master English and at the same time act the character of Midori, whom she found great empathy for."

The biggest concern for both Youki and Russell was the love scene they were required to do together. Says Lahiff, "In directing the love scene, I felt it was important that we saw Midori taking the initiative. This is part of her journey and transformation in trying to change her fate."

Russell had played a somewhat submissive character as a gay man in *The Sum of Us*, but he had never assumed that role with a woman, at least not as an actor. "Russell was keen to know how I intended to shoot it and invited me around one night to his apartment, where he cooked dinner for me—lobsters, if I remember correctly—and I went through my storyboards," says Lahiff.

What had concerned Russell about the scene was that Midori would be on top during the lovemaking and would undress him, instead of him undressing her. He would take his clothes off and she would remain clothed. In other words, for the purpose of the scene, he would be the girl and she would be the guy, a thematic reversal that was necessary to demonstrate her awakening as a free woman.

When the time came to film the scene, it took place without a hitch. "While both Russell and Youki weren't getting on, it in no way affected the playing of these scenes," says Lahiff. "One of my favorite scenes in the film is the rather poetic scene after the lovemaking, where we see a sensitive and gentle side to Russell, which is rarely seen in his other films. Another scene that I am particularly fond of, for the same reasons, is the scene where Colin meets his father, Cam, played wonderfully by Ray Barrett, who is moved wistfully by seeing his son again after such a long time."

Heaven's Burning begins with Midori entering a large Australian hotel with her new husband, Yukio. Later, at dinner, they talk about combing their savings to buy an apartment. Midori seems unusually quiet, uninterested in her situation. When he leaves with a business associate, she takes the elevator to their room. Slowly, it becomes apparent that they are there on their honeymoon.

While Yukio is occupied with business, Midori mysteriously disappears from the hotel, but not before calling the desk clerk to say that she is being kidnapped. Yukio is crushed by the disappearance of his wife. As the mystery deepens, the police trace her to a motel, from which she called a man in Japan. The police are honest with Yukio: the man she called is someone with whom she has had a relationship. They tell Yukio they planned to run away together, but he got cold feet at the last minute.

Colin makes his first appearance with a group of Afghan gangsters, who hire him to drive their getaway car during a bank robbery. As fate would have it, Midori is in the bank to withdraw money when the robbers arrive. After the robbery is botched, she is grabbed as a hostage and carried outside, where Colin is waiting in the getaway car. They elude police and go to a secluded location, where the Afghans decide to kill Midori so that she cannot testify against them.

Colin intervenes and shoots both robbers, killing one and wounding the other. He drives off with Midori and tries to get rid of her, but she follows him until he agrees to take her with him. Short of money, they rob a bank, thus escalating the story into a Bonnie and Clyde–type adventure.

Meanwhile, police examine photos from the bank robbery and identity Midori. They also find a letter to her husband that she lost in the confusion. It acknowledges what the police have already discovered and asks for her husband's forgiveness. Later, police return with another incriminating photo, one that indicates that she has partnered up with Colin. Police tell Yukio that it looks like they are working as a team.

Angered by Midori's apparent infidelities, Yukio shaves his head and decides to look for her himself, intending to kill her for shaming him with another man. For that, he must take a number: the Afghans, enraged by the way Colin turned on them, want to kill her traveling companion.

Colin and Midori—pursued by the police, Yukio, and the Afghans—leave the city and head out into the countryside, where they run into prejudice outside a truck stop. Colin is beaten by a man who hurls insults at him for being with a woman of another race.

On the road they almost run down an accordion-playing man in a motor-driven wheelchair. Feeling guilty for roughing up a cripple, they give him a lift to the next town. That night, while they are lying in separate beds in a motel, Midori says, "I really like this—I feel like I'm alive."

"Good," Colin answers.

"I like you very much. Do you like me?"

"Yes, I do."

The next morning, while Midori is out shopping, the Afghans catch up with them. Finding Colin alone in the motel, they torture him by nailing his hand to a desktop. Says one of the gangsters, "An eye for an eye and a hand for a hand." They make it clear that they are going to kill him, but before they can, Colin gets loose and shoots both of them.

Knowing the police are probably not far behind, the couple seeks refuge at Colin's father's farm, where the only love scene in the film takes place. The next morning, they set out for the coast. Shortly after they leave, Yukio shows up at the farm and shoots Colin's father when he refuses to divulge where they have gone.

Just as Bonnie and Clyde had a violent demise, so do Midori and Colin, but not before dealing with Yukio, who comes out a loser in his final showdown with Midori.

Heaven's Burning is an unusual film in many respects. It has all the markings of a conventional thriller, but at its core it is a satire that is saturated with varying levels of black comedy, some of which deal with the prickly issue of racism directed against Asians.

The latter consideration, according to Lahiff, is why the film did not do well at the Australian box office. *"Heaven's Burning* is not a Hollywood-style film," explains Lahiff. "It's a film that was meant to provoke people in a left-of-center way. People either love it or hate it, so I guess I've achieved that!"

In some ways, Lahiff is not a typical filmmaker. With a bachelor's degree in physics from Adelaide University, he worked for five years as a project manager in the computer industry before quitting his job to enroll in Flinders University to study film. After earning his master's, he worked extensively in the Australian film industry as both a director and producer of short films and documentaries.

Racism was a serious issue for him, which was why he injected it into *Heaven's Burning.* He took a second crack at the subject in 2002 with a film titled *Black and White.* Based on a true story, it dealt with a landmark murder trial that took place in 1958, in which a young lawyer defends an Aborigine on a murder charge and comes up against the prejudice and corruption ingrained within the Australian legal system.

Going into 1997, Russell was on a roll. He had two films in the can, *L.A. Confidential* and *Heaven's Burning*—and more scripts to choose from than he could keep track of. One of the things about Russell that baffled people was the way he chose his projects. After *The Quick and the Dead, Virtuosity,* and *L.A. Confidential,* Hollywood observers assumed that Russell would stick with big-budget films, but he dashed those assumptions by choosing a very low-budget ($1 million) film for his next project.

Breaking Up was easily the most unusual film he had ever made. Directed by Robert Greenwald, it had only two characters—Steve, a photographer who thinks in images, and Monica, a teacher who probably thinks too much. The entire film is built around angst-driven conversations between Steve and Monica as they struggle to define their relationship in terms of their separate needs and expectations.

Russell was asked to play Steve, of course. It was a challenging role in several aspects—for one, it is essentially a dialogue between two characters with no action to speak of. There were pages upon pages of lines for Russell to memorize, and he wasn't given long to do it. Because it was a low-budget film, there was no preproduction period for rehearsals and conversations with the director. The entire film took only twenty-eight days to shoot. That meant that Russell had to cram for it like a college-student, with lots of late-night sessions built around gallons of black coffee.

Just as people were scratching their heads over Russell's decision to be in the film, they were perplexed by Robert Greenwald's decision to direct it. Since 1990, he had built a career as a producer of serious television films, beginning with *Hiroshima: Out of the Ashes* and *Forgotten Prisoners: The Amnesty Files*. By the time he took on *Breaking Up*, he had produced seventeen projects, many of them winning prestigious awards.

As a director, his interests seemed to go in the opposite direction. Although he directed a fair share of serious dramas, including *The Burning Bed,* which starred Farrah Fawcett, he also directed fluffy television films such as *Katie: Portrait of a Centerfold* and *Flatbed Annie & Sweetiepie: Lady Truckers*. Prior to *Breaking Up*, he had only directed three previous feature-length films—the musical *Xanadu,* starring Olivia Newton-John, *Sweet Hearts Dance,* and a thriller titled *Hear No Evil.*

Whatever his reasons for taking on *Breaking Up*, he approached the project with enthusiasm. Although the subject matter was among the oldest in recorded history, he was convinced that he could add something new.

For the part of Monica, he chose Mexican-born actress Salma Hayek. It was a risky choice. She had appeared in seven movies prior to *Breaking Up*—most notably *Desperado*, for which she received rave reviews—but no one had yet viewed her as a leading-lady type. Thus far, her image was that of a dark-eyed siren, an actress who could project her sensuality from the screen in heart-stopping increments. It was felt that she was too inexperienced, perhaps even too "ethnic," for a leading role. Not since Dolores Del Rio had Hollywood producers and directors taken a Mexican actress seriously.

Of course, none of that mattered to Greenwald. It says something about his approach to directing that he would pair a Mexican with an Aussie to tell a story of modern romance in New York City.

"Day to day, just working on it, was pretty challenging to try and tell that type of a story, which is really uncomfortable subject matter for most people anyway," Russell told the *Austin Chronicle*. "Trying to stay true to the reality of those characters, you know, because they're both in their own ways sort of charmless people, copping out by taking a secondary option, right? They've met the person who is the passion of their life, but it's kind of too difficult."

Russell didn't feel his character was a very likable person—"I saw him as such a dick, you know?"—but he felt the audience would look past the character's imperfections and see that he's very much in love with a woman who has imperfections of her own.

Whatever Monica's faults, they did not attach themselves to Salma, at least not in Russell's eyes. He was very attentive to her, often presenting her with small gifts, especially if she had a bad go of it the previous day. "She's got to be one of the greatest performers I've worked with," Russell told *Detour* magazine. "She's fantastic. She's really, really cool in the movie. I think a lot of opportunities have passed by, maybe because some people can't see through race and color. She can really turn it on, man."

Breaking Up begins with Steve and Monica talking about their relationship, though not to each other. They are seated in chairs in different rooms, taking directly to the camera as if it were an interested bystander.

In a reference to their relationship, Steve says, "Sometimes you don't know you're in pain until it goes away." As a couple, they can neither live with each other nor live without each other. There seems to be only one solution: after being together for more than two years, they decide to break up.

"Wake up in the morning and the dream is over. So what?" says Steve. "I'm still here. You're still here. We're still here. OK? So maybe we should…maybe we should just not see each other anymore."

"That's what I said," says Monica.

With that, she moves out of his apartment. He's fine with that at first, then he goes nuts missing her. They make up, then break up again.

"I've been thinking," says Monica. "There used to be reasons for people to be together, to stay together—stability and security and even kids. I don't need you for those reasons. I can get all of those things on my own."

Monica ponders that dilemma, finally deciding that if there are no longer any real reasons for couples to stay together, there must be "unreal reasons" such as "fantastic things like happiness and good company and comfort and understanding and emotional support."

Steve's fear is that if the relationship doesn't last, he will have lost part of himself. "I've got to hang on to what I have besides this," he says. "Who I am away from this? 'Cause if this isn't going to last—and this is all I have and it doesn't last—who am I?"

Monica asks him what he's so afraid of.

"I'm afraid that I won't ever love anybody as much as I love you."

By the end of the movie, Steve and Monica discover what real-life couples discover the hard way—that *talking* about a relationship hardly ever makes a difference in the final outcome, for there are always other factors at work.

When the film was released, Russell went to Austin, Texas, for its premiere.

While there he did an interview with Marc Savlov of the *Austin Chronicle* in which he turned on the charm.

"In person, his earthy good humor belies the imposing, shotgun rage he exposes in so many of his film characters," observed Savlov. "You get the feeling, all things considered, he'd much prefer to be at home on his farm outside of Sydney instead of making the interview rounds. Still, he's gracious to a fault, and it's easy to see why so many people are convinced the actor is on the verge of cinematic superstardom."

Russell liked Austin, which probably had something to do with his pleasant demeanor during the interview. The city is a blend of rough edges and bold dreams, and the people who live there possess the same mix of Old West and big-city perspectives that is so familiar to Australians, who balance the sensibilities of the outback with those of a thriving metropolis. Russell was also impressed by Austin's music and recording scene. It was exactly the sort of place that he could see himself fitting into.

Critics didn't hate *Breaking Up*, but they didn't love it either. Writing in *Boxoffice*, Ian Hodder observed: "[This] is a good movie, but it doesn't have enough zingy lines or story innovations to rise above the level of prototypical romantic comedy. Steve and Monica can't live with or without each other, but moviegoers in search of chuckles and romantic insight can take or leave this cinematic coupling."

Atlanta Journal-Constitution critic Eleanor Ringel thought that the film, written by Pulitzer Prize–winning playwright Michael Cristofer, went too far in allowing the audience to experience the couple's emotional claustrophobia. "Cristofer is so rigorously honest about his characters that we're uncertain whether to root for them. An hour and a half is a log time to spend with people you're not sure you want to end up together."

Breaking Up did nothing to enhance Russell's career (it was only released to three theaters), but it did seem to result in Salma Hayek receiving more serious attention as an actress, even if the roles she was subsequently offered fell short of stretching her capabilities. Salma looked back on the movie as an important turning point in her career, and she had nothing but good things to say about Russell because of that.

"[Russell] was the first person that I felt respected me as an actress," she told *Premiere* magazine. "And afterward he would come up to me all the time at parties and say, 'What are you doing with your life? You are the best actress I've ever worked with. I've seen the shitty stuff you're doing and it makes me so angry!'"

Movies like *The Quick and the Dead* and *Virtuosity* gave Russell added clout at cocktail parties, even though neither film was a box-office success, but that did not mean he was in a position where he could count on getting every role he wanted. On the contrary, he sometimes lost roles that he very much wanted.

Harvey Weinstein, the influential head of Miramax Films, tried to talk Russell into signing a four-film deal, but Russell balked, mainly because he felt he would lose control of the characters he would be playing. To convince the actor that he would have the best scripts to choose from if he signed with Miramax, Weinstein sent him seven scripts that he considered the top of the line. To his surprise, Russell was very critical of all the scripts except one, prompting Weinstein to tell the actor that he was never going to go anywhere in the business with that attitude.

The script that Russell liked was for a comedy titled *Shakespeare in Love*. Directed by British-born filmmaker John Madden, it had Gwyneth Paltrow playing the female lead. Told by Russell that he thought the script was fantastic, Weinstein set up a meeting between the actor and Madden, perhaps against his better judgment.

The meeting was a disaster. "I met with this English bloke who was involved at the time—a great filmmaker, actually, but f– – him, too—and he said his instincts told him I wasn't right for the character," Russell explained to *Entertainment Weekly*. "I told him his instincts were f– –ing s– –. Obviously we didn't get on very well."

Before *Heaven's Burning* was released, it was selected for a showing at the Toronto International Film Festival in September 1997. That would have been good news if the festival had not also been chosen to launch *L.A. Confidential*. To Lahiff's disappointment, Russell did little to promote the Australian film and focused most of his efforts on *L.A. Confidential*.

"I feel Russell saw *L.A. Confidential* as his big break and wanted to nurture that film," says Lahiff. "When they were both selected for the [festival], Russell was very careful to promote *L.A. Confidential* at the expense of *Heaven's Burning*."

He did more than that: he actually spoke out against *Heaven's Burning*, telling reporters that it turned out to be less of a political satire and more of a thriller than he had anticipated when he read the script. Agreeing with him about the movie was *Toronto Sun* critic Bruce Kirkland, who thought the film had little satirical content. "All that said," he observed, "*Heaven's Burning* is still a hell of a B-movie romp thanks to the charismatic Crowe."

Author James Ellroy helped attract attention to *L.A. Confidential* by traveling with Russell and other cast members to the Toronto festival, where a press conference with the cast was arranged.

The first question went not to the actors or director but to Ellroy. The reporter wanted to know if the author had any ambitions to ever direct a film. When Ellroy answered that he had no interest, the reporter persisted with, "Come on, James, how do you know you don't want to direct a film until you've directed a film?" To Russell's delight, Ellroy shot back with, "Listen, pal, I've never fucked a porcupine, either!"

After the publicity tour ended, both Russell and Guy Pearce headed back to Australia. Pearce went to direct his first film and decided to stay in order to be closer to his family. Russell went back to unwind at his ranch and to enjoy the company of his family, but he had no intention of staying, for he now had Hollywood at his beck and call—or so it seemed.

Not long after arriving in Australia, Russell made a quick trip to New Zealand to visit family members, While in Auckland, he gave a press conference where he talked about *L.A. Confidential* and the cost of fame. The *New Zealand Listener* described Russell as having a "strong, dominating presence. The dynamic of fame, the relationship between star and acolytes, seems nakedly obvious and he is giddy and pumped up because of it."

Russell told his fellow New Zealanders that he didn't understand why people were offended by his ambition. "You've got to have ambition, regardless of what your job is," he said. "Shit, if the guy that's going to operate on me for heart surgery isn't ambitious to be the greatest surgeon, then get the f– – away from me!...The only problem is, in my job, ambition from a public's point of view is seen as this nasty, narcissistic pastime."

When Russell returned to Australia, the first thing he did was to get his band up and playing again. They wrote new songs, they rehearsed the old songs they already knew, and they put their heads together to figure out what to do next. For all his recent success as an actor, Russell was still a musician at heart.

One day, out of the blue, he received a call from Danny DeVito, who was in Australia promoting a film he had directed titled *Matilda*. "What do you want to do?" asked DeVito. "You want to hang out and stuff?"

At the time, Russell was in a studio rehearsing with his band, so he told the diminutive actor that he was tied up with the band, perhaps thinking that DeVito would understand that he was busy. No chance of that: DeVito invited himself to the rehearsal, according to a story Russell told Jay Leno on the *Tonight Show*.

"Oh, well, we really don't do anything," Russell said to DeVito, giving him fair warning. "We just kinda stand around arguing, looking for the new material and stuff, you know?" DeVito said not to worry about it, he would be fine.

When DeVito arrived at the studio, he was escorted to a room that Russell described as "dirty and stinky." Russell said, "You want a soda, you want a cigarette or whatever?" DeVito answered no, they should just carry on with whatever they were doing: "I'll just sit here and listen."

After the first song, DeVito spoke up: "Hey, how about giving me them cigarettes?"

"I thought you didn't smoke."

"I need them for something."

Russell handed him a pack of cigarettes and watched as DeVito fished out two weeds and broke the filters off, then asked, "You guys gonna sing any more songs?"

"Yeah," answered Russell.

With that, DeVito stuck the filters into his ears. Then, brandishing an elfish grin, he instructed them to proceed with the music. As he learned that day, the making of beautiful music is not always a pretty sight.

When *L.A. Confidential* was released in September 1997, it was greeted by glowing reviews. Roger Ebert gave it a four-star review in the *Chicago Sun Times*. "One of reasons [the film] is so good, why it deserves to be mentioned with *Chinatown*, is that it's not just plot and atmosphere," he wrote. "*L.A. Confidential* is seductive and beautiful, cynical and twisted, and one of the best films of the year."

Writing in the *San Francisco Chronicle,* Mick LaSalle called *L.A. Confidential* "one of the best crime dramas to come along in years." The film, he said, offers "in its sort-of heroes, White and Exley, what might be the most noble response possible in a corrupt world: an on-your-feet integrity. Not the kind where you can ever feel completely good or sure, just pretty good and pretty sure."

Time magazine critic Richard Schickel wrote: "If you have to spend time in a labyrinth, these are the kind of guys to do it with—tough, canny realists who can follow a tangled thread to daylight....The film's look suggests how deep the tradition of police corruption runs. And that, paradoxically, makes it as outrageous (and outraging) as tomorrow's headlines will surely be."

Unfortunately, the film's box office did not reflect the critics' enthusiasm. Four months after its release, it had grossed only $42 million—a lot of money, to be sure, but less than what *Titanic* had grossed in the first two weeks of its release. Director Curtis Hanson blamed the slow ticket sales on Warner Brothers' marketing efforts. "In my opinion, the original marketing campaign was a misstep," Hanson told the *Los Angeles Times.* "It was cops and guns. That's not what the movie is. It was labeling the movie in a very diminutive way."

As *L.A. Confidential* lingered in three hundred theaters going into 1998, a very encouraging sign for a four-month-old film, Warner Brothers took Hanson's criticism to heart and made a major effort to provide the film with its second wind by expanding its coverage to more than eight hundred theaters.

Warner Brothers' decision made Hanson happy and he praised the studio for admitting it had made a mistake in its initial marketing efforts. That was Hanson's interpretation of the studio's abrupt turnabout, but it was not necessarily a correct one. Warner never publicly admitted making a mistake, because executives there did not feel they had botched the initial marketing effort.

The studio's decision to place the film in more theaters was based on a new marketing assessment. Because of the critical acclaim the film received, executives felt that it stood a good chance of getting one or more Academy Award nominations. They flooded theaters with the film in January in the hope that it would attract renewed attention when the Oscar nominations were announced in February.

The gamble paid off in a big way. To everyone's surprise, *L.A. Confidential* received an astonishing nine nominations, including Kim Basinger for best actress in a supporting role, Curtis Hanson and cowriter Brian Helgeland for best screenplay based on material from another medium, Hanson for best director, and the film itself for best picture, a category many consider the most important.

Neither Australian actor in the film, Russell Crowe or Guy Pearce, received nominations, confirming in Russell's mind the existence of a built-in prejudice against foreign-born actors. He didn't bother to attend the awards ceremony in late March. If he had, he would have seen Hanson and Helgeland take home an Oscar in the writing category, and he would have seen Basinger beat out Joan Cusack, Minnie Driver, Julianne Moore, and Gloria Stuart for best supporting actress.

"O my God, yes!" Basinger shrieked when she went to the stage. "I just want to thank everyone I ever met in my entire life."

L.A. Confidential went on to gross another $22 million, bumping the total U.S. gross to $64 million and giving the studio a nice return on its $35 million investment. Hanson felt that it was due to his call for more aggressive marketing efforts, and the studio felt that it was due to its plan to capitalize on the film's Oscar potential. Who was right? At that point, with millions coming into the coffers, everyone was too happy to quibble over small details.

The first thing that came to Russell's mind when he read the script for *Mystery, Alaska*, was that the role that he was earmarked for required him to be able to ice skate, something he never tried to do. That would have been enough to discourage most actors, but not Russell, who doesn't feel that he's doing his job as an actor if he doesn't overcome some major obstacle—physical, emotional, intellectual, or philosophical—to prepare for a new role.

Toward the end of November, he headed up into the mountains of California with skates in hand. Six weeks later, he felt he was proficient enough on the ice to be convincing in the film. He returned to Australia for Christmas, then flew to Canmore, Alberta, in early January to start work on *Mystery, Alaska*.

The film was directed by Jay Roach, a graduate of the USC School of Cinema-Television, who had only two previous credits as a director. Ordinarily, that would not be an encouraging statistic to an actor on the rise, but because one of those two films, 1997's *Austin Powers: International Man of Mystery*, was an enormous success, it overrode any concerns Russell might have had about working with a green director.

The film also had another thing in its favor: it was written by Sean O'Byrne and David E. Kelley, the latter being the successful writer-director of television's *Ally McBeal, The Practice,* and *Picket Fences*. If ever a project had money written all over it, it was *Mystery, Alaska*, or so it seemed to everyone concerned.

Russell was asked to play the role of Sheriff John Biebe, a star player on the Mystery, Alaska, amateur hockey team. In truth, it is more than a team; it is the town's reason for existence. Playing his wife, Donna, was thirty-year-old Mary McCormack, a veteran of nearly a dozen feature films and television series, including Howard Stern's *Private Parts* and *Deep Impact*.

Hank Azaria played Charles Danner, a sportswriter and former Mystery resident who comes home to announce that he has arranged for Mystery's team to play an exhibition game with the New York Rangers. Rounding out the cast were Burt Reynolds as Walter Burns, a pompous judge; Lolita Davidovich as Mary Jane Pitcher, the mayor's promiscuous wife; and Ron Eldard as Matt "Skank" Marden, one of the team's best players.

Mystery, Alaska begins with a man skating through what looks like Alaskan wilderness with a hockey stick in hand. A small village comes into view. Another man is taking shots with a hockey stick. Sheriff John Biebe tries to start his car but can't: it's too cold for the spark plugs to ignite. The snow is very deep, piled up in big drifts. As Biebe reaches down to pick up his young son, the boy speaks an obscenity. With his car dead, Biebe drives a snowmobile to the sheriff's office.

There is no immediate crime on the horizon, but the entire village is excited over a *Sports Illustrated* article, written by Charles Danner, that paints a rosy picture of the town's hockey team. The article says that the team is good enough to rival any in the National Hockey League.

As the excitement over the article builds, Biebe is called into the mayor's office and told that he can no longer play on the team because he skates too slowly. He is made an alternate. His demotion comes as a shock to Biebe, a player many considered the best on the team. Hockey is the most important thing in the world to him—apart from his family, of course—and he grieves over his loss of status in the community.

Still, life must go on, and Biebe suddenly finds he has a crime to deal with. While he investigates a freak incident in which one of the team's young players shoots a visitor in the foot, a helicopter arrives carrying Charlie Danner, the author of the magazine piece. Because he is the former boyfriend of Biebe's wife, Donna, the sheriff is not happy to see him. Says Biebe, his voice chilled with sarcasm, "Twice in one year, Charlie. What do you want this time?"

Charlie tells him that the New York Rangers want to come to Mystery to play the local hockey team. That is big news indeed. Since nothing remotely like this has ever happened in Mystery, the mayor calls a town meeting to decide if they want to accept the offer. "Do we really stand a chance?" asks a woman in the audience. "'Cause if all that's gonna happen is that we get laughed at, I'm not for that."

Charlie tells the gathering that they wouldn't stand a chance in a regulation hockey rink, but they had a good chance of winning on a pond, since that is where they are used to playing. Amid cheers, the town decides to take the Rangers on.

After the meeting, the mayor asks Biebe to coach the team. He is reluctant because he considers himself more of a player than a coach, and he feels hurt by his dismissal from the team, but eventually he decides to do it.

As if the town didn't have enough problems getting ready for the upcoming game, the team's star center goes on trial for shooting the visitor. The case is heard by the town's only judicial officer, Judge Walter Burns, whose son plays on the team. Even though the hockey player clearly was guilty of the shooting, the jury declares him not guilty, an obvious gesture of support for the team. Judge Burns tells spectators that he is embarrassed by what has happened in his courtroom.

When a television producer comes to town and tells the residents that they are going to call the team the Mystery Eskimos, everyone is horrified. "We aren't Eskimos," protests the mayor. The producer, in an effort at compromise, responds that perhaps the name Mystery Boys would be better.

Feeling that he has gotten in over his head as a coach, Biebe asks Judge Burns if he would consider replacing him. Burns was a star player in his youth, and Biebe considers him more knowledgeable than himself about the mechanics of the game. Burns says he just isn't interested.

After the town has gone to a lot of trouble to prepare for the event, Charlie learns that the Rangers have changed their minds because of a dispute with the players' union. The townspeople figure that the game is a dead issue, but then they hear that the team's owners plan to take the union to court. Mystery sends a local lawyer, Bailey Pruitt (played by Maury Chaykin) to New York to represent the community in the dispute. "We do have our pride," says Pruitt to the judge. "And maybe it's sometimes a little too connected to how well we play hockey."

Pruitt gets so excited about his cause that he has a heart attack and dies right there in the courtroom. Perhaps influenced by Pruitt's dying appeal, the judge rules in Mystery's favor, and the game is back on.

After the funeral, Biebe again asks Judge Burns to coach the team. This time he says yes. The switch enables Biebe to get back on the team as a player.

The night before the game, the Rangers arrive by helicopter and are warmly greeted by the entire town. The game builds into a major event with satellite dishes, news networks, and dozens of trucks and vans popping up all over town.

To spice things up a bit, the mayor brings in Little Richard to sing the national anthem. At the last minute, the mayor goes into Little Richard's trailer and asks him to please sing the song as slowly as possible. Knowing that the Rangers are not accustomed to severe cold, he hopes that the Mystery team will gain an advantage by keeping their opponents on the ice for a long time.

The story ends with lots of excellent hockey, during which the town salvages its dignity and comes to terms with the outside world. The Rangers are so impressed with the team that they offer farm contracts to two of Mystery's best players.

When the film wrapped, Russell was eager to get to a warmer climate. Most days of production saw the actors and crew working in temperatures of twenty to thirty degrees below zero. Russell told reporters that the intense cold did weird things to his beard and to the hairs inside his nostrils.

Critics seemed to agree with Russell that there was just a bit of weirdness in the air. "It's a pity *Mystery, Alaska* is not a better movie," wrote *Cincinnati Enquirer* critic Margaret A. McGurk. "It works so hard to make everybody happy that pointing out its faults seems a mite mean-spirited. Still, there's no getting away from the fact that what we have here is basically a TV show with dirty words—and a not very inventive TV show at that."

For *Los Angeles Times* critic Kenneth Turan, Russell's performance was one of the best things about the film. "Though a comic cameo by Mike Myers as a hockey legend turned TV commentator is highly effective, it is Australian Crowe, a previous non-skater, who gives the film's standout performance," he wrote. "Almost unrecognizable from his breakthrough in *L.A. Confidential*, Crowe is one of those blessed leading men who can convincingly disappear inside a variety of roles."

With a headline like "Penalty Box Is the Place for 'Mystery, Alaska,'" you might think there would be nowhere to go in the actual review but up. Unfortunately, *Detroit Free Press* critic Terry Lawson has a bad sense of direction: "The best thing about *Mystery*, save the uncredited cameo by a friend of director Jay Roach as a hockey commentator, is also the saving grace of Kelley's shows: strong and sympathetic female roles, played here nicely by Davidovich, McCormack and Judith Ivey. But when the best thing in a movie about a male hockey team is the women, something is clearly offside."

Moviegoers seemed to agree with the critics. The film, which cost $28 million to make, only grossed $9 million in the United States, making it one of the biggest flops of 1999. No one blamed Russell for the film's failure, but it is not the sort of thing that an aspiring leading man wants on his resume.

The first thought Russell had after receiving the script for a film titled *The Insider* was that the director had made a mistake or confused him with someone else. The three male leads were real-life people whom he had seen on television—*60 Minutes* reporter Mike Wallace, who had one of the most famous faces in television; *60 Minutes* producer Lowell Bergman, and Jeffrey Wigand, the tobacco company whistleblower who became a central figure in one of most publicized class-action lawsuits in American history. He couldn't see himself playing any of those characters, especially Wallace, who was supposed to be in his seventies, and Wigand, who was in his fifties and overweight.

However, because he thought the script was magnificent and because he wanted the director to keep him in mind for future projects, he agreed to a meeting with Michael Mann. When Mann told Russell that he wanted him to play Jeffrey Wigand, Russell didn't take him seriously. In a conversation lasting more than four hours, he told Mann that he should probably offer the role to some out-of-work, middle-aged actor who would look the part. With that, Mann reached out and patted his hand on Russell's chest, right over his heart. "I'm not talking to you because of your age," he said. "I'm talking to you because of what you have in here."

Russell melted on the spot. That was exactly the kind of talk he loved to hear from a director. At that point, he would have walked five miles over broken glass for Michael Mann. Russell told him that he would love to be Jeffrey Wigand, even though it would require some dramatic alterations in his physical appearance.

They agreed that a makeup artist could easily handle the age factor but not Wigand's weight. In real life he had a stocky, fleshy look that would be impossible to finesse with makeup and padding. Realistically, that meant that they had two choices: Russell could play a slimmed-down version of Wigand, or he could gain weight—lots of weight—and shoot for a real-life resemblance. He chose the latter and went on an eating binge, consuming mainly cheeseburgers and bourbon, stuffing himself until he gained an astonishing forty-eight pounds.

The Insider began as a magazine article titled "The Man Who Knew Too Much," written by Marie Brenner for *Vanity Fair*. It was about Jeffrey Wigand, a $300,000-a-year tobacco company executive who took a job as a high school chemistry and Japanese teacher after being fired from his corporate position. After being contacted by *60 Minutes* producer Lowell Bergman, he did an interview with

Mike Wallace in which he accused tobacco company executives of committing perjury when they testified before Congress on the dangerous effects of cigarette smoking.

Before the interview could be aired, however, it was pulled by CBS on the grounds that it would put the news organization at legal risk. That was the official position. The truth was that the CBS network was for up for sale, and there was a fear among executives that a multimillion-dollar lawsuit from the tobacco companies might diminish the value of the stock.

As that drama unfolded, another one took place in the state of Mississippi, where Attorney General Michael Moore had asked a small-town lawyer named Richard Scruggs to file a lawsuit against the tobacco industry on behalf of the state to recover money paid out by the state Medicaid commission to treat smokers.

Moore had three good reasons for approaching Scruggs: first, they had attended the University of Mississippi law school together, and they had a good personal rapport; second, Scruggs had successfully sued the asbestos industry from his law office in Pascagoula, Mississippi, winning millions in class-action lawsuits; and thirdly, Scruggs is the brother-in-law of Mississippi Senator Trent Lott, the former majority leader of the United States Senate and one of the most powerful men in Washington.

It was into that atmosphere of big business and big money that Jeffrey Wigand stumbled, becoming a major player not only in the public debate on tobacco and the national health but in a public reassessment of a respected television news organization that buckled when its integrity was put to the test.

"I thought it would be interesting to do something that was a totally situational drama," director Michael Mann explained in an interview with the website Reel.com. "What drew me to the characters was the degree in which they are multifaceted. I found that really quite exciting, that they're not stock heroes....A real man like Jeffrey Wigand, I identify [with] him more closely. He's more accessible, he's real. He's filled with flaws, he has mixed motivations, he acts imperfectly—there's no single catalyst."

Mann was also attracted to the story because he had never done anything remotely like it. Known for his work in the television series *Starsky and Hutch* and *Miami Vice*, he had branched out to bigger projects with a broader vision. He cowrote and directed *The Last of the Mohicans*, which was released in 1992, and he cowrote and directed the psychological thriller *Heat*, starring Al Pacino and Robert De Niro, which was released the following year.

When the time came to cast *The Insider*, Mann went directly to Pacino to play the role of Lowell Bergman. It was a part with little outside action, which meant that the actor had to absorb the dramatic events around him and project them to the audience through the strength of his personality. Who better to tackle that challenge than Pacino, regarded by many critics as one of the greatest actors in film history?

Mann had a relationship with Pacino because of their work together on *Heat*.

Pacino had appeared in five films since then, including *Donnie Brasco*, but Mann had not done a movie in over four years, and in some respects his creative sensibilities were still with Pacino in *Heat*. The actor was not only tremendously talented, he was a comfortable fit for a director who felt he had something to prove.

In many respects, the role of Mike Wallace was the hardest to cast, primarily because his face was so well known to television viewers. Mann considered several people for the role, finally settling on veteran Broadway and film actor Christopher Plummer at the suggestion of Pacino, who was a fan of his work.

Plummer accepted with great relish. "Well, the part of Mike Wallace drew me to the movie because I thought what an outrageous part to play," he told *Entertainment Tonight*. "Most of my life I have played a lot of famous people, but most of them were dead, so you have a poetic license....But here is somebody who is visible to the public, and I have been watching him since the early fifties....He has created a great monster of a character in himself, which is a delight to play."

For the role of Wigand's wife, Liane, Mann went with forty-six-year-old Broadway actress Diane Venora, a veteran of two dozen television series and motion pictures. She was attractive, yet she had just enough of that ordinary-woman, suburban-wife look to her to be convincing.

Before production began, Russell asked for a meeting with Jeffrey Wigand. He didn't particularly like the scientist and sensed that the feeling was probably mutual, yet he left the meeting determined to honor Wigand as a man. "I have respect for him, for what he did, and he understands how serious I am about my job," Russell told the *London Evening Standard*. "[But] sometimes I read articles about actors and they talk about how they have to fall in love with their characters, and I think that's just a bunch of bollocks. I can't think of anything more stupid: when you fall in love, you forgive a great deal and lose your objectivity."

By the time Russell reported for filming, he was very much Jeffrey Wigand, not just because of the added forty-eight pounds or the hair that he had colored and thinned but because of his attitude toward the character. He knew his transformation into the character was complete when he found himself rocking several times back and forth just to get out of the car. He felt as if he were living inside someone else's body.

Perhaps because of the extra weight, Russell found it exhausting to put in a full day's work. Each day after the wrap, he went home and crashed. He had no energy for parties, no time for romance. All he thought about was getting the job done, then getting enough sleep to be refreshed when he returned to work the next morning.

For a change, Russell got along well with everyone in this film. His onscreen wife was not in the least intimidated by his reputation as a wild man. "An actor, by his very nature, if he's good, has a temperament," Venora told the *Boston Globe*. "He has to live in an open wound all day long because he may have to use that in five minutes. Now, if you did that in normal life, you'd get killed, but on the screen it allows him to let you into his heart. That takes transparency of soul, true nakedness of soul. It takes talent, and this guy Crowe is an ace."

What impressed Russell most about working with Al Pacino was the realization that they used totally different approaches to their characters. Russell prepares thoroughly before every scene, sometimes to the point of obsession, so that he understands the "truth" of his character and encounters no surprises on the set. Pacino takes an opposite approach, discovering the "truth" of his character while the camera is rolling.

One day Russell asked Pacino about his technique. Pacino explained that in the beginning he approached films as if they were live stage productions—situations where he had some level of control over what the audience saw. Then, after he had made a few films, he realized that he was always surprised at what directors chose to use in their final edits. They didn't always pick what he thought was important.

For that reason, he explained to Russell, he decided to act his scenes in the moment, giving directors as many choices as they thought they needed. It was not in Russell's constitution to be that flexible or trusting in front of a camera, but he watched with fascination as Pacino nailed scene after scene by throwing himself into the moment, working the angles with consummate skill.

Just as Russell learned from the actors he worked with, so did he learn from the directors, perhaps none more so than Michael Mann. The first scene that Russell shot with Mann was of Wigand walking through a doorway. He ended up doing it seventeen times over a two-day period—just walking in and out of the doorway.

Finally, Russell exploded. "Michael, don't spend the first ten takes looking at the fucking shadow on the wall," he said, according to *Empire* magazine. "Don't even call me until you've worked out where the fucking shadow is. Don't waste this stuff, because I'm working from take one. I don't care who you've worked with before, mate. I don't need a warm-up. I'm ready. And if we go into double figures, then someone's gonna have to fucking die!"

Mann parried Russell's verbal abuse by adopting a technique that boxer Muhammad Ali had used very effectively in the ring—the rope-a-dope. Mann covered up until Russell had vented his anger, then came back with his best shot. He told Russell that he had the best Ferrari on the road. "So, what are you gonna do?" Mann asked. "Are you going to leave it in the garage, or are you gonna get in and drive it?"

Seeing Mann in a different light, Russell drove and drove and drove.

The Insider begins with two blindfolded men being driven through the streets of an Iranian city by armed men. When the car reaches its destination, the men are led into a building, where one of the men—*60 Minutes* producer Lowell Bergman—is placed in a chair in front of a Muslim guerrilla leader. Bergman has not been taken hostage; he is in Iran to arrange an interview for Mike Wallace.

From there, the scene switches to an office building, which Jeffrey Wigand is leaving, briefcase in hand. He goes home, where his daughter is watching cartoons on television. Later, his wife arrives and voices surprise at seeing him home early from work. After his daughter has an asthma attack, which requires emergency treatment, Wigand tells his wife that he was fired from his job.

Back in America, after successfully arranging the *60 Minutes* interview, Bergman takes delivery on a package of documents that was obviously sent to him by a disgruntled employee of the Philip Morris tobacco company. When he calls around to find someone who can translate the scientific jargon in the documents, he is given the name of Jeffrey Wigand, the former head of research with Brown & Williamson.

The two men talk on the telephone, and after several rejections, Wigand agrees to meet with Bergman. He tells him that he can read the documents and comment on them because they are not from his former company, but he cannot talk about anything involving Brown & Williamson because he signed a confidentiality agreement with the company as part of his severance package. That is fine with Bergman, whose main concern at this point is the Philip Morris documents.

After that meeting, Wigand is called in by his former employer, Thomas Sandefur, who asks him to sign a broader confidentiality agreement. He makes several statements that Wigand takes as threats if he does not sign. Wigand is outraged. "On top of the humiliation of being fired, you threaten me, you threaten my family. It never crossed my mind not to honor my agreement," he says. "Well, fuck you!"

After he storms out of the office, one of the lawyers present says, "I'm not sure he got the message," to which Sandefur responds, "Oh, I think he did!"

Later, Wigand calls Bergman and accuses him of betraying him. He thinks his former employer called him into the office because he heard he was talking to *60 Minutes*. Bergman denies betraying him. They talk for a while, and it becomes obvious that Wigand wants to talk to Bergman about his research.

Bergman meets with Mike Wallace and other *60 Minutes* staffers to see if they can come up with a plan to get Wigand to talk on the record. For that to happen, they would have to protect him from a possible lawsuit. They conclude that the only way that Wigand's free speech could be protected, in view of the confidentiality agreement, would be if he were required to give testimony in the class-action lawsuit then being pursued against the tobacco companies.

To that end, Bergman calls Richard Scruggs, the Mississippi attorney who had filed the lawsuit on behalf of the state of Mississippi. He asks Scruggs if he could use Wigand's testimony in his court case, so that it would then become public record. Scruggs answers in the affirmative, elated at the prospect of having an expert witness.

As the days pass, Wigand receives death threats, which so anger him that he agrees to do the interview with *60 Minutes*. He also agrees to talk to Scruggs about testifying in his lawsuit. Bergman arranges for Wigand and his family to receive private security, but that is not enough for Wigand's wife, Liane, who tells her husband she can't stand the stress much longer.

Wigand flies to Mississippi to meet with Scruggs and Mississippi attorney general Michael Moore, who plays himself in the movie. At the airport, he is served with papers from a Kentucky court ordering him not to testify. He decides to ignore the court order and testify anyway at a sworn deposition. When Wigand returns home, he discovers that his wife has left him and taken the children with her.

Just as Wigand's life becomes more difficult, so does Bergman's. *60 Minutes* is warned by an attorney from the CBS corporate office that they are at risk for "tortuous interference" if they air the interview with Wigand. There is more at stake than journalistic integrity, as Bergman later learns, because CBS is up for sale to Westinghouse and corporate officials feel that a messy lawsuit with Brown & Williamson might jeopardize the deal. As a result, CBS decides to kill the interview.

A series of behind-the-scenes skirmishes take place, with Bergman masterminding a plan to bring the network's decision to the public's attention while working at the same time to protect Wigand's credibility as a witness.

Those efforts eventually pay off, and Wigand's interview is aired, but by then it is too late for both Wigand, whose life has been destroyed in the process, and Bergman, who decides that he has no choice but to resign from *60 Minutes.*

By the end of 1998, Russell was back in Australia doing what he enjoys the most—kicking back on his ranch and playing music with his band. He used his downtime to launch a new album, *Gaslight*, which had been recorded in bits and pieces over the past two years at studios in Los Angeles and Sydney.

The band's previous album, *What's Her Name?*, released in 1997, was not an entirely pleasant experience, for there had been marketing problems with the record label. "We've done tours with two different record companies and both times have acquiesced to the way they wanted to do things because, you know, you're starting a relationship from a business point of view, you don't want to necessarily rock the boat," Russell told the *Daily Telegraph.* "So you do what you're asked and it gets you nowhere."

Russell and the band decided to offer *Gaslight* for sale only through the Internet and by mail order. They might not sell many albums to the general public, but they would be able to control sales and feel confident that the people who had supported the band over the years would be able to find the album without difficulty.

Gaslight contained eleven songs. "Wendy," written by Russell, was recorded live-to-eight-track in 1995 at an apartment in Los Angeles. "Eternity" was an older song for which Russell had written the lyrics in 1987 and Dean Cochran had written the music in 1993. It is a lonely song that reflects the mood of Russell's struggling years, when he was living off $3.50 a day earned singing on the street.

"Nowhere," written by Russell and Kevin Durand, was recorded at Hollywood Sound. The idea came to Russell after talking to a girl in Louisville, Kentucky, who wanted to go to Los Angeles simply because she had heard so much about it. For Russell, her obsession exemplified the magnetic attraction the city has on some people.

"What You Want Me to Forget," written by Russell, is what he calls a "romp and stomp; it's an up-tempo song based on a conversation he had with his father.

Three Crowe-Cochran compositions on the album—"Oblique," "What's Her Name?" and "The Legend of Barry Kable"— were recorded live at Melbourne's Esplanade Hotel.

Russell wrote "David" after two mistaken-identity incidents with strangers. The first occurred after a man showed him a *Life* magazine story about a thirteen-year-old ballroom dancer from Sydney named Russell Crowe. The second occurred when a passenger on an airplane showed him a story in *USA Today* about a Florida snake trainer named Russell Crowe who was found guilty of abusing his snake. The stranger asked, "Is this you?" to which Russell answered, "No."

Other songs on the album include "Circus," written by D. Walker, and two additional compositions by Russell—"Chocolate" and "She's Not Impressed." Not included on the album but released on a CD single were two more songs written by Russell—"The Photograph Kills" and "High Horse Honey," the latter a thinly disguised swipe at actress Sharon Stone.

Australians seemed perplexed by the album and by the fact that Russell and the band were content to perform in hotel pubs and give interviews to local newspapers. He was a huge star in Australia at that point. Why was he taking a local approach to his music and an international approach to his films? Was he just mucking around with his music, treating it like a backyard game of rugby, or was he making a serious effort?

"I take it seriously," he told a reporter for the *Courier*. "I wouldn't do it on the basis of something to do on my summer holidays. It's another creative expression. If you have any respect for what I do as an actor you know I'm not a fucking soap star. I don't have an empty attitude to what I do as a screen performer. I do work that has content to it. If you acknowledge that, give me the opportunity to show you the same artist coming to you in a different medium."

Russell showed extraordinary patience in dealing with music writers based in small towns along Australia's Gold Coast, where the band performed in hotels and small clubs. When they insulted him with off-center questions about his music, it was generally out of ignorance or lack of musical sophistication, and he allowed their comments to pass unchallenged. The point he expressed time and time again was that he was not trying to make slick music of the type that was dominating radio. He wanted his music to make listeners uncomfortable so that it would have an impact on them. They could embrace it or they could shove it away in disgust; either way was fine with him.

"When I'm playing with these three guys it's a powerful thing," he told Lisa Zanardo of *Go!* magazine. "We're the real McCoy, and I don't care if people don't like a song, because I didn't write it for them…I wrote it for me."

For the first time, during the Christmas of 1998, Russell began to crystallize his concept of music. To him, it was the narrative content of the song that was of primary importance, not the beat or the melody or the heat generated by a slashing guitar solo. If a song doesn't have a story, he concluded, it doesn't have Russell.

SIX

MEG LEAVES THE
GLADIATOR DOWN UNDER

Russell was sloshing about on the set of *The Insider*, the forty-eight extra pounds he had gained making him feel soft and pudgy as a donut, when he received a call from his agent, George Freeman, who told him that DreamWorks was interested in talking to him about a big-budget film named *Gladiator*.

The first thing that came to mind was that Hollywood hadn't made a film like that in years. Was it *Ben-Hur* or *Spartacus* that was the last sword-fighting epic out of the gate? He couldn't remember, but it must have been at least forty years since anyone tried to make a film like that—not in his lifetime, anyway. From a career standpoint, it didn't sound like a smart thing to do. For that reason, he didn't respond immediately.

Russell told director Michael Mann about the telephone call, and Mann encouraged the actor to talk to DreamWorks about it. As a result, he called Walter Parkes, who ran the DreamWorks production department, and spoke to him about the project. Russell suggested that Parkes send him the script, but Parkes told him that the script wasn't finished and they were afraid that if he read what was down on paper, he would say no.

What they wanted to do, Parkes explained, was pitch it to him, which is Hollywood shorthand for having a sit-down meeting at which the project is described verbally. That thought made Russell cringe. He responded, "If you don't have a script, don't pitch it to me."

Parkes refused to take no for an answer. Before Russell could terminate the conversation, he blurted out three selling points: "It takes place in 185 A.D., the director is Ridley Scott, and you would start the film as a Roman general." There was a pause, then Parkes asked, "Can we pitch it to you?"

"Yeah," answered Russell, duly impressed.

But even before the meeting with Scott, Russell began to have second thoughts. He talked to Mann about it, and the director told him that he shouldn't pass up an opportunity to work with Ridley Scott, primarily because of his skill with a camera. Insiders call Scott one of the best "shooters" in the business, a director with an uncanny ability to sniff out the most dramatic visual presentation for his films.

Russell took Mann's advice and met with Scott, who described the film to him in great detail. It was a successful meeting, and before the two men parted they agreed to do the deal based on a handshake, leaving the messy legal work to the agents and lawyers.

His new role presented quite a challenge to Russell, for after his work on *The*

Insider he was faced with losing the forty-eight pounds he had gained for that film. Before getting started on a weight-loss program, he went to see a doctor, who told him that his cholesterol was dangerously high.

Even so, he wasn't worried about it. He had five months to get back in shape. It had taken only six weeks to gain the weight. Surely it could be lost in the same amount of time. Thinking he would lose the weight by simply going back to his old lifestyle, Russell went on a low-fat diet for about three weeks.

When that didn't work, he enrolled in a ten-day program at a health spa, only to withdraw halfway through the program so that he could return to his ranch in Australia. But before getting down to business, he joined a group of friends, collectively named La Famiglia (Italian for family), and set out on a four-thousand-mile, four-week motorcycle trip around Australia. The idea was to see how it felt to lead an army of men on an expedition.

Traveling on Hondas, Harleys, and Ducatis, the group, which included Russell's bandmates, a Los Angeles costume designer, and one of Russell's childhood friends, went from Darwin to Alice Springs and then all the way back down to Sydney.

To document the trip, Russell invited independent filmmaker Brendan Fletcher and his crew along for the ride. The previous year, Fletcher had filmed a music video for Russell and his band that was built around a song titled "Circus." Russell asked him to film the motorcycle trip because he felt it could be used in a documentary. "It was a pretty full-on experience," Fletcher told *HQ* magazine. "When you enter into a project with [Russell] you certainly enter into a project where you're up to be pushed."

Back at the ranch, Russell took an old-fashioned approach to losing the weight. He got up at dawn each day, rode horses and wrangled the nearly three hundred head of Angus cattle on his ranch, did chores around the farm, practiced sword fighting, and worked out in the gym near his barn. Now in his mid-thirties, he found that while it was not easy to lose the weight, it was possible if he stayed physically active.

Director Ridley Scott had made some very successful films, including *Thelma & Louise, Blade Runner,* and *Alien,* but he had never attempted anything remotely like *Gladiator.* For it to work, he had to breathe life into a genre that had been dormant for forty years. He had technological advantages that had not been available to directors in that era—computer-generated crowd scenes, for example—but he would have to walk a cinematic tightrope that afforded him little room for error.

Casting would be his biggest challenge, for today's audience had grown up with a different set of standards for superheroes than had previous generations. The film's main character, General Maximus Decimus Meridius, had to be larger than life, which was why Scott felt he needed Russell Crowe to play the role. Maximus had to be physically imposing, and he had to possess an inner rage that was palatable. None of the other actors he considered for the part had that combination.

In casting the other parts, he went for a blend of new actors, such as Joaquin

Russell Crowe, Danielle Spencer and Robert Hanimone in "The Crossing." (Photo by Photofest)

Russell Crowe and Danielle Spencer during their love scene in "The Crossing" (Photo by Phototest)

Russell Crowe in "Proof." (Photo by New Line Cinema)

Russell Crowe's first album. (photo by REX)

Russell Crowe and Charlotte Rampling in "Hammers Over the Anvil." (Photo by Photofest)

Russell Crowe and John Polson seconds before the kiss in "The Sum of Us." (Photo by Photofest)

Russell Crowe as Bud White in "L.A. Confidential." (Photo by Peter Sorel, Monarchy Enterprises)

Russell Crowe and Salma Hayek in "Breaking Up." (Photo by Magdalene Kispal/Monarchy Enterprises/Photofest)

Director Craig Lahiff, left, gives direction to Russell Crowe in "Heaven's Burning." (Photo courtesy of Craig Lahiff)

Youki Kudoh with Russell Crowe in a scene from "Heaven's Burning." (Photo courtesy of Craig Lahif)

Filming Michael Mann's "The Insider" with Al Pacino (© Corbis/Sygma)

Russell Crowe receives his first Oscar at the 73rd Annual Academy Awards. Left to right, Benicio Del Toro, Marcia Gay Harden, and Julia Roberts. (Photo by Long Photography/Photofes)

Meg Ryan and Russell Crowe in "Proof of Life." (Photo by Ralph Nelson/Castle Rock Entertainment/Photofest)

Meg Ryan and Russell Crowe in "Proof of Life." (Photo by Frank Connor, Castle Rock Entertainment)

Russell Crowe and Jennifer Connelly in "A Beautiful Mind." (Photo by Universal Studios/Photofest)

Phoenix as Emperor Commodus and Connie Nielsen as his sister, Lucilla, and seasoned veterans, such as Richard Harris as Emperor Marcus Aurelius (who better to deliver an illusion of imperial fatalism?) and Oliver Reed as the jaded former gladiator Antonius Proximo.

The film was shot in the spring and early summer of 1999, with production beginning in England, then moving on to Morocco and finally Malta, where most of the action sequences were filmed. Scott assembled more than 260 cast and crew members, and he led them as if they were a small army.

When Russell reported for work, it was obvious that he had not only lost the weight he had gained for his previous movie, he had buffed up and added muscle in new places. Emotionally, he looked self-possessed, hungry for victory—like a general who was eager to lead an army to war. He had prepared himself for the role by reading books about the Roman Empire, the structure of the military, and hand-to-hand combat. Two books he found especially helpful were *A Day in the Life of Ancient Rome* and Marcus Aurelius's *Meditations.*

The fight scenes, which were bloody, extravagant, and filled with the digital energy inherent in video games, were very difficult to bring off to the satisfaction of both Russell and Scott. Battle scenes that were supposed to be shot in one day ended up running on for ten or twelve days.

After one grueling series of staged battles, Russell and the other actors were given a day off. He spent the day playing soccer, which prompted a note from a studio executive asking him not to play soccer in case he got hurt. Russell fired back a written response saying that if he could wrestle with four tigers, he could bloody well play a game of soccer with his friends. He signed the note, "Love, Russell."

Russell received lots of injuries while making the film, but none came from playing soccer. He broke a bone in his foot, fractured a hipbone, and had the tendons of both biceps pop out of his shoulder sockets. Perhaps because of his willingness to sustain injuries on the set, Djimon Hounsou, who played Maximus's fellow gladiator Juba, described Russell as a man's man, someone he would want on his side if he were riding off into a real-life battle.

Russell and Scott fought constantly during filming, with Russell usually arguing things from his character's point of view, but Scott didn't buckle under the pressure. He was patient with Russell without surrendering his authority as director. Their first argument centered on Maximus's accent. Since the script said he was from Spain, Russell thought he should sound Spanish, like actor Antonio Banderas. He lost that argument, and Maximus, like the other characters, emerged with an English accent that Russell later described as "Royal Shakespeare Company two pints after lunch."

Another argument they had, though it took place only inside the corridors of Scott's own mind, was over Maximus's sex life. Scott didn't feel he should have one, so he axed the passionate love scenes between Russell and actress Gianina Facio, who played Maximus's wife in the film. Facio was Scott's real-life girlfriend at the time, and she later told reporters that the scenes were not filmed because

Scott was afraid she and Russell might take the scenes off-camera.

Russell didn't limit his advice about how the film should be made solely to the director. He shared his thoughts with the other actors, often giving them pointers on how a particular scene should be played. Two actors he was especially generous with, as far as advice was concerned, were Joaquin Phoenix and Connie Nielsen, who played brother and sister in the film.

"From both Connie and Joaquin, I demanded they remain completely involved and protect their own part of the narrative," Russell told *Talk* magazine. "It's a very scary situation for a young actor like Joaquin. He's got himself out at the end of the branch and he's swinging in the breeze and counting the leaves, not knowing whether he's doing the right thing in his heart." Phoenix, who once compared Russell to a big brother who is "giving and gracious," welcomed the attention.

Scott didn't necessarily consider Russell to be gracious, but he found him to be giving, at least insofar as the film was concerned. The actor would do anything he asked, just as long as he was given an explanation for what it meant to the film. If a direction did not make sense to him, he usually resisted with the full-blown Crowe fury.

One occasion when Scott was probably glad that Russell took a stand was prompted when a studio executive flew in from Hollywood to suggest that the film have a happy ending. Russell went ballistic. He later told *Empire* magazine that he took a stand to make certain that the film did not "end up as a fucking grape-chewing fucking toga party. I mean, c'mon, Maximus has to die, right? What's he going to do if he doesn't? Open a pizza parlor outside the Coliseum and sell fucking autographs?"

As *Gladiator* begins, the Roman emperor Marcus Aurelius is ending a twelve-year campaign against the barbarians of Germania. In the final battle, General Maximus, the emperor's most trusted military leader, wins an impressive victory. Afterward, the emperor asks the general how he can reward him for his service to Rome.

"Let me go home," answers Maximus, whose wife and son await him in Spain.

The emperor says nothing in response at that time, but he later calls the general back into his tent to tell him that he is dying. He has seen only four years of peace during his twenty-five-year rule and he wonders how he will be viewed by history.

For that reason, he wants Maximus, not his son Commodus, to succeed him as emperor in order to free Rome of the corruption that has taken hold in the emperor's absence. Maximus is stunned by his request, for he has never even visited Rome and there is nothing he wants more than to return to his family.

The emperor gives him time to think it over, but so sure is he of the general's decision that he calls Commodus into his tent to inform him that he will not become emperor. He tells his son that he has decided to transfer power to Maximus so that he can maintain order until Rome can again become a republic.

Outraged by that news, Commodus embraces his father, pressing his face so tightly into his tunic that he suffocates him. After the emperor's death is reported to the troops, Commodus sends for Maximus and offers him his hand as a test of his loyalty, but Maximus, suspecting foul play, refuses his hand and walks away.

One of Commodus's first decisions as emperor is to order Maximus's execution. The general is taken to a wooded area, far from the sight of his troops, but before the execution can take place, he escapes and flees to Spain, where he hopes to join his family. Unfortunately, Commodus has ordered their execution as well, and the soldiers have a head start on Maximus.

When he arrives at his home, he discovers that both his wife and son have been brutally murdered and burned, along with all the buildings on his farm. Weakened by the ordeal and depressed by his family's murder, he is captured by slave merchants and transported to Africa, where he is forced to become a gladiator.

Maximus proves to be so fearless a gladiator that when his owner, Antonius Proximo, takes him to Rome to fight in the Colosseum, he tells him that he will give him his freedom if he wins the crowd.

Maximus does more than win the crowd, he wins the admiration of Emperer Commodus, who does not recognize Maximus because he is wearing a helmet. Playing to the cheering crowd, Commodus strolls out onto the field to meet the gladiator who has won the hearts of his constituents. After a brief exchange, Commodus orders the gladiator to remove his helmet. He is shocked to see that it is Maximus, the man he had ordered killed. Says Maximus to him, "I will have my vengeance in this life or the next."

Not understanding what is at stake, the crowd urges Commodus to spare the gladiator's life. Since it would be politically damaging to go against the crowd's wishes, he gives a thumbs-up, indicating that Maximus will be allowed to live.

Later, Commodus asks his sister, Lucilla, "Why is he still alive?"

"I don't know," she answers.

"He shouldn't be alive," says Commodus. "It vexes me."

Lucilla arranges a secret meeting with Maximus. He tells her that her brother murdered his family. Desirous of power herself, she urges Maximus to work with the senators to overthrow her brother. He refuses and asks her to leave.

The next day, with tigers nipping at his heels, Maximus fights the only undefeated gladiator in Rome—and defeats him after a brutal battle. Faced with a growing sense of mortality, Maximus agrees to a clandestine meeting with Senator Gracchus, leader of the opposition. Reluctant to get involved in politics, he tells the senator, "I will kill Commodus. The fate of Rome I leave to you."

When Commodus learns of the plot, he arrests Gracchus. Fearful for her own safety, Lucilla buys Maximus's freedom and helps him to escape so that he can gather his army together and challenge Commodus's power. But Maximus does not get far before he, too, is captured. Instead of ordering Maximus killed, Commodus himself decides to fight Maximus in the Colosseum, in full view of the crowd.

"You would fight me?" asks Maximus.

"Why not? Do you think I'm afraid?"

"I think you've been afraid all your life."

To insure his victory over Maximus, Commodus inflicts a painful knife wound on the gladiator moments before they step into the arena. Already wounded, Maximus fights with a passion never before seen by Commodus. It is with that fierce battle that Maximus's odyssey—and Rome's fate as a republic—comes to a spectacular resolution.

In May 1999, several weeks before production on *Gladiator* wrapped, sixty-one-year-old Oliver Reed, who played Maximus's handler, Antonius Proximo, became ill in a pub and fell over dead. Director Ridley Scott was able to use a body double and more than a little computer wizardry to complete Proximo's part, but Reed's death meant that Scott would have to revise the script. As originally written, the script called for Proximo to live; Reed's untimely death meant that his character would also have to die.

Russell was stunned by Reed's death—it was the first tragedy of that nature he had ever experienced while making a film—but he considered Reed's work on the film to be the best of his career and viewed it was a fitting memorial to a man who had made a major contribution to cinema.

Once he packed away his swords and armor, Russell flew back to Australia to nurse his wounds. *Gladiator* was easily the most physically demanding film he had ever made, and it left him with real injuries that required time to heal. That was fine with him, for it gave him an excuse to spend time with the horses, cattle, chickens, and snakes that inhabited his ranch. He would be the first to admit that he is a terrible rancher, simply because he won't allow any of the animals on his land to be killed, not even for food.

By the time *The Insider* was released in November 1999, Russell was well rested and ready to promote the film. To his delight, it was an immediate hit with the critics. Mick LaSalle, writing in the *San Francisco Chronicle*, saw the film as an issue-oriented drama that goes for the big punch. "What gives *The Insider* its extra dose of urgency is the big question swirling around it: Do we live in a democracy or an oligarchy?" he wrote. "In considering that, *The Insider* takes its place in the tradition of Frank Capra's *Mr. Smith Goes to Washington* and *Meet John Doe*."

Chicago Sun-Times critic Roger Ebert gave the film a three-and-a-half-star review. "Pacino's performance underlies everything," he wrote, barely mentioning Russell Crowe. "He makes Bergman hoarse, overworked, stubborn and a master of psychological manipulation who inexorably draws Wigand toward the moment of truth....*The Insider* had a greater impact on me than *All the President's Men*, because you know what? Watergate didn't kill my parents. Cigarettes did."

David Edelstein, writing for the Internet magazine *Slate*, thought the film showed insight into what happens to corporate whistleblowers when corporations also control the media. "*The Insider* is a big, overlong, and rather unwieldy piece of storytelling, but the story it has to tell is so vital that it cuts through all the dramaturgical muddiness," he wrote. "It's a terrific muckraking melodrama—it will get people fuming."

Of course, the film angered both the tobacco companies and *60 Minutes,* particularly Mike Wallace and executive producer Don Hewitt, both of whom were made to look weak and unprincipled. Both men lashed out at director Michael Mann, accusing him of distorting their roles in the controversy.

"They're saying our movie hurts '60 Minutes.' What nonsense!" Mann told the *San Jose Mercury News,* pointing out the obvious—that the damage to the television newsmagazine was self-inflicted. "The show and Mr. Wallace have been respectfully dramatized in this film. The fact that they complain is a little strange. What is the alternative? That this episode be hidden and forgotten, that we revise history?"

For all its flaws—and they were few, all things considered—*The Insider* did perform a valuable public service by reminding people of the nefarious behind-the-scenes power that corporations can exert on government and private institutions. It is also the first motion picture to tackle the sensitive issue of how television journalism has restructured itself as entertainment fare at the expense of journalistic integrity.

The big winners in Jeffrey Wigand's story were not necessarily those who had been damaged the most by the tobacco companies, nor even those who went out on a limb to make the movie. Lawyer Richard Scruggs's class-action lawsuit against the tobacco companies was expanded to all fifty states, eventually leading to an historic $246 billion settlement that made Scruggs a multimillionaire and pumped billions into state coffers for use on issues of public concern.

In November 1999, after doing the obligatory interviews to promote the film, Russell returned to his ranch in Australia to unwind. Interviews always made him tense. When he heard that a friend named Mark Lizotte was performing not far from his ranch at a nightclub in the small village of Coramba, about a ten-minute drive from the coastal town of Coffs Harbour, Russell and his brother, Terry, decided to attend.

At about 3 A.M., according to the *Sydney Morning Herald,* Russell became involved in a melee in which the actor argued heatedly with an eighteen-year-old woman outside the nightclub, punched and bit a man on the neck, then kissed a man who tried to calm the actor down. Russell was not prosecuted, and he thought that was the end of the matter. But unknown to him, a security camera operated by a next-door bar captured the episode on videotape. It would later come back to haunt him.

In January 2000, a little more than two months after *The Insider* was released, Russell returned to Los Angeles to attend the Golden Globe Awards, for which he was nominated in the best-actor category for his role in *The Insider.* Also nominated were Michael Mann, in the director's category, and the film itself, which was nominated for best picture, along with *American Beauty, The End of the Affair, The Hurricane* and *The Talented Mr. Ripley.*

Since it was Russell's first American awards ceremony, he made certain that he had a controversial date. Accompanying him to the ceremony was new mother

Jodie Foster, who held hands with Russell going in and out of the venue, prompting the tabloids to speculate that he might be the baby's father (she has never identified the father).

It proved to be a disappointing night for Russell. He lost to Denzel Washington for his role in *The Hurricane*, Mann lost to Sam Mendes for his work on *American Beauty*, and *The Insider* lost in the best picture category to *American Beauty*.

Russell returned to Australia beaten but not broken. He had not won an award, but he was thrilled to have been nominated. It was the first tangible evidence he had seen that his work was being recognized.

When the 1999 Oscar nominations were announced the following month, no one was surprised that Michael Mann was nominated in the best director category, or that *The Insider* was nominated for best picture, along with *American Beauty*, *The Sixth Sense*, *The Green Mile* and *The Cider House Rules*. But everyone was surprised that Russell Crowe was nominated for best actor, beating out Al Pacino for the honor.

When Russell returned to Los Angeles for the ceremonies in March 2000, he seemed more sociable than on previous visits. With him was his thirteen-year-old niece, Chelsea, his official "date" for Oscar night. Children had been on his mind lately. He told *Glamour* magazine: "Explaining why you want children is a bit like explaining why you want to live—you want to pass things on, watch them grow, they make you laugh. It's one of the best things in life."

When he attended events without Chelsea, he seemed in a decidedly "unfamily" frame of mind, more the old randy sea dog people had come to expect, though it was unclear whether that was because of his extended exile at his ranch or because of a lull in his love life. At any rate, according to *Us* magazine, he attended a pre-Oscar party at the home of Ed Limato, the head of International Creative Management, Russell's management agency, at which he "brazenly hit on" Winona Ryder when she was still involved with actor Matt Damon.

At the awards show, Russell was asked to present the award for best art direction with best-actress nominee Julianne Moore, which he did without ruffling any feathers. But for most of the show, he sat in the audience glowering at the television camera whenever it swung his way. Producers staged an *Insider* song parody that prompted Russell to scowl, as did the clip that promoted the film in the best-picture category.

It ended up being another bad night for Russell. He didn't win the best-actor Oscar (Kevin Spacey did for his role in *American Beauty*), nor did Michael Mann or the movie itself win. It was a complete washout for *The Insider*, leaving some observers wondering what message the academy wanted to send to the public.

So far, 2000 was proving to be one of the busiest years in Russell's career. In May, less than two months after the Academy Awards show, *Gladiator* was released, setting the mighty promotional machine back in motion. Russell was optimistic about the film, primarily because of his own reaction at the screening. He didn't like to see himself in films—he still had not seen *The Insider* at this point, though that would later change when director Michael Mann practically dragged him into a theater—but when he saw *Gladiator* he jumped up and down like a child attending his first action movie.

Most critics agreed with him. *Time* magazine's Richard Corliss said the film had the smell of a hit. "Crowe could be a nicer fellow but hardly a better actor," he wrote. "To *Gladiator*, a film in need of a star and a working-class hero, Crowe brings strength and honor."

Desmond Ryan, writing in the *Philadelphia Inquirer*, considered it a stunning triumph. "*Gladiator* is full of arresting splendor and technical virtuosity on a plane beyond the imagining of the makers of this kind of epic in the 1960s," he wrote. "But its impact as a movie flows from Russell Crowe, who is that rarity: a great actor who is fully up to the demands of playing a man of action."

Chicago Sun-Times critic Roger Ebert gave the film only two stars. He gave Russell credit for being "efficient" in his portrayal of Maximus, but he thought that most of the other actors seldom got beyond "reliable" or "passable." His biggest beef was with the movie's art direction. "The film looks muddy, fuzzy and indistinct," he wrote. "Its colors are mud tones at the drab end of the palette, and it seems to have been filmed on grim and overcast days....I would have traded any given gladiatorial victory for just one shot of blue skies."

Regardless of what the critics said about the film, it was the moviegoing public that had the last word. By the time the film completed its run, it had grossed nearly half a billion dollars worldwide, making it one of the most successful films in history. For director Ridley Scott, who had spent a little over one hundred million dollars making *Gladiator*, and for Russell Crowe, who had put his heart and soul into the film, it was the type of vindication that only money can buy.

Perhaps it's not the reputation that he cherishes most, but director Taylor Hackford has proved to have a knack for pairing sexy male and female stars who deliver steamy onscreen chemistry. He was the brains behind Richard Gere and Debra Winger in *An Officer and a Gentleman*, Keanu Reeves and Charlize Theron in *The Devil's Advocate*, and Jeff Bridges and Rachel Ward in *Against All Odds*.

When the time came to cast *Proof of Life*, the first two actors who came to his mind were Meg Ryan and Mel Gibson. Ever since her 1989 hit *When Harry Met Sally*, which she followed up four years later with *Sleepless in Seattle*, Meg had been every director's first choice for a love-interest role. The camera loved her, as did audiences, who seemed to perceive her as the perfect girlfriend for just about any situation.

But *Proof of Life* was not a traditional love story—Meg would play Alice Bowman, the wife of an American engineer kidnapped by terrorists in a fictional South American country—and Hackford wondered whether she would be able to define her character while holding her footing in a plot that was as emotionally fluid as shifting sand. He met with her to discuss the script, and she impressed him with the way she defined her character using elements of her own personality.

For Meg, it was an opportunity to display her versatility. The thirty-nine-year-old actress felt that her previous film, *You've Got Mail* with Tom Hanks, had typecast her as a romantic-comedy lead, and the prospect of going down in cinematic history as the Queen of the Chick Flicks did not especially appeal to her.

"I've done something like thirty movies and only seven have been romantic comedies," she complained to *Entertainment Weekly*. "But I was getting locked into that. It was starting to get irritating." For that reason, *Proof of Life* looked like a godsend.

With Meg signed to do the movie—she received fifteen million dollars, her largest paycheck to date—Hackford focused on finding his leading man. He sent the script to Mel Gibson, but the actor passed on the grounds that it just wasn't right for him. Hackford's second choice was Russell Crowe. Impressed by Russell's depiction of Bud White in *L.A. Confidential,* he got in touch with Michael Mann, who had directed Crowe in *The Insider,* and Ridley Scott, who had directed him in *Gladiator.*

At that point, neither film had been released, so both directors invited him into their editing rooms to view portions of the films. Hackford was impressed that Russell could portray two totally different leading men—one very physical and imposing and the other very cerebral and unpredictable. The role of hostage negotiator Terry Thorne in *Proof of Life* would require him to display both qualities, though with more of a middle-of-the-road approach.

When he met with Russell, Hackford knew he had the right man. The actor loved the script and was eager to tackle the role, especially when Hackford told him that he could use his Australian accent. But to Hackford's surprise, the studio gave him a hard time over his selection. *The Insider* and *Gladiator* had not yet been released, and studio executives did not think Russell was a big enough star to play opposite Meg Ryan. Hackford stood his ground, though, and got the actor he wanted.

Proof of Life was based on a story that appeared in *Vanity Fair* about a professional hostage negotiator. It focused on the realities of the "new world order." As giant corporations expanded their influence from country to country, the risks to their high-level employees were increased.

In recent years, a rash of kidnappings for cash by revolutionaries and terrorists had revealed the inadequacies of local governments to deal with the problem. As a result, a new breed of hostage negotiator emerged—men with paramilitary training who had the expertise to deal directly with kidnappers to secure the release of their hostages. These men were hired guns who worked for the corporations involved and kept their distance from local police officials.

Some of the scenes in *Proof of Life* were shot in London and Poland, but most of the film was filmed on location in Ecuador. That suited Hackford just fine, because he had studied international relations at the University of Southern California in the 1960s and he was familiar with the politics and terrain of South America, where he had served for a time as a Peace Corps volunteer.

Russell wanted to do many of his own stunts, so Hackford allowed him to tackle whatever the actor felt he could handle. In Poland, during cold, bitter weather, Russell hung from a hovering helicopter; in Ecuador he traveled fourteen thousand feet into the mountains during the rainy season to film scenes in a jungle setting.

Because the hour-and-a-half ride from a hotel to the jungle set was so dangerous, with chunks of roadway washing away on a daily basis and Ecuadorians driving recklessly all over the road, Russell spent many nights in his trailer on the mountaintop, where he squirreled away food from the caterer and built a barbecue grill out of an oil drum so that he could do his own cooking. For self-protection, he kept a Leatherman in his pocket, a multipurpose tool with a serrated knife blade that is used by British special-service soldiers to cut the throats of their enemies.

Hackford was amazed at Russell's toughness. The conditions in the jungle were so stressful that one week the director had to have nearly three dozen men carried out. "You can take stars to a place like this and they can say, 'To hell with this,'" Hackford told *Movieline* magazine. "But Russell went in and did it. He's thorny. He challenges you right back—and he keeps everything alive."

Proof of Life begins with Terry Thorne, who works for a company that rescues kidnapped business executives, making a report on a kidnapping in which a ransom was paid to secure the release of a man abducted by Chechen rebels. It was a messy operation, and in the end Terry had to rescue the hostage from Russians soldiers who came upon the transfer and engaged the Chechens in battle. Since the company for whom the hostage worked was willing to pay the ransom, it was possible to get the hostage back with minimal difficulty—a modern-day reality of the corporate bottom line.

Halfway across the globe, an American engineer named Peter Bowman is trying to build a dam for an oil company that considers him a do-gooder and his work a necessary evil that allows the company to exploit a South American country's oil reserves. He is married to Alice Bowman, a former hippie who has a low opinion of the oil executives for whom her husband works.

When rebels kidnap Bowman and demand a three-million-dollar ransom, Terry is sent to negotiate his release. After he arrives, the oil company discovers that Bowman is not covered by insurance, so Terry is told his services are no longer needed. Alice's feelings about the oil company are confirmed when she is told that no ransom will be paid to secure his release. If she wants to see her husband again, she will have to raise the money herself and negotiate her own deal.

Because he has fallen in love with Alice during the brief time he spent with her, Terry returns to volunteer his services as a hostage negotiator. Through a series of telephone calls, he is able to negotiate the price down to $650,000, an amount that Alice and her husband's sister attempt to raise through contacts back in the States.

Unfortunately, before the money can be raised, the rebels tell Terry that the deal is off because Bowman now knows too much about their operations. Terry calls in a friend he has worked with in other rescue operations, and the two men put together a plan to extract Bowman from the rebels.

During the stress of the negotiations, Alice discovers that she has feelings for

Terry. One day, as she watches Terry load weapons onto a helicopter, she says, "I've never seen you nervous," to which he responds, "Yes, you have," and then kisses her.

At that point, the question for moviegoers is not whether Bowman will be rescued—everyone knows that will take place, though at what cost is not made clear—but whether Alice and Terry will ride off into the Ecuadorian sunset together.

Soon after production began, it became clear to everyone associated with the film that Russell and Meg were interested in each other in a romantic way. They held hands and cuddled and looked at each other with starry eyes. No one was really surprised, since both actors had a habit of falling in love with their costars.

For Russell, that trend had begun with Danielle Spencer in *The Crossing* and continued through a string of on-set romances, most of which didn't last any longer than it took to make the movie. For Meg, it began in 1985 with Anthony Edwards, her costar in the film *Top Gun*. After the film wrapped, she moved in with Edwards and lived with him for a time. Then she met actor Dennis Quaid on the set of *Innerspace* and fell in love with him. They lived together for a while, then eventually got married.

By the time she reported for work on *Proof of Life*, she was thought to have one of the strongest marriages in Hollywood. She had a son, Jack Henry, born in 1992, and she seemed to enjoy a happy relationship with Dennis, one that never made the tabloids.

All that came to an end in June 2000, when she and Russell flew to London together to film additional scenes for *Proof of Life* at Pinewood Studios. On board the flight was a New York businessman who recognized the actress, even though she tried to disguise herself by wearing shaded glasses.

The businessman was excited about having a famous actress aboard the flight, especially one who had such a squeaky-clean reputation. She was the closest thing to a national sweetheart that America had. Imagine his surprise when he realized that the man sitting next to her was Russell Crowe and not her husband, Dennis Quaid.

As the businessman looked on, the two actors seemed to relate to each other more as a couple than as friends. "He was leaning over her, kissing her on the neck and stroking her hair—and it went on that way the whole flight," the businessman told *People* magazine. "They were definitely very affectionate and flirtatious. It was certainly more than you'd want your wife or girlfriend doing with another man."

So impressed was the businessman with the boldness of their affair that he told reporters about it when the plane landed in London. The incident made headlines around the world. Within days after Meg returned to Los Angeles, publicists for both Dennis and Meg announced that they were separating after nine years of marriage. Shortly after that, Dennis filed for divorce. Friends and family members told reporters that they didn't have a clue that anything was wrong in the marriage.

It was a busy summer for Russell. In between trips to and from London to finish scenes for *Proof of Life,* he flew his band members to Austin, Texas, to begin work on an album. He also started work on a new film with Jodie Foster titled *Flora Plum* and pursued his romance with Meg.

At times, there were conflicting reports on the romance. Russell and Meg were spotted at a Los Angeles café, where they were said to be giggling and carrying on like teenagers. Photographers snapped shots of Russell kissing Meg while holding her face in his hands.

On another occasion, the two were seen together at a David Bowie concert in London, after which they went backstage to meet the singer. Not long after that, Meg kissed Russell goodnight and returned to her hotel, citing an early morning shoot the next day. Half in jest, a twenty-six-year-old BBC researcher named Jennie invited Russell to attend a crew party at a Liverpool Street hotel. To her surprise, he said yes and suggested that they go to the party in his limousine.

When they arrived at the hotel, he led her to a quiet corner and ordered drinks. They talked for about an hour; then, according to witnesses, he put his arm around her waist and slipped his hand beneath her T-shirt. They left the bar at 2:30 A.M., and Russell stretched out on the back seat of his limo so that he could put his head in Jennie's lap and extend his feet out the window. They kissed and talked on the ride to his hotel, but when they arrived, Russell told her that he was going to call it a night because he was tired.

"Jennie was a bit hurt so she tried to make a joke by saying he was no one special," reported the *Daily Mail.* "He looked furious and said, 'No, I am a somebody, I worked f– – hard to be. I am not a nobody.' Then he asked his chauffeur to take her home and said goodnight."

The next morning, Meg discovered what Dennis had felt like when he read about her affair with Russell in the newspaper, because she read about Russell's late-night fling with Jennie in the *Daily Mail.* By the time Meg returned to Los Angeles she was telling friends that her affair with Russell had cooled, although they were still affectionate with each other in public. At that point, Russell seemed to be the one with the deepest emotional investment in the relationship.

Truthfully, their relationship had reached its high point while they were filming *Proof of Life.* They saw each other every day and laughed at each other's jokes. They lived in a makeshift movie world far from home, making up the rules for their romance as they went along. With their return to the real world, they found it more difficult to spend time with each other because of their conflicting schedules.

One of the things that keep Russell apart from Meg was his Austin, Texas, recording session with Thirty Odd Foot of Grunts. The session was booked in the summer of 2000, after Russell accepted an offer from Artemis Records, an independent label based in New York City, to release an album consisting of both new material and songs previously recorded by the band. It would be titled *Bastard Life or Clarity.*

Artemis Records is not a major player in the industry, but it has done well with artists and groups that have gone out of favor and then rebounded with new material. Country singer and guitarist Steve Earle is an example, as is the pop group Boston. None of the major record labels in the United States had ever shown any interest in Thirty Odd Foot of Grunts, but Artemis liked the band's material and thought that Russell's celebrity would give them just enough edge to successfully promote the album.

Austin was a good place for the band to record, for several reasons. Russell felt comfortable there, primarily because of its urban-cowboy ambiance but also because it is the only American city outside of New York and Los Angeles that nurtures both a music and a film industry. In an average year, Hollywood will do about one hundred million dollars worth of business in Austin, making films such as *Spy Kids, Where the Heart Is, The Getaway,* and *The Great Waldo Pepper.*

For years, Austin has been a recording center for electric blues, alternative rock 'n' roll, and left-of-center country artists who didn't feel comfortable in Nashville, New York, or Los Angeles studios. Russell is fond of saying that his music cannot be defined, that it has to be savored—rubbed onto your soul like a miracle salve. Probably ninety percent of the artists that record in Austin say the same thing about their music, which is why Thirty Odd Foot of Grunts felt so much at home there.

Arlyn Studios seemed as good a place as any for the band to lay down its tracks. Located in the old Austin Opera House, in the heart of the downtown area, the nearly twenty-year-old studio offered top-of-the-line equipment and more than six thousand square feet of recording space.

Over the years, co-owner Lisa Fletcher, a Mississippi native (and Ole Miss graduate) who was raised on the nuances of Southern hospitality, has welcomed an eclectic mix of recording artists to her studio, including Bonnie Raitt, Willie Nelson, the Indigo Girls, the Fabulous Thunderbirds, Jimmie and Stevie Ray Vaughan, and Neil Young.

The makeup of Thirty Odd Foot of Grunts had changed somewhat over the years—only guitarist and songwriter Billy Dean Cochran had been with Russell from the beginning—but the rhythm section of Garth Adam on bass and Dave Kelly on drums had put in about five years with the group. The newest members were Dave Wilkins on guitar and Stewart Kirwan on trumpet. Kirwan, the only member of the band with a degree in music, also sang lead with his own group, Cracksquad.

Bastard Life or Clarity was produced by Kerry Tolhurst, an Australian who had first traveled to the United States in 1976 with a pioneering band named the Dingoes. That visit expanded into a three-year stay, during which he signed a deal with A&M Records and toured with Tom Petty and the Heartbreakers. For the past several years, Tolhurst has divided his time between homes in New York and Melbourne.

Under Tolhurst's watchful eye, Russell and the band recorded about two dozen songs at Arlyn Studios, only ten of which made it onto the album. "Sail Those Same Oceans," a rhythm-heavy ballad that features session player Ian McLagen on keyboards, was written for Russell's first serious girlfriend, Danielle Spencer. It is about how his ambition to be a star in Hollywood affected their relationship.

"The Legend of Barry Kable," a slow narrative about a homeless man whom Dean Cochran met while working for a rescue mission in Sydney, first appeared on the band's *Gaslight* album. Dean first shared the lyrics with Russell after a performance at a Coffs Harbour hotel named the Hoey Moey. Russell added some lyrics of his own and made suggestions regarding the song's structure.

Another song recycled from the *Gaslight* album was "Wendy," written about a woman Russell got to know while working in a New Zealand resort. The woman did a ten-day-on, four-day-off shift at the resort. At work, she was flirtatious and affectionate with the guests, but when her young son appeared at the start of the four-day-off shift, she transformed herself into the perfect mother. The track features a viola and some solid trumpet work by Kirwan.

Russell and Wilkins cowrote "The Night That Davey Hit the Train," based on conversations that Cochran had with actor Daniel Pollock, who costarred with Russell in *Romper Stomper*. A heroin addict, Pollock was killed after the film wrapped, when he stepped in front of a train.

Russell wrote "Judas Cart" about his niece, Chelsea, who after living with his parents and his divorced brother, Terry, for seven years, left to be with her mother again. It befell Russell to drive her back to her mother's home. The look of devastation he saw in Terry's face as he drove away with his daughter stuck with him for a long time and made its way into the song.

Perhaps because the first line of "Somebody Else's Princess" refers to unrequited love for a red-haired, blue-eyed woman, there are some who think it was written about Nicole Kidman. But Russell denies that and swears it was written about a publicist who once promoted one of the band's tours.

Cowritten by Russell and Cochran, "Memorial Day" was inspired by the World War II experience of Russell's grandfather. Other songs on the album include "Things Have Got to Change," "Hold You," "Sail Those Same Oceans," and "Swept Away Bayou," the last featuring some impressive fiddle work by Lili Haydn. One song that didn't make it onto the album was "Other Ways of Speaking," which Russell wrote for new friend Jodie Foster.

During a trip to London that summer, Russell did a telephone interview with the *Austin Chronicle*, during which he was asked a question that often occurs to first time listeners of the band's mix of folk and rock: How do you describe your music?

"Well, instead of going through some elaborate kind of description, I just tell people it's folk music," he responded. "In most people's heads, that makes them think of some kind of dusty, acoustic setting, which obviously isn't really what the band is about. But I don't think there's any more accurate description of what we do. It's folk music, with true stories....Some of them are a little oblique and maybe you can't necessarily follow the story A to Z, but that's not a bad thing either. It just makes you think."

While recording in Austin, Russell and the band gave a two-hour concert at

Stubb's Bar-B-Q, a popular music venue that packed in more than two thousand of the actor's fans for the event. Russell drank beer and chatted with the audience during the performance, at one point explaining that "Sail Those Same Oceans" was written about his experiences with Danielle. He laughingly told the crowd that she was working on an album of her own, but he doubted that any of the songs were about him.

Reporters described the enthusiastic audience as predominantly female, which is probably why Russell received such a hearty round of applause when he stripped down to a sleeveless tank top to sing his encore song. Meg did not go to Austin to attend the concert, but she was very much on his mind, as evidenced by his onstage comments about her. Between the recording sessions and flying to Los Angeles to visit her, he began training for Jodie Foster's film, *Flora Plum*, which would require him to commute to Orlando, Florida.

Flora Plum was important enough to Foster that she turned down a hefty paycheck for the starring role in *Hannibal*, the sequel to the *Silence of the Lambs*, to sit in the director's chair. The film is about a circus freak who feels sorry for a penniless waif, Flora Plum, and takes her under his wing with the intention of making her a trapeze star. In the process he falls in love with her and discovers that she is not the angel he once thought she was.

Foster had directed two previous films, *Little Man Tate* (1991) and *Home for the Holidays* (1995), and *Flora Plum* was just the type of offbeat romance she could relate to as a director. Since Foster was also a coproducer on the film, she supervised the casting herself. For the title role, she chose Golden Globe–winning actress Claire Danes, who agreed to take time off from her studies at Yale to do the film. And for the role of the freak, she picked Russell Crowe.

Foster apparently asked Russell to take the role in January, leading some people to wonder if her "date" with him at the Golden Globes had been a tradeoff for him taking the role. At his suggestion, she went to Austin to scout possible locations for the film, perhaps in the belief that it would make it easier for him to work on his album while making the film. However, none of the sites in and around Austin worked out, and she decided to start filming in Orlando.

Two weeks before shooting began, Russell called Foster with some bad news: he had injured his shoulder while rehearsing one of the climbing scenes he would be required to do in the film. He said that he would have to return to Australia immediately for emergency surgery and that he had no idea when he would be able to resume work on the film.

Foster was devastated. She felt especially sorry for Danes. Not only had she dropped out of college to make the film, she had spent eight weeks training for her work on the trapeze. Foster had no choice but to stop production. From that point on, she had two new choices: she could hold off resuming production until Russell had healed, or she could recast the role with another actor. Though it would mean putting a twenty-four-million-dollar production into limbo, she decided to wait for Russell.

No sooner had the actor left the country than rumors circulated that he had faked the injury to get out of being in the movie. So many people were quoted as saying that he looked fine that he was forced to address the rumors. "People say to me, 'You look all right,'" he told *Heat* magazine. "Well, what the fuck did you expect to see, you idiot? It's inside my fucking shoulder. Because some people say it like I'm lying, like this is a big ruse. Walking around to pick up a beer is one thing, but I need to be able to do the chin-ups with one hand. That to me is recovery—it's not just being able to put your jacket on in the morning without wincing."

When the rumors persisted, he posted gory photographs on a website, claiming they were taken during the surgery. He offered no verifiable proof that the photos were of his shoulder operation, but skeptics had no proof that it was otherwise. His biggest defender throughout the controversy was Jodie Foster, who said the film would be rescheduled when Russell was feeling better.

That never happened, of course. A year and a half after halting production, Foster jump-started the project and made it clear that Russell would not be rejoining the cast. "Times have changed," she told *TV Guide*. "Russell has gone on to do other things, and he's not necessarily—for whatever reason—the right person for it anymore."

After returning to Australia in September, Russell kept a low profile. Whether it was to nurse his alleged wounds or simply to rest after an exhausting year, he did little other than to enjoy life on his ranch and commute to Los Angeles to visit Meg.

By that time, Meg was talking more openly to the media about her marriage to Dennis Quaid. The marriage was in trouble long before she ever met Russell, she told *USA Today*: "The public and the press tuned in way after....I'll never talk about what went down and neither will Dennis." She denied stories published in the tabloids that Dennis had been unfaithful to her.

By the time *Proof of Life* was released in early December 2000, the offscreen romance between Russell and Meg had taken a back seat to more pressing Hollywood issues. Director Taylor Hackford was greatly relieved; the last thing he wanted was for their love life to overshadow a film they had put so much work into.

Perhaps because of the offscreen romance, the critics savaged the film. Under a headline that proclaimed the Ryan-Crowe film romance flat, *San Francisco Chronicle* critic Wesley Morris took aim at the real-life romance: "While [Meg] chain-puffs, the smoke-aholic Crowe only gets through a fraction of a pack. It turns out to be an awesome thing for his acting...he takes long drags on Ryan instead. He appears to want her so profoundly that there ought to be Meg-flavored Nicorette. For her, though, the cigarettes are a prop, a stand-in for what she really wants."

Writing in *Time* magazine, Richard Corliss felt that the film was superior entertainment, but he had a difficult time getting past the big romance. "The all-American blonde is now a Jezebel, her cuddlings with Crowe sprayed across gossip-mag covers and on tabloid-tale TV shows," he wrote. "The eventual film looked destined to be remembered as Exhibit A in the trial of adulterous love."

Los Angeles Times critic Kenneth Turan heaped praise on Russell's acting abilities, and he felt that the climatic action scenes were "briskly done," but he, too, had a difficult time moving past the starring couple's real-life affair. "It may be unfair, but it's inevitable that *Proof of Life* is going to be seen, at least in the short run, through the lens of the offscreen romance that developed on location," he wrote. "The affair that unleashed a flood of tabloid headlines is simply too fitting a viewpoint to resist in our scandal-and-celebrity-crazed age."

Before the release of the film, Hackford had been optimistic. Asked by *Movieline* if the offscreen romance would affect the box office, he replied: "I'd like *Proof of Life* to be seen and judged on the film—not on some paparazzo view of the world. On the other hand, name identification of *Proof of Life* is rather strong at the moment—and that helps."

Hackford's mood darkened considerably after the film was released, for it quickly became clear that it was going to be a box-office failure. The worldwide gross for the film was only fifty-one million dollars, much less than the sixty-five million dollars he'd spent making it. Hackford blamed the poor box office on the controversy generated by the offscreen romance, and he accused Russell and Meg of ruining the movie.

The comments made Russell furious. At a London press conference, he said, "The guy's an idiot—seriously, what a knob. The film is what the film is. I don't think truly the relationship had a negative effect on the movie."

After the promotional tour was over, Russell returned to his ranch in Australia. He tried to talk Meg into joining him there for Christmas, but she was reluctant to leave her son during the holidays or to take him away from his father at a time when the family was still in an upheaval over the impending divorce. Instead, she urged him to come to Los Angeles for Christmas. He declined, saying that he had always spent Christmas with his parents and felt a need to be with them during the holidays.

As Christmas approached, Russell and his parents planned an enormous celebration for family and friends that would begin two days after Christmas and continue on into the New Year. The holiday itself they spent alone, enjoying one another's company. They were having lunch on Christmas Day when the telephone rang.

Told it was Meg calling from Los Angeles, Russell rose from the table and accepted the call. It was not what he expected. Meg told him that the relationship just wasn't working out and that she felt it would be best if they didn't see each other again.

"He was devastated and went straight to his room," a close friend told *New Idea* magazine. "He virtually didn't leave his room for two days. His mother was really worried, but by the time his friends started arriving for the party he had composed himself. He joined in the drinking, swimming and barbecues, but Meg's name was never mentioned."

Russell didn't talk about Meg again—at least not publicly—for nearly a year. In December 2001, he broke that self-imposed ban in an interview with *Entertainment Weekly*. "We fell in love," he said. "It happens—thank God. It was an incredibly intense period of my life and obviously of her life. She's a magnificent person. If anything, I owe her an apology for not being as flexible as I might have been. I don't think I'll ever make that mistake again."

Russell was thirty-six years old when Meg broke up with him. Despite all of his affairs over the years, he had only fallen in love twice—first to Danielle and then to Meg. That was not much to show for nearly two decades of manhood, and the pain of that realization bore deeply into his concept of self, reviving old fears of inadequacy. He didn't have what he most needed in life, and that only fed the rage inside him.

SEVEN

FINDING REDEMPTION IN
A BEAUTIFUL MIND

Faced with Meg's devastating rejection, he turned to the person who had always been there for him during times of stress—Danielle Spencer. After emerging from his room on December 27, he called her at her home in Sydney and asked if she would make the seven-hour drive to Coffs Harbour to be with him.

Danielle was unable to go immediately because she had made other plans for the holidays, but she did make it up to the ranch before the week-long celebration ended, and she stayed after the other revelers left. Russell's friends briefed Danielle on his breakup with Meg, but she never asked him any questions about it and he never brought the subject up. Instead, they fell back into the rhythm of their early relationship, before they became lovers, when they talked for hours on end, took long walks, and read books while in each other's company. There was something about Danielle that soothed the anger inside Russell and allowed him to be a peace with himself, at least for the moment.

Shortly after Danielle left the ranch, Russell returned to Los Angeles to attend the presentation of Golden Globe Awards. The nominations had been announced three days before Christmas, and Russell was pleased to learn that he had been nominated in the best-actor category for his role in *Gladiator*. Also nominated were Ridley Scott for best director, Joaquin Phoenix for best supporting actor, and Hans Zimmer and Lisa Gerrard for best original score for a motion picture. Russell and Meg had planned to attend together if he received a nomination, but he ended up going with two burly, tuxedo-clad men, the discomfort clearly showing in his face.

Those who thought his discomfort was due to the heartbreak he felt were only half right. Shortly before leaving for America, Russell was told by American authorities that they had uncovered a plot to kidnap him. The FBI advised Russell to maintain a high level of security, and the agency arranged for two agents to accompany him to the Golden Globes.

Russell did not win the best-actor award—nor did Ridley Scott and Joaquin Phoenix win in their categories—but Zimmer and Gerrard did take home awards for best original score. It was a disappointing night for everyone involved with *Gladiator*, and it did not bode well for the upcoming Academy Awards (tradition has it that the Golden Globes are a good indicator of how the Oscars will be distributed).

At some point during the awards show, Russell encountered rock star and sometime actress Courtney Love. They talked for a while, both agreeing that post-ceremony parties were a bore; then they left together to go to Russell's hotel suite.

Russell was depressed over his breakup with Meg, but Courtney, who had not had a satisfying or sustained relationship since the death of her husband, Nirvana frontman Kurt Cobain, was in more of a total life funk because of a lawsuit with her record label.

Universal Music Group had sued her to recover damages for five undelivered record albums. Love was outraged because the original deal she had signed in 1992 was with Geffen Records. Through a series of buyouts, Geffen was absorbed by the Universal Music Group, and Love's contract was given to Universal's subsidy label Interscope Records. She released two albums with Interscope—1994's platinum CD *Live through This* and 1998's slower-selling *Celebrity Skin*—but she was unhappy with the way they marketed the second album and refused to do any additional albums.

On the evening she returned to Russell's hotel with him, she was preparing to file a countersuit claiming that she owed Interscope nothing since she had never signed with that label. She was outraged that she could be treated like a piece of property—transferred from one company to another at will. That didn't happen with lawyers or doctors or plumbers. Why was it all right for big companies to do that with recording artists, songwriters, or authors?

If Russell thought he was going to be consoled that evening because of his breakup with Meg, he was wrong, for Love's needs were much greater than his own. Love was distraught and unfocused, roaming from subject to subject, her emotions flowing like a river. Russell didn't really know what to do with her, so he encouraged her to organize her thoughts.

"I'm a gentle soul, so we sat down and found a way for her to express what she was feeling, which was writing it down," Russell later told *Entertainment Weekly.* "And she got to the point where what she was writing was really upsetting. But it was brilliant. She's a poetess."

They spent the remainder of the evening writing poetry and song lyrics, and doing major damage to a bottle of tequila. They never had sex, according to both Russell and Love. However, by the time Russell returned to Australia, the tabloids were filled with salacious stories of their evening together. As the weeks went by, the tabloids reported that Love was pregnant, and Russell was fingered as the probable father.

Russell gave interviews denying that he had ever had sex with Love. He probably should have consulted with Love before making those statements, because she interpreted them as meaning she was not worthy of sex. His denials threw her into a rage.

"You know, Ben Affleck went on a talk show and said he made out with me at a party, and there's nothing further from the truth," she told *Entertainment Weekly.* "Did I issue a press release saying we didn't f– –? It's embarrassing that Russell was embarrassed….Am I a sexual pariah?"

As the tabloids continued to stroke the story, Russell hunkered down even more resolutely at his ranch in Australia. Then, in February 2001, the Academy of Motion Picture Arts and Sciences announced its nominations for that year's

Academy Awards.

Gladiator received an astonishing twelve nominations, including Russell Crowe for best actor, Ridley Scott for best director, Joaquin Phoenix for best actor in a supporting role, and the film itself for best picture. Other nominated categories included best costume design, best effects, best sound, best art direction, best cinematography, best editing, best music and best writing. It was the second year in a row that Russell had been nominated for an Oscar, but he was still stunned by the announcement, for he had lowered his hopes the previous month after not receiving a Golden Globe.

Amid the excitement over the nomination, the realization crept in that Russell would have to return to Los Angeles and face reporters, many of whom would still be interested in asking him questions about his evening with Courtney Love. There was also the possibility that Love would confront him over his denials of a relationship. Recent newspaper quotes that were attributed to her indicated she was still fuming.

Again he turned to Danielle. He telephoned her and asked what she was doing on a certain night (which just happened to be Oscar night). She told him she wasn't sure, that she would have to check her appointment book. He promised to call back in a day or so. When he got back to her, she told him she was free that night. It was not until then that he asked her to be his date for the Academy Awards ceremony. She was thrilled.

Russell also asked his mother and father to accompany him to the awards show. Because of the large number of nominations the film received, he felt good about his chances this time around. In the event he did win, he wanted to do something special to demonstrate his love for his family. He asked his grandmother, Joy, if he could take his grandfather's World War II medal with him to Los Angeles and wear it on stage if he were to win an Oscar. Joy told him that she felt that his grandfather would be honored.

With his plans for the Academy Awards in place, Russell hit the road, ending up in an unlikely place—Nashville, Tennessee. In town to check out the city's recording facilities for future Grunts sessions, he strolled downtown one night and saw an old girlfriend's name on the marquee of the Wildhorse Saloon.

Australian-born Jamie O'Neal, who recently had scored a No. 1 hit on the country charts with her debut single, "There Is No Arizona," was in the nightclub performing in the Country Music Seminar's annual New Faces show.

Russell approached the doorman and asked, "Now that wouldn't be Jamie O'Neal of Melbourne, Australia, now would it?"

"Yes, I believe it would," answered the doorman.

Ebullient over his discovery, Russell went inside and found O'Neal backstage. She was astonished to see him. They had dated in the early 1990s, while she sang backup for Australian pop star Kylie Minogue, but they hadn't laid eyes on each other since then. They chatted until it was time for her to go on stage, at which point she asked him if he wanted to get up and sing a song.

Russell didn't say yes and he didn't say no: He simply intoned the words,

"Folsom Prison Blues." That was answer enough for O'Neal, and when she completed her set, she introduced Russell to the audience and plugged his album *Bastard Life or Clarity.* Wearing black leather pants and a fashionably untucked black shirt, Russell took the stage to play acoustic guitar and sing the song that Johnny Cash made famous.

With that, he faded into the night and headed back to the bright lights of Los Angeles, convinced he had tapped into the Music City mother lode, if only for a moment.

Unfortunately, a cloud still hovered over the upcoming Academy Awards ceremonies. The kidnap plot was still under investigation and the actor was still in danger. Rumors of the plot had begun to surface in the media, and the FBI broke its silence and answered questions posed by newspaper reporters.

"The threat was for a kidnap and that was apparently to possibly occur here in the United States, but beyond that I really can't get into specifics," said Los Angeles special agent Matthew McLaughlin. "Specifics of that we are avoiding talking about right now—we have personnel and resources in place that could be compromised, so we want to make sure we can take care of everybody."

A police source described Russell as "genuinely scared" by the plot to kidnap him, but the actor downplayed the threat when he arrived in Los Angles with Danielle and his family for the pre-Oscar festivities.

"I don't think those blokes have thought it out," Russell told reporters after the annual Oscar nominees lunch. "Quite frankly, if they had to spend that much time in a small room with me...one of them might end up saying, 'Look, pass the hat around and for a couple of hundred dollars you can take him off our hands.'"

Twelve FBI agents stuck with him throughout his appearances that week, but he didn't allow that to slow him down. His worst nightmare was not that he would turn a corner and suddenly encounter the kidnappers, but rather that he would come face-to-face with Courtney Love. He could hardly turn to the FBI agents and scream out, "Drop her!"

The dreaded encounter occurred at one of the pre-Oscar parties, where there was lots of drinking and loud music. They spoke privately for a while and everything seemed fine, but then the music of her late husband Kurt Cobain flowed over the PA system and Courtney became upset, shouting to all those around her that Kurt was the greatest rock star who had ever lived.

Russell tried to console her, but emotionally she seemed totally withdrawn into herself. At around 3 A.M., Russell notified his bodyguards that he was ready to leave, and they called for his limousine. Russell and Courtney walked out the door together, but as Russell headed for the limo, she became distracted by a group of rowdy fans on the sidewalk and stopped to talk to them for a moment.

When Courtney turned around, she saw Russell leap into the limousine and sit next to a striking blonde who seemed happy to see him. Courtney pressed her face against the window and angrily demanded to know if the blonde was his Australian girlfriend. It was a frightening moment for Danielle, who could see the rage in Courtney's eyes. Courtney is a big woman with long arms, and when she is upset she looks intimidating, like a lioness slashing into the air. Russell didn't want to be rude to her, but when she began pounding on the window, shouting unpleasant things to Danielle, the order was given to drive off.

Later, he expressed his disappointment about Courtney to a writer for *Entertainment Weekly*. He was fine with Courtney, he maintained, until the moment she stepped over the line and shouted at Danielle. "Now I see her in a different light," he said.

When Russell arrived at the Oscar ceremonies with Danielle on his arm, the press corps started buzzing. Who was she? No one had ever seen her before. Was she Russell's girlfriend? If not, why did the two of them enter the building holding hands? Reporters looked around for Meg Ryan so that they could get a comment, but she was a no-show at the ceremonies, having wisely opted to watch on television. With little to go on, the reporters eventually determined that the blonde in the stylish black gown was an Aussie whom Russell had imported especially for the occasion.

One of the reporters who spoke to Russell as he entered the building was Joan Rivers. She later complained that the actor had a bad case of body odor, leading her to conclude that he did not use deodorant.

The seventy-third Academy Awards was a glamorous affair, with stars everywhere the eye could see. Russell and Danielle sat close together, holding hands, as host Steve Martin poked fun at himself and the actors who were in attendance. It all seemed funny enough to Russell until Martin told the audience that actress Ellen Burstyn had put on thirty pounds and twenty years for her role in *Requiem for a Dream*. Even then, Martin joked, "Russell Crowe still hit on her."

Russell gripped Danielle's hand tightly and glowered at the comedian. He couldn't understand why Americans made fun of him. He had only experienced two great loves in his life and one of them was sitting at his side. Why did they have to embarrass him in front of Danielle?

Martin tried to make it up to Russell when he introduced him to present the award in the film-editing category. "I'd like to call [him] a close personal friend," Martin quipped, "but he asked me not to."

"G'day folks, how are ya doing?" Russell told the audience, "On this list are people who have thrilled me, astonished me, and protected me." He paused, allowing people to wonder if he was going to present an award to the FBI; then he explained that he was talking about film editors.

As it turned out, *Gladiator* surprised all the pundits, who predicted that it would not do well because of its demographic appeal to young males. Most of the academy voters were in their fifties and sixties. Why would they vote for a movie that catered to teenagers? But before the night was over, *Gladiator* racked up five wins, including the all-important best-picture category. Russell looked truly surprised when he heard presenter Hilary Swank call out his name as the winner for best actor.

When that happened, Joaquin Phoenix, who was seated directly behind Russell, jumped to his feet and embraced him. Russell turned and kissed Danielle on the mouth, then walked to the stage amid thunderous applause, his grandfather's medal clearly visible on his jacket, placed directly over his heart and attached by a bright red ribbon.

"I'd like to thank my mom and dad, who I just don't thank enough, I guess," he told the audience, after dedicating the award to his grandfather and uncle. "But really folks, I owe this to one bloke, and his name is Ridley Scott…If you grow up…in the suburbs of anywhere, a dream like this seems kind of vaguely ludicrous and completely unattainable. This moment is directly connected to those childhood imaginings. And for anybody who's on the downside of advantage and relying purely on courage, it's possible."

Russell seemed on top of the world, but then when he went backstage after making his acceptance speech, his mood quickly darkened. When a female reporter asked him how he got into the skin of his character, Maximus, he said with more than a little impatience, "I'm an actor. I read the script, I learn the lines, and I put the costume on."

The adoring reporter insisted that he did more than that.

"Let's move on," he snapped. "Next question."

When Russell returned to his seat, he did a double take on his mother, for there was something wrong with her face. Finally, after staring at her a moment, he figured out that one of her eyelashes had fallen off. She told him that she had cried so much during his acceptance speech that her eyelash had dropped to the floor.

That night Russell bypassed all the post-Oscar parties with the exception of one—the Governors Ball, which featured Elton John. Russell took his mother to that party so that she could meet the British pop star, one of her favorite recording artists. Russell arranged for them to be photographed together; then he called it a night.

When he returned to the hotel, all his friends were waiting for him, even though it was early in the morning. They stayed up talking for a while; then he went to bed and arose at 6 A.M. to catch a flight to New York so that he could start on his next film.

The following day, Danielle flew back to Australia with Russell's mother and father. "It was one of those things that I knew would cause a bit of trouble for me," she told the *Sydney Morning Herald*. "But I've watched the Academy Awards all my life and I just couldn't resist the invitation.…There's a magic when you are watching on TV in your lounge room but when you're actually there, there's the nuts and bolts of the organizing and people running around frantically. A bit of the sheen goes off. But it was pretty fascinating. It's like a once in a lifetime experience."

The idea for *A Beautiful Mind* began with an article in *Vanity Fair* magazine about a Nobel Prize–winning mathematician named John Nash. It was a heartwarming story about a genius's long struggle with mental illness, and his eventual triumph. Feeling that the story, which was prompted by Sylvia Nasar's book *A Beautiful Mind*, would make a good motion picture, Graydon Carter, the magazine's editor, pointed the article out to Hollywood producer Brian Grazer.

When he read it, Grazer thought it would make a terrific motion picture, so after consulting with his business partner, director Ron Howard, he asked Universal Pictures to purchase the rights to the book for their production company, Imagine Entertainment. Howard read the magazine story and was impressed, but at that point he made no claim on being the director because of other projects that were in the works.

"I think the article really did present the possibilities of a terrific drama," Howard told the *Hollywood Reporter*. "There's no question about it. But it was a complex next step to a screenplay."

When screenwriter Akiva Goldsman—whose credits include *The Client, Batman Forever*, and *A Time to Kill*—heard about the rights purchase, he asked his agent to set up a meeting for him with Grazer. He had read the biography in galleys, long before the magazine article appeared, and he was convinced it would make a great movie.

Goldsman knew he had his work cut out for him to convince Grazer that he was the right person to do the screenplay. He had written some very successful screenplays, but none of them had a deep intellectual foundation. A screenplay about a genius's struggle with schizophrenia would have to be handled with intelligence and a subtlety of detail not required in the other scripts he had written.

Not surprisingly, Grazer wanted to know what made Goldsman qualified to write such a script. The reply stunned him. Years ago, Goldman's parents—his mother is a child psychologist—had founded one of the first group homes for emotionally disturbed children in Brooklyn. That meant that he grew up in a home filled with children who had been diagnosed with schizophrenia or other mental illnesses. As a youngster, what impressed him most was the way the disturbed children always had reasons for their aberrant behavior. No matter how crazy their behavior looked to others, it always made sense to them.

Every writer feels in his heart that there is one book, play, poem, article, or screenplay that he or she was put on earth to write. For Goldsman, that one vehicle was the screenplay for *A Beautiful Mind*. He felt so passionately about it that he begged Grazer to allow him to write the script. Faced with such emotion, Grazer felt he had no alternative but to hire him.

When Grazer read the first draft, he was ecstatic, for Goldsman had done a masterly job of allowing the reader (or viewer) to experience Nash's descent into madness. Howard felt the same way and insisted on directing it himself. He saw it as a challenge. He had directed several films with serious themes, including *Apollo 13* and *Cocoon*, but he had also dabbled in the frivolous with *Splash* and *Parenthood*.

A Beautiful Mind was more than a film to Howard; it was also a possible turning point in his career. He was one of the most respected directors in the world, yet he had never won an Oscar or received the critical recognition he deserved. To many, he was still little Opie on the *Andy Griffith Show*.

The first real test of his ability to make the screenplay come to life was in casting. To play the role of John Nash, he needed someone who could be impressive in his early twenties and then be able to advance convincingly into his sixties. The actor would have to be intelligent enough to deal with Nash's high intelligence, volatile enough to express his bouts with schizophrenia, and creative enough to help define his character.

Howard sent the script to several actors, but it was Russell who intrigued him the most. *Gladiator* had not been released at that point, but Howard had seen *The Insider* and thought that Russell had given an inspired performance. Besides having a high reputation as a character actor, Russell was said to be as manic as John Nash himself.

When Russell received the script, he was in Austin recording with his band. It was a steamy night, but he took the script and went out onto the back porch of his rented home and read it from cover to cover. It gave him goose bumps, so he went back through it, making notes in the margins as he played with the dialogue. If he thought the dialogue was off base in a particular situation, he wrote down lines that would work better for him. By the time he finished making notes, he was certain he wanted the role.

Howard scheduled a meeting with Russell and was astonished to discover that the actor had already done more research on the character than he himself had done. By the time they finished talking, Howard was convinced that Russell was perfect for the role.

With Russell aboard, Howard turned his attention to casting the other roles. Since the movie was also a love story about Nash's courtship of his wife, Alicia, and her support for him during his illness, it was important to find an actress who could be intelligent, strong, determined, and attractive enough to satisfy the expectations of the theatergoing public.

Howard chose Jennifer Connelly, a thirty-one-year-old actress with two dozen movies to her credit, including *Mulholland Falls* (1996), *The Rocketeer* (1991), and *Labyrinth* (1986). He was familiar with her work because of a movie she had appeared in that he had produced (*Inventing the Abbotts*). The quality that he liked most about her was her ability to offer surprises during her performance. He felt that she and Russell would make an excellent screen couple, which was confirmed when she did a screen test with Russell at Howard's New York office.

When Connelly met Russell for the first time at the reading, she did not feel he was overly polite, but she was impressed by his presence. "When he first walked in I thought he was…energetic," she told *Vanity Fair.* "You feel him come into the room.…He's kind of charismatic and interesting to watch." At he end of the reading, Russell surprised her by walking her to the elevator and offering to have his driver take her home.

For the supporting roles, Howard went with Ed Harris to play William Parcher, the shadowy government agent; Christopher Plummer to play Dr. Rosen, the psychiatrist; Paul Bettany to play Charles Herman, Nash's roommate; and Judd Hirsch to play Helinger, Nash's faculty advisor at Princeton University.

When Russell returned to Australia to have surgery on his damaged shoulder, he communicated often with Howard by telephone and e-mail, offering suggestions about his character. One thing that Russell felt was important was that his scenes be shot in sequence. Movies are not traditionally shot that way, because it is too expensive. Instead, directors tend to group scenes that can be filmed in sequence to take advantage of location, lighting, and thematic similarities. Russell felt that if he played the young Nash one day and the older Nash the next day, it would dilute the intensity of his performance. He wanted to start at the beginning of the story and go straight through to the end.

Howard understood his point and convinced the studio that such a schedule was necessary to make the quality movie they all wanted. Russell's points were well taken, but it was more than a production issue for the actor: It was Howard's first test as the film's director, one he passed with Opie-like ease.

Just as Russell had done his homework on Nash, so had Howard done his homework on Russell. "One of the things that I learned from talking to the directors who'd worked with him before was that he could be kind of difficult," Howard told the New Zealand pop-culture magazine *Pavement*. "Then Russell said to me, directly, early on, 'I can be kind of noisy but I don't mean to be a rude bastard. Talk to me, hear me out, because I have my ideas, too.' So that's what I did. I applied that advice whenever things seemed tense. I'd give it a moment but I'd also open up a conversation. I found that using that approach worked and that Russell wasn't that unreasonable a person if you listened to him."

Before filming began, Russell viewed videotaped interviews with Nash so that he could get a feel for the man himself. He didn't meet with him, as he did with Jeffrey Wigand for *The Insider*. Instead, he wrote out questions he wanted Nash to answer and he asked Howard to videotape the replies.

Watching the videotapes, Russell was fascinated by Nash's hands, which the actor felt looked graceful because of their long, tapered fingernails. As a result, Russell allowed his own fingernails to grow so that his fingers would appear longer. When they didn't grow fast enough, he had tips glued to the ends of his fingers.

Russell had been obsessed with his hands for years. He thought his fingers were unattractive, or at least not attractive enough to belong to a world class actor. In an interview with Diane Sawyer for *PrimeTime*, he shyly held up his hands for her to examine. "They're not graceful—little scratches and everywhere little pits and scars," he said. "I was actually just looking at them the other day before I got on the plane and I realized, I started laughing, 'You ain't got Hollywood hands, boy.'"

Insanity was a subject that troubled Russell deeply. He was intrigued by the historical correlation between madness and genius, all the more so since people were constantly telling him that he was a genius. "It's a romantic notion that there's a link between madness and genius and certainly no amount of intelligence can protect you from insanity," he once told London's *Sunday* magazine. "Like everybody else, I've had my moments when I've felt I've been losing my grip."

Russell's mother had told him once that he was crazy as a child, though she didn't use language quite that blunt. Growing up, he had always felt a little out of the loop. Was he was crazy? It would certainly explain his frightening outbursts, his propensity for violence, and his occasional binge drinking. If so, was he crazy because he had a rage burning inside him, or did he have the rage burning inside him because he was crazy?

Besides studying the videotaped interviews with Nash, Russell wandered the streets of New York City, seeking out street people who were emotionally unstable. One man on East Ninety-second Street particularly impressed him with his conversations with numerous imaginary companions. Russell spent time talking to him and other street people he came across, noticing their mannerisms and the conviction with which they described their alternate realities.

Production began the day after Russell received an Oscar for his role in *Gladiator*. That meant he had to leave town quickly and bypass all the star-studded events, but that was fine with Russell, who didn't much care for stuffy cocktail parties. He was ready to get to work, but not before rattling his director's cage.

After arriving in New York, Russell drove down to Bluefield, West Virginia, the small town where John Nash was born, so that he could walk around and get a feel for what Nash's early years might have been like. Unfortunately, a big snowstorm blew in after he arrived and complicated his return to New Jersey, where an early morning meeting was scheduled with Ron Howard.

Russell drove all night to make it back in time for the meeting, but there was no time to change clothes. "I get out of the car and I'm still in my leathers, which I'd put on in anticipation of riding the bike prior to the snowstorm hitting, you know," he said in an interview with CNN's Larry King with Ron Howard sitting beside him. "So I've got hair like this, a beard substantially longer than this. And when my beard's a little bit longer, my IQ drops rapidly, you know....So, I'm getting out of the car...and it was like, 'Good day, Ron—let's do a movie.'"

To which Ron Howard countered, "I thought I was impassive and welcoming. But I looked panicked, right?"

"It was definitely rising panic," said Russell.

When shooting began, Russell was given a surprise of his own when the real John Nash, who still works at Princeton, showed up on the set unannounced. Russell introduced himself and asked what he thought was a simple question: "Would you like a cup of coffee or would you prefer tea?" Nash responded with a fifteen-minute monologue about his feelings about coffee and tea. Then, at the end of his speech, he told Russell that he really didn't care for either and would prefer to just sit down and watch. Russell and Howard were so impressed by the monologue that they worked it into the script.

Most of the film was shot in New Jersey, with locations at Belleville, Princeton, and Bayonne, but some scenes were done in New York City, at Manhattan College and Fordham University. Russell was on his best behavior, primarily because Howard remained ever alert to the nuances of his changing moods, which sometimes could range through shades of gray to pitch black in the course of a single conversation.

Russell and Howard got along remarkably well, with none of the explosive blowups that had characterized the actor's previous films. That is not to say there were no embarrassing moments. During a break in the filming of a scene on the campus of Princeton University, Russell looked up and saw a female student taking his picture from a second-story window. Angered, he flipped his middle finger at her, looking every bit the egomaniac.

The incident made the student newspaper, *The Daily Princetonian*, and was subsequently picked up by national news services. The student, Meredith Moroney, was appalled at Russell's behavior. "I wasn't out on the street, harassing him" she told *The Trentonian*. "I was on my own turf, not interrupting, not bothering him. Now I believe the rumors he's an a— —." Howard defended his star by saying that it was out of character for him. He assured the other students that Russell was not a "bad guy."

Toward the end of the shoot, while filming the scene where Nash accepts the Nobel Prize, Russell proved that, despite the bad publicity about his dark moods, he did have an actual sense of humor. Noting that the extras who had been hired to make up the audience were looking tired and listless, he feared they would appear bored when the camera panned them. At the critical moment, when they were supposed to applaud, he whipped out his Oscar and waved it in the air, off-camera of course. The audience went wild, which was just what was needed for the scene.

A Beautiful Mind begins with a speaker addressing a class of mathematics students at Princeton University. John Nash sits apart from the others, looking awkward and ill at ease. Later that day, at an outdoor party, Nash tells a fellow student that there must be a mathematical explanation for how bad his necktie is. Another older student, Martin Hansen, mistakes Russell for a server at the party.

As Nash moves the furniture in his apartment around, his roommate, Charles Herman, introduces himself. They go up on the roof and share a flask of whiskey. Nash admits that he doesn't like people and "they don't like me."

Nash skips classes to try to discover an original idea that will make him famous, and he solves mathematical problems by writing on the library windows—behavior that does not inspire confidence among those around him.

One day his friends talk him into going to a pool hall for relaxation. There he meets a girl at the bar and embarrasses himself and his friends by saying, "I don't exactly know what I'm required to say in order for you to have intercourse with me, but could we assume I've said all that?" He tells the girl, "Essentially, we're talking about a fluid exchange, right? So could we just go straight to the sex."

For that unsolicited bit of honesty, Nash receives a stiff slap across the face.

Nash's advisor tells him he's in trouble because he's not attending class and hasn't presented an idea for a paper. However, at the end of the year he presents a brilliant thesis that wins accolades from his advisor.

Five years later, at the Pentagon, Nash keeps an appointment with top generals who want him to help break an enemy code. He solves the problem but notices a man watching him from a distance.

Nash works for a research company that requires him to teach a university class, something he is reluctant to do. He meets his wife-to-be in class when she solves a problem involving noisy workmen outside the window.

One day, as he leaves a building, William Parcher, the man who looked at him so intently in the Pentagon, stops to introduce himself. He tells Nash that he works for the Department of Defense. After a brief conversation, he takes Nash to a restricted area on campus, where people are working on special projects. Parcher shows him film of a factory in Germany where the Nazis worked on a portable nuclear bomb; he explains that after the war the factory fell into the hands of the Russians.

Parcher asks him to help the government decipher codes hidden in magazines and newspapers by enemy agents who use that method to communicate with each other. He is recruited as a spy and given a drop-box location to use for communicating with the government.

When Nash begins his courtship of Alicia, he is distressed to notice that shadowy men are following him everywhere he goes. As the days go by, he discovers secret messages in magazine after magazine. He uses the codes to plot enemy locations on a map. After he writes his reports, he stuffs them into an envelope and leaves them in a drop box outside a large house with a gate.

One day he is befriended by a little girl, the niece of his former roommate, who comes back to visit him on occasion. He tells his roommate that he has met a girl and asks if he should marry her. That night he meets Alicia in a restaurant, drops to his knee, and in his own inimitable fashion, asks her to marry him.

Considered acceptably eccentric by his wife and friends, Nash hides his secret world of violence and intrigue from everyone around him. Ever so slowly, he descends into madness, his mind poisoned by schizophrenia, and only by sheer will power is he able to overcome the disease and claim the prestigious Nobel Prize for economics.

Once Danielle Spencer returned to Sydney, speculation began that she and Russell were again a couple, but she discouraged that kind of talk, saying they were simply friends. Always more at ease with the media than Russell, she deflected their questions about the relationship by pointing out that she had a boyfriend in Sydney and was not interested in resuming a romantic relationship with Russell.

More of a concern to Danielle than gossip about Russell was the release of her first album, *White Monkey*, a collection of pop songs that she had worked on for three years. She wrote the songs herself and played piano, Tori Amos style, on all the tracks.

The first single, "Jonathan White," featured Danielle on the cover dressed in black; the second single, "Blast Off," had a picture of her looking sadly at a distant fire. EMI Records in Australia released both singles in spring 2001, but neither made it to North America, even though the label has a strong promotional presence in the United States.

"Ideally I'd like to go between acting and music," she told the *Sydney Morning Herald*. "Obviously, the music has to take priority right now because you have to focus solidly on something like getting a record out. And the fact that it's my project and I've written it means I'm obviously very personally invested in it. So I want to do everything I can to make it work. But acting is obviously there and I'd always want to go back to it, so it's a matter of choosing your times to focus on either one or the other."

Coinciding with the release of her singles in Australia was the release of Russell's album in the United States. *Bastard Life or Clarity* had received a great deal of positive press upon its earlier release in Australia, and Russell was optimistic that it would find a receptive audience in America.

To his surprise, the local Australian press focused on the content of the songs, speculating in particular about the inspiration of the relationship songs. Was "Wendy" written about Meg Ryan? He told reporters it was written about the woman he observed at the New Zealand resort, and there is no reason to doubt him. Was "Somebody Else's Princess" written about Nicole Kidman? He stuck to his story that it was written about a publicist, but there is every reason to doubt that was the case.

Some Australian reporters wondered aloud if he was perhaps going soft, with so many relationship songs on the album. "I'm an expert at unrequited love," Russell sheepishly confessed to *Weekend* magazine. "I have, however, over a while, worked that out."

After wrapping production on *A Beautiful Mind*, Russell focused all his attention on putting together an American tour to promote the album. To no one's surprise, Danielle was added as the opening act, a decision that was probably made when she accompanied him to the Academy Awards ceremony. She saw it as an opportunity to promote *White Monkey*, even though EMI Records had no plans then for an American release.

In early July, Russell headed back to Australia to visit his family, but on the way he detoured to the Fiji Islands, where actress Nicole Kidman was vacationing with her two children. They had a friendship that dated back to their early years as struggling actors in Sydney. Nicole is fond of saying that she finds few things sexier than a man's hands working the frets of a guitar. She has never identified any particular hands, but the speculation is that she is referring to Russell.

When Nicole's divorce from Tom Cruise made headlines earlier in the year—and her pregnancy and subsequent miscarriage raised questions in the tabloids about the child's paternity—Russell reestablished contact with her and offered to console her.

Russell and Nicole arrived separately at the Wakaya Club, an exclusive resort on Wakaya Island, where they stayed for about a week. Tourism officials on the island confirmed that the Aussie actors were there at the same time but reported that they checked into separate quarters. After the Fiji vacation, they were spotted in Sydney at a private screening at Fox Studios. Despite the appearance of a brewing romance, both Russell and Nicole denied that they were anything more than friends.

Russell returned to the States in August to launch his band's tour. It was an enormous success, with tickets selling out quickly, but the reaction to Russell's album was tepid. Almost all the magazines and newspapers that typically review new CDs passed on covering it, due, no doubt, to perceptions that the band was nothing more than a plaything for a rich actor.

One exception was the *St. Petersburg Times*, where Janet K. Keeler gave the album a positive review. "There is something so personal about these songs that what would normally be distracting is not," she wrote. "Storytelling is the strong suit here with driving roots-rock the backdrop. TOFOG has managed to do something that seems almost impossible these days: make original, meaningful music."

With so many reviewers either prejudiced against the album because of Russell's fame as an actor or befuddled by its eclectic content, I turned to someone whose judgment I trusted—the legendary Scotty Moore, who along with Bill Black and Elvis Presley, invented what we now call rock 'n' roll on a hot July night.

When Russell listened to those first Elvis Presley records, the ones that made him want to pick up a guitar and join the rockabilly caravan, it was Moore's innovative guitar licks that led the way. All these years later, what could be more appropriate than for the master to evaluate the music of a third-generation disciple?

Moore, who had just returned from a tour in Europe, said he would be happy to listen to *Bastard Life or Clarity* and review it for this book. For a week he played the CD, sometimes listening to it head-on, other times allowing it to play in the background as he did chores at his home outside of Nashville.

At first he was baffled. The music didn't seem to fit any particular category. Then one morning he was eating his pancakes and watching television when he saw guitarist Mark Knopfler on Regis Philbin's show. Then it hit him. "He's from Scotland—that's still his roots—and he does what this guy [Russell] is doing."

By that, he meant that Knopfler, formerly of Dire Straits, worked his Scottish roots into a more contemporary sound. It was the same thing that Russell was attempting with his music, "To me, it's more folkish than anything else," Moore said of Russell's CD. "The songs were all well done. I can hear a little Irish, a little Scottish—that's the only bag I could put it in. I couldn't put it in rock 'n' roll."

Moore complimented the production and the musicians, adding that he thought the trumpet work was tastefully done. "There's something in [Russell's] way of portraying things that is fine," he explained. "I just don't know who his audience is. I sit here at the house and noodle around on stuff that will knock me out, but I know I'm not going to waste my time putting it on a record because I don't know who the audience is. It's my impression that they're doing their own thing, and if someone doesn't like it, to hell with them. Sometimes an audience is created by doing things that way. Maybe there's an audience [for their music] that's been overlooked."

Interestingly, the same newspapers that passed on reviewing the CD made an effort to review the live concerts, rationalizing that the shows were news events that required coverage, while the album was an artistic statement that was probably best ignored.

Reviews of the concerts varied greatly. "[The band's] themes were thirty or more feet from memorable all night long," wrote Tom Moon for the *Philadelphia Inquirer*. "As he bounced around the four or five serviceable notes of his tenor range with his portentous lyrics, Crowe practically begged for this age-old career advice: Don't quit your day job."

After attending a concert at Irving Plaza in New York, Ann Powers concluded that Russell might have been a rock star had fate given him a different twist. "Ignoring the womanly screams that greeted the brawny Mr. Crowe's every sip of tea, one could hear a seasoned, very straightforward, very Australian band fronted by a singer with a compellingly crusty baritone," she wrote for the *New York Times*. "The group's sincerity and competence was unquestionable. This would be the perfect band for a movie about classic rock."

Most critics failed to mention Danielle's contribution to the tour. That wasn't the case with Sandra Barrera of the *Los Angeles Daily News*, who pointed out in her review of a House of Blues concert that Danielle, "who bears a striking resemblance to Kirsten Dunst," received applause when she sat at the keyboard and, accompanied by cello, acoustic guitar, and a backup vocalist, sang material from her upcoming album.

Despite rumors of a Crowe-Kidman romance, Danielle found herself drawing close to Russell again. He told her that he and Nicole were only friends, and she believed him. She broke up with her boyfriend and braced for another romantic relationship with Russell. "We have a lot in common, we both love acting and music, and we sort of understand each other," she explained to *Hello* magazine. Asked if she thought Russell was still in love with her, she responded, "You'll have to ask him that."

When the tour ended, they returned to Sydney and started house hunting. After making the rounds, they selected a nine-million-dollar mansion that had once belonged to Lachlan Murdoch, the son of media king Rupert Murdoch. The four-bedroom house, which overlooks Sydney Harbour, has stained-glass windows, marble fireplaces, a conservatory, a heated pool, and chauffeur's quarters. It offers a splendid view of the harbor and has the added advantage of being within sight of Nicole Kidman's mansion.

Describing their new relationship to friends as a trial marriage, Russell and Danielle moved into the house in December 2001. Both sets of parents, according to reports, were enthusiastic about the commitment that Russell and Danielle, now in their late thirties, made to each other by deciding to live together.

"Russell and Danielle have never stopped caring about each other," Danielle's father, Don Spencer, told the *Daily Mail*. "Russell might not be everyone's cup of tea, but he's always been fabulous to Danielle." He said he hoped the arrangement led to marriage because Russell has "all the right qualities—he's very loyal, straightforward and unbelievably generous."

One of those qualities—loyalty—would be put to the test in the new year, but for the moment, everyone was optimistic about the couple's chances of success.

In early December, Russell returned to the States to promote *A Beautiful Mind*. Director Ron Howard told *Entertainment Weekly* that it was a role Russell was born to play. "He's not entirely unlike Nash," Howard explained. "He's highly intelligent and he has this self-confidence that you could define as arrogance—all qualities which Nash was supposed to embody."

For the most part, reviewers were enthralled by the movie. *Washington Post* critic Stephen Hunter paid tribute to John Nash's genius in his review, but he also tipped his hat to the actor who portrayed him. "Russell Crowe is fabulous," he wrote. "His Nash is quite a concoction: a mixture of arrogance and fear, all locked in a giant, clumsy body, with a wit that was deadly when it could be provoked into paying attention."

Steven Rosen, writing in the *Denver Post*, said Russell gave an "outstanding performance" that would, along with the contributions of the director, the screenwriter, and the cinematographer, make the movie "as talked-about as any late-year release."

San Francisco Chronicle critic Edward Guthmann said that Russell executed an "Olympian leap" from his previous role as Maximus: "Crowe, beefy and solid, isn't the first actor one might imagine in the part of a world-class math nerd, but his intensity is such, and his talent so large, that he pulls us into Nash's world."

As the critics spun their opinions, rumblings began to surface that the film had not addressed the issue of homosexuality, as described in the biography. Howard responded to criticisms by saying that the issue would have distracted from the dramatic thrust of the script. Besides, he pointed out, Nash had repudiated accusations that he engaged in homosexual activities while battling schizophrenia.

Others pointed out that even if Nash had homosexual experiences, he was crazy at the time and could hardly be held accountable for that, any more than he could be held accountable for talking to imaginary people. Homosexual organizations were hypersensitive about any association with schizophrenia, because at the time the story took place, homosexuality was still listed in abnormal-psychology textbooks as a disease not far removed from schizophrenia in its causation and development.

Russell admitted to reporters that the issue was airbrushed to a certain extent, but he said it was for a valid reason—to provide an overview of the man's life. Even so, he claimed to have made an effort to make it a part of the story, however subtle. "I mean, watch the movie—half the time I'm eyeing up other guys in the corridor," he told *Empire* magazine. "Besides, come on, moviemaking is very Freudian. Any little gesture is a stone into a pond, mate. There's a future resonance at play here. So our level of sensitivity to the bisexual aspect should be applauded, not machine-gunned."

Backing up Russell on that point is Anthony Rapp, who played Bender, an aspiring physicist who meets Nash in graduate school. Rapp, who is openly gay, told the *Advocate* that Russell brought "some subtextural bisexual stuff to different moments, particularly with Paul Bettany, who plays his friend."

In one scene, Nash is walking down a hallway when he encounters a fellow student approaching him. He looks at him with intense interest, after which the student turns around and says, "Wow, what was that all about?"

The gay issue is one that Russell has exploited ever since he played a homosexual man in *The Sum of Us*. When *Gladiator* was released, it surprised no one that Maximus, with his bulging biceps and skimpy loincloth, became a hero among homosexuals. There were news reports that gay men flew to Los Angeles from all over the world to be on hand for the film's Hollywood opening. Russell didn't care whether his fans were gay or straight, as long as they bought tickets to his films.

Over the years, Russell has chosen roles in which his characters were either strongly gay or strongly heterosexual. He has been comfortable playing either role. What makes him uncomfortable are characters who are uncertain about their sexual preference.

Perhaps with that in mind, *PrimeTime's* Diane Sawyer once drew him into a conversation about masculinity by asking him who he thought was the most masculine actor in films. "I don't know, because I read masculinity in different ways, I think," he answered. "Ed Harris is a pretty masculine actor, you know? But at the same time a very gentle soul. You know, you have to have that combination."

Russell laughingly told Sawyer that his "poetic soul" is a source of amusement to his friends in Australia, especially when they are out riding horses. They would be on the ranch, he explained, calling out the names of their horses—"Come on, Thunder"—as they galloped across the pasture, only to hear Russell, without an ounce of shame, call out the name of his favorite horse—"Come on, Honey!"

When the Golden Globe nominations for 2002 were announced in December 2001, a collective gasp erupted in Australia, for Aussies were prominent in most major categories. Russell was nominated for best actor in a drama (*A Beautiful Mind*), Nicole Kidman for best actress in a drama and in a comedy/musical (*The Others* and *Moulin Rouge*), Baz Luhrmann for best director (*Moulin Rouge*), and Rachel Griffiths for best supporting actress in a television series. *A Beautiful Mind* was named in the best-film category, and *Moulin Rouge* made the list for best comedy/musical.

Russell was still in America promoting *A Beautiful Mind* when the nominations were announced. He worked harder on the film's behalf than he had for any of his other films, primarily because he felt it was his most challenging role to date. But juxtaposed with the desire to do all he could to help the film was the added pressure of the interviews themselves.

There was not much that Russell feared, but certainly at the top of his list was the news media, for they alone had the power to ask him revealing or embarrassing questions. His family never asked him questions, and neither did Danielle. Fans cowered before him, offering him praise and gifts, as did the Hollywood elite. Only the news media went toe to toe with him and asked the hard questions.

At a press conference held a couple of weeks before the Golden Globe Awards were presented, Russell seemed to be wrestling with himself, as he held his temper in check while fielding questions about his sanity and his temperament.

Asked if he would talk about moments during which he felt insane, he bit his lip and said, "I know where you're going—next!" Asked if he thought he was misunderstood, he replied, "No, I don't think I'm misunderstood, but I think I'm misconstrued. I think it's very easy to offend people with the truth."

At another joint interview, held early in the year, he growled and snarled at a journalist who asked a follow-up question to an answer he had just given about a scene in *A Beautiful Mind*. "Didn't we just go through all that?" Russell demanded, his voice tinged with anger. Then he asked the journalist if he had a tape recorder. "Well, you can listen to it later to get the answer—fuck!"

Journalist Desmond Sampson, who attended that interview to write an article for *Pavement* magazine, felt that interviewing Russell was like going on an "emotional roller-coaster ride." Wrote the New Zealander: "Ultimately, it feels like we've just endured three rounds in the ring with Crowe, rather than enjoyed half an hour chatting with him in a swanky hotel room. It's a truly dissatisfying experience, perhaps more so because of the expectations of meeting a fellow Kiwi who has achieved so much."

The more interviews Russell gave, the more people began to question his emotional stability. In the beginning, when he was fresh and unknown, his eccentricities had been viewed as a charming aspect of his personality. Perhaps all Aussies were like that, people reasoned. Wasn't that Crocodile Dundee fellow also crazy as hell? It took Russell's playing the part of a schizophrenic in *A Beautiful Mind* to open people's eyes to his sometimes-strange, sometimes-violent behavior in public.

Despite his enormous success, Russell often seems consumed by an inner rage that he is constantly struggling to keep in check. Those looking for explanations for his behavior have been baffled. The traditional precipitators for the type of rage that haunts Russell are usually found in early childhood trauma, such as sexual abuse, the death of a parent, or the endurance of a painful disease that separates the child from his friends. But the actor apparently had an uneventful childhood in all those areas.

Russell's rage seems to have begun during adolescence. Adults don't suddenly awaken one morning filled with rage without reason; it usually can be traced back to childhood or adolescence. When we examine Russell's adolescence, the factors that emerge with the most resonance are his difficulties accepting his mixed-race heritage and his slow social development, especially with girls his own age. Either of those factors, left to fester, is enough to fuel the rage that has followed him into adulthood.

Of course, the irony of Russell playing John Nash in *A Beautiful Mind* is that the scientist allegedly engaged in behavior that Russell himself has displayed over the years in full public view—temper tantrums, experiments with homosexuality (in films if nowhere else), and declarations of grandeur. The only difference is that no one outside Russell's circle of family and friends knows whether he has heard voices or conversed with imaginary people.

January 2002 turned out to be a brutal month for Russell. After he endured interview after interview to promote *A Beautiful Mind*, his nerves frazzled by way too much human contact, Russell went to Park City, Utah, to attend the Sundance

Film Festival, where *Texas,* his documentary about Thirty Odd Foot of Grunts, would be shown for the first time.

The film covers the band's activities from 2000 through 2001, with the focus on rehearsals and recording sessions in Sydney, London, and Austin, Texas, plus some actual concert footage from several performances at Stubb's Bar-B-Q in Austin. Russell is listed as the coproducer of the film, along with Brett Leonard, his director on *Virtuosity,* and his friend Brendan Fletcher is listed as one of two cinematographers.

Russell started filming the band long before he had a distribution deal. Miramax studio chief Harvey Weinstein picked it up after Russell arranged a private showing of the finished product. "It's very raw and very rude and puts me in an incredibly bad light," Russell told *Ralph* magazine. "So [Weinstein] bought it."

Texas was shown at midnight on January 17 in a theater that seated fewer than two hundred people. Wearing a red flannel shirt and blue jeans, Russell entered the theater alone and took a seat in the fourth row.

Several hours earlier, Nicole Kidman's new film, *Birthday Girl,* was shown in a different theater. At a prescreening party for Kidman's film, the actress was teasing a reporter to come closer so that he could smell her pesto breath when Russell rudely stepped between them. "Sorry mate," he said, "But we go way back." With that, Russell planted a big kiss on Nicole's mouth, immediately after which a studio photographer snapped a picture of the two Aussies in a tight embrace.

Russell answered a few reporters' questions before leaving the theater, but it seemed obvious that he was disappointed in the film's reception. That disappointment was heightened by the fact that the film won neither an award nor the hearts of critics.

Variety reviewer Dennis Harvey was made somewhat uncomfortable by a screening audience made up mostly of screaming females who sometimes mouthed the words of the songs. Concluded Harvey, "Curiosity factor aside, this technically rough souvenir offers pretty much what you would expect: a not especially interesting look at a workmanlike band that probably would never have gotten past the Aussie club circuit if not for a quirk of celebrity fate. Commercial prospects are correspondingly modest."

A few days later, at a special screening at the Paramount Theatre in Austin, Texas, enthusiastic fans packed in knee-deep to witness TOFOG's cinematic debut. However, for Kate X. Messer, who reviewed the film for the *Austin Chronicle,* it was "two hours of mildly annoying torture." Wrote Messer, "As a straightforward love letter to fans, it's sweet. The filmmakers avoid exploiting the mostly forty/fifty-something group of devoted bra-flinging female fanatics for yuks, and in these days of T&As and *Girls Gone Wild,* that is somehow noble."

Russell could be forgiven if he left Utah with the sinking feeling that the documentary was not going to live up to expectations. There was no buzz about the film at the festival, and he left without the kind of backslapping endorsement from critics he had hoped for. The next morning, he flew back to Los Angeles, where he appeared on CNN's *Larry King Live* with director Ron Howard to talk about *A*

Beautiful Mind.

Russell ended up talking about his love life, thanks to King's heroic persistence. When King asked him if he was now in love, Russell answered in the affirmative, though he resisted King's efforts to have him say her name.

"Is this something that could be the big one?" King asked.

"Well, we'll just see," answered Russell. "I'm not one for making predictions or, you know, that sort of thing. It's somebody I've known for a very long time. And we're just together. It's as simple as that, you know."

Everyone assumed he was talking about Danielle, which won him accolades from the Oprah Winfrey set, but as the months went by, it became apparent that he just as easily could have been talking about Nicole.

Two days after the King interview aired, Russell and Danielle entered Merv Griffin's Beverly Hilton Hotel, where the Golden Globe Awards ceremony was held, with a minimum amount of fanfare. Russell glared at the reporters who approached him, and Danielle, wearing an elegant black gown, smiled with what could be described as cautious optimism.

Unlike Russell, the other Australians at the Golden Globes were eager to be seen. Baz Luhrmann and Rachel Griffiths were happy to talk to anyone with a microphone or reporter's notebook, as was Nicole Kidman, who arrived with her mother and father. Though obviously nervous, Kidman was gracious and garrulous, working the crowd with inquiring eyes and a radiant smile. Before the seating was assigned, the Australians asked if they could all be seated at one table, but officials turned them down on the grounds that they would be "too rowdy."

As it turned out, the Aussies took home their share of trophies. Russell won for best actor, beating out Will Smith, Kevin Spacey, Billy Bob Thornton, and Denzel Washington. Nicole Kidman lost to Sissy Spacek for best actress in a drama but won for best actress in a comedy or musical. Rachel Griffiths won for best supporting actress in a television series, and Baz Luhrmann took home the award for best comedy or musical.

Accepting his award, Russell thanked John and Alicia Nash "for living such an inspirational love story," but he cautioned viewers to remember that *A Beautiful Mind* was "just a movie," even though it "gives us the belief that in our lives, something extraordinary can always happen." He also thanked Ron Howard: "I want to thank him for setting a platform every single day that allowed his actors to be adventurous, take risks, and explore. I also want to think him for his humility, his consummate skill, and his honor as a man." Then he gave a thumbs-up. "Thanks Ron!"

Exhausted by two months of promotional efforts on behalf of *A Beautiful Mind* and, to a lesser extent, *Texas,* Russell took Danielle to Rome in February, where they vacationed before going to London for the British Academy of Film and Television Awards and then back to America in March for the Academy Awards.

In Rome, they behaved like giddy teenagers and tossed coins into the Trevi Fountain, an Italian tradition for new lovers. Not only did Russell want to reward

Danielle for standing by him in Hollywood, he wanted to help soothe the pain she felt over the poor performance of her album, *White Monkey*. The CD had received a great deal of publicity in Australia, but sales were sluggish in that country. The situation was much the same in North America, though without the good reviews. Under the headline "Debut Disc Nothing to Crowe About," *Toronto Sun* critic Jane Stevenson wrote that "some artists get recognition for reasons other than their music...[Spencer's] intentions are good but the execution somehow falters."

Rome changed everything for Danielle. It was where she fell in love with Russell all over again. She was the happiest she had been in a long time. She could hardly wait for Valentine's Day, for it had always been her and Russell's most special date. One Valentine's Day, Russell had rented a guesthouse in the Australian wine country, about one hundred miles from Sydney, where they had one of the most romantic times of their relationship. For that reason, she was anxious to find out what he had in store for her in Rome. Knowing him, it could be just about anything: nothing was off limits.

Everything seemed to be going fine until the day before Valentine's Day, when they received news of the Academy Award nominations. Russell was nominated in the best-actor category for *A Beautiful Mind*, along with Sean Penn, Will Smith, Denzel Washington, and Tom Wilkinson. Also receiving nominations were Ron Howard for best director, Jennifer Connelly for best supporting actress, and, of course, *A Beautiful Mind* for best picture.

When Russell learned that Nicole Kidman had received a best-actress nomination for her role in *Moulin Rouge,* he called to congratulate her. Since the screening at Sundance, she had been in Trollhattan, Sweden, filming *Dogville* with director Lars von Trier. Russell had stayed in contact with Nicole while she was in Sweden, sometimes calling every day, but when he called from Rome to congratulate her, she told him that she would be spending Valentine's Day alone for the first time since her marriage to Tom Cruise.

To Danielle's surprise, Russell flew to Sweden on his private jet to spend Valentine's Day with Nicole. They had dinner at her hotel, dining on champagne and caviar, according to the hotel manager. Then Russell returned to London. Perhaps to make it up to Danielle, he reportedly bought her a twenty-nine-thousand-dollar Cartier watch before leaving Rome for London. Photos of the couple taken shortly after they left the jewelry store show a very somber Danielle, her eyes hidden behind sunglasses.

When the day rolled around for the British Academy Awards (BAFTA), Danielle was at Russell's side, though her customary smile was notably absent. She told reporters she had no problem with Russell's longtime friendship with Nicole. Russell himself appeared more somber than usual, his jaw set tight and his lips pursed into a tiny patch of pink beneath his scruffy beard.

Also attending the awards show was Nicole Kidman, who arrived alone and sat at the table next to Russell and Danielle. There was a bit of polite chatter between the two tables, but when Danielle got up to go to the bathroom, Nicole slipped over to Russell's table and sat down in the seat vacated by Danielle. Russell's arm was around Nicole when Danielle returned, so she made herself comfortable on Russell's lap.

Russell seemed to use the two women as buffers against the other guests. Earlier in the week he had attended a charity-award ceremony sponsored by *Variety*, where, after learning that actress Joan Collins was a previous recipient, he reportedly told organizers they could shove his award up their ass. He also attended the music industry's Brit Awards and snubbed the other guests, but not before bullying an adoring fan who snapped a picture with a digital camera.

As expected, Russell won the BAFTA for best actor for his role in *A Beautiful Mind*. When he took the stage to accept the award, Russell thanked several people and recited the Patrick Kavanagh poem "Sanctity." Then he left the venue with Danielle to watch the one-hour-delayed broadcast elsewhere. He was horrified at what he saw, for unknown to Russell, the poem was edited out of his acceptance speech.

Later, when he returned for the BAFTA postproduction dinner, he appeared sulky to those in attendance. According to Dominic Mohan, a reporter for the *Sun*, producer Malcolm Gerrie was having a conversation with recording artist Sting when Russell made his appearance. Noting Russell's facial expression, Sting told Gerrie that he should be careful because it looked like Russell was after "somebody's blood."

True enough, Russell was unhappy over the deletion of the poem by the show's editors. He made his way backstage to a storage room and ordered his burly bodyguards to fetch Gerrie. When Gerrie was ushered into the storage room, Russell pushed him against the wall, jabbed his finger into the producer's face, and according to one published report, screamed, "You f— —ing piece of shit, I'll make sure you never work in Hollywood." With that, Russell kicked over several chairs and stormed out of the room.

With the British press nipping at their heels, Russell and Danielle fled to Australia, where the actor started receiving reports from his studio that his outburst might cost him an Oscar. It's bad enough when actors lose their tempers with fans or exhibit bizarre behavior in public, but when it happens at an awards show and results in threats against a producer, it enters the very different realm of career suicide.

As the growing storm approached Hollywood in the weeks leading up to the Academy Awards, Russell was advised to do what he could to lessen its impact. He decided to telephone Gerrie and offer him an apology.

"I couldn't believe it was him," Gerrie told the *Sun*. "I heard this distant voice saying, 'I'm ringing to say I'm so sorry about what happened.'…I told him I didn't get any satisfaction out of the whole situation and if he wanted to make it up to any of my family he could speak to my son, who has been getting a bit of stick at school."

Russell then spoke to Gerrie's son and told him all about making *Gladiator*, especially the part about working with the tigers. Russell then offered to buy Gerrie "a few pints of Guinness" the next time he was in London. Gerrie told the *Sun* that the actor sounded "humble and genuinely apologetic."

With that nasty bit of business out of the way, Ron Howard, Brian Grazer, and executives at Universal Pictures, the studio that financed and distributed *A Beautiful Mind*, all sighed with relief. However, the respite would prove to be short-lived.

American electronica musician Moby was in a Sydney nightclub in March when he went to the bathroom and found the door blocked. He nudged his way inside and was confronted by Russell, who had the small room packed with his friends. Russell grabbed him and threw him against the wall, Moby told the *Sydney Morning Herald*. "He started berating me for being an American. He was like, 'You stupid American, your country, you think you own the world.'"

That was all Ron Howard needed—an Oscar-nominated actor who hated Americans. Coming as it did only six months after the September 11 attack on New York City and Washington, D.C., it had the potential to do major damage to his efforts to make Russell look desirable as a possible Oscar winner. But the incident with Moby was only the beginning of his problems.

In the days leading up to the awards ceremony, rumors started circulating around Hollywood that John Nash, the character portrayed by Russell, had made anti-Semitic statements at various times in his life. Since the movie industry has a long history of Jewish involvement, it was the sort of rumor that could sink an Oscar campaign.

Ron Howard did what he could to salvage the situation. "If there's an attack strategy, that's an impolitic tool," he said in a press release. "It's not about reminding people of your virtues, it's about undermining the other candidate's credibility. That's a shame." Howard's greatest difficulty in dealing with the whisper campaign came from the fact that the statements apparently were true: Nash had made anti-Semitic remarks when he was in the throes of paranoid schizophrenia. But he was crazy during that time, Howard argued, and made all sorts of outrageous statements.

Nash and his wife Alicia went on television to talk about the rumors. They denied that Nash was anti-Semitic or gay. They pointed out that he was ill at the time he was alleged to have made the comments and sometimes had "strange ideas during certain periods of time."

One of the most thoughtful comments about the controversy came from film critic Roger Ebert, who told a *Tonight Show* audience that Nash was "schizophrenic—you can't hold him to the same standard as a healthy person…at the time he made those statements, he thought he was a Palestinian secret agent."

As Oscar night approached, there was a feeling around Hollywood that Howard and his film were in big trouble, not just because of the Jewish issue but because of the scuffle that Russell had with the BAFTA producer. Russell came across as a dimwitted thug, and that simply was not the sort of image that most academy members, most of whom were in their fifties and sixties, wanted to present to the world.

The seventy-fourth Academy Awards presentation was held on March 24,

2002, at Oscar's elegant new home, the thirty-three-hundred-seat Kodak Theatre, located only a block away from the Hollywood Roosevelt Hotel, where the first Oscars were awarded in 1929.

When Russell and Danielle arrived at the theater, they were photographed holding hands. Wearing a strapless gown and a matching choker, Danielle smiled broadly and stayed close to Russell. Two weeks earlier, they had hosted a private party in Sydney in honor of Russell's favorite rugby team, South Sydney. "There's no doubting the love between Russell and Danielle," observed a reporter for the *Sunday Telegraph*, who added that "the couple barely left each other's side."

Also in attendance was Nicole Kidman, who arrived wearing a frilly pink gown. She steered clear of Russell and Danielle, but she attracted attention by flirting with *Spiderman*'s Tobey Maguire, who is eight years her junior. Nominated in the best-actress category for her role in *Moulin Rouge*, she was considered a favorite, despite going up against Sissy Spacek, Halle Berry, Judi Dench, and Renee Zellweger.

Russell was asked to present the award for best actress, and he saw it as the opportunity of a lifetime. Who better to hand Nicole her first Oscar than himself? When the time came, he left Danielle at their front row seat and went backstage to wait his cue to take the stage. For some reason, his tux didn't feel right. The jacket fit fine, but the pants seemed a size too large. Only minutes before his cue, he dashed into the touchup artists' room and asked if someone could pin his pants. By the time he walked into the spotlight, he was pinned up tighter than a baby's diaper.

Russell seemed genuinely shocked when he read out the winner's name—Halle Berry, for her performance in *Monster's Ball*. Also shocked was Nicole, who looked as if she couldn't quite believe her ears. The strangeness of the moment was then amplified by Berry's acceptance speech, a rambling, emotional salute to the African-American actors who had preceded her in the industry.

Despite all the controversy, *A Beautiful Mind* was a big winner that evening. Ron Howard won for best director (it was his first Oscar), Jennifer Connelly won for best supporting actress, Akiva Goldsman won for best screenplay adaptation, and *A Beautiful Mind* won for best picture. Of the major players, only Russell Crowe walked away empty-handed, defeated by Denzel Washington, who won for his role in *Training Day*.

In a reference to the number of African-American winners that evening, emcee Whoopi Goldberg quipped that there had been so much mud thrown during the lead-up to the awards that everyone involved ended up black. In a reference to Berry's win, Denzel Washington told the audience that Oscar had killed "two birds with one night."

Clearly, academy members did not hold John Nash's anti-Semitic remarks against Ron Howard or the film itself. But just as clearly, academy members decided that it was inappropriate for Russell to win Oscars two years straight. One academy member probably spoke for many when he told *Entertainment Weekly*, "When you get right down to it, [Crowe's] an obnoxious human being and an arrogant prick. I know I shouldn't base my voting decisions on that, but, hey, we're all human."

Russell made a graceful exit from the theater and kept his mouth shut about the awards, but it must have galled him that both he and Nicole were beaten by African-Americans who had given what many people felt were lesser performances in their respective roles.

Faced with giving the awards to Australians, one of whom was a "prick" and the other of whom seemed a little too eager to win for her own good, academy members decided to use the occasion as a payback for African Americans. It was not a rational decision, but coming as it did, close on the heels of the terrorist attack in New York, it was probably a proper decision.

Race is a hot-button issue with Russell. He often speaks out against racial prejudice, but in real life he has no black friends and does not publicly identify himself with black issues, an unusual stance for someone involved in rock 'n' roll. He seems to have a split personality on the issue of race, one that is directly related to his Maori heritage. He despises people who put down others because of their race, but he knows how they feel because he felt the same way growing up in New Zealand. He is capable of holding two contrary positions at the same time   an unusual talent, to be sure, but one that sometimes nurtures his creativity. As a creative stimulant, self-loathing can be every bit as powerful as love or hate.

When Russell was first approached about playing Captain Jack Aubrey in *Master and Commander: The Far Side of the World*, an adaptation of author Patrick O'Brian's twenty-volume series of seafaring tales set during the Napoleonic Wars, he was cool to the idea. He had never read any of O'Brian's books, and he wasn't overly impressed with the script he was sent, so he turned it down, even though one of his favorite Australian directors, Peter Weir, was at the helm.

"What kept me up at night was thinking, 'what am I doing?'" Russell told the *New York Times*. "Do I really want to give up a chance to work with Peter Weir, something I used to dream about doing?"

The more he thought about it, the more curious he became about the project. The only thing standing between him and working with Weir was the script, so he gathered up a sampling of O'Brian's books and read up on Captain Jack Aubrey. As a result, he fell in love with the character and told Weir that he would join the cast if the script was fleshed out and augmented with a few new scenes, including one that showed Aubrey's relationship with the young midshipmen on board.

Weir was delighted to accommodate a fellow Australian. The fifty-eight-year-old director had been involved with several successful films over the previous thirty years, including *The Truman Show* and *Dead Poets Society*, but he had not made a film in six years, and he was eager to flex his directorial muscle in a movie that would have box-office appeal. Coming off his hit with *Gladiator*, which had grossed half a billion dollars, Russell Crowe was box office personified. Also cast in the film was Paul Bettany, who had appeared with Russell in *A Beautiful Mind*.

No sooner did shooting begin in Mexico on June 17, 2002, than Russell was in the headlines again, this time because of the video that was made during the brawl that allegedly took place outside the Coffs Harbour pub. According to Australian press reports, Russell got into a fight with one man and kissed another man, in addition to getting into an altercation with a woman.

After the incident, two local men, Philip Cropper and Malcolm Mercer, allegedly contacted Russell and offered to sell him the incriminating video for a little over one hundred thousand dollars. Russell interpreted it as a blackmail scheme and tipped off the police, who tapped the two men's telephone calls.

As a result, the men were arrested and charged with attempting to extort money from Russell in exchange for destroying the video. They went on trial the same week that Russell started filming *Master and Commander*, but the proceedings only lasted a few days. The presiding judged ordered the jury to acquit the men on the grounds that the prosecution had failed to prove that they had demanded money in return for destroying the video. "There seems to be not much doubt in this matter that money was an object," the judge ruled, "but what [the prosecution has to prove is that] there was a demand for money and that demand was supported by a threat."

Russell was out of the country at the time of the trial and could not be called as a witness, which was just as well, since the last thing he needed was to be questioned under oath about the incident. Even so, it was more unflattering publicity about a life seemingly out of control.

That month, while Russell was working in Mexico, Danielle went to England to celebrate her grandmother's eightieth birthday and to do what she could to promote her album, *White Monkey*. While there, she stayed at her aunt's home in Yorkshire and slept in the bedroom of her cousin Niki Waldegrave, who was a reporter with the *Sunday Mirror*. When Waldegrave asked her well-known cousin for an interview and a couple of photographs, Danielle was hardly in a position to say no.

In the resulting story, Waldegrave reported that Russell called Danielle twice a day during her visit, with each call lasting an hour or more. Waldegrave asked her cousin if she could be the only journalist present at her supposedly imminent wedding to Russell, but Danielle laughed the question off. "I'm not engaged…I'm not married and I'm not pregnant," she declared, "although I'm sure that by next week, somewhere in the world, someone will be saying I've done all three."

When talking to her cousin, Danielle was most generous in her comments about Nicole Kidman. "The truth is Nicole and I are friends," she said. "It's a shame people have to keep bringing up her friendship with Russell as a negative thing because it's actually really nice. She has had so many ups and downs lately and I think it's great that Russell has been there through it all. I don't have a problem with it."

While Danielle was in England, Nicole took a helicopter to Rosarito, Mexico, where Russell was on location. Their relationship had shown signs of heating up the previous fall, when Russell appeared on the *Ray Martin Show* in Australia and described Nicole as a princess. The host then read him a quote in which Russell said that Nicole was the most beautiful woman in the universe. "Did I?" Russell responded. "Did I say that? If she's watching, yes, of course, I say that about Nicky just about every day."

Two weeks later, when Nicole appeared on the same show, the host showed her a clip of Russell making the statements. Nicole responded, "Now you've got to ask me about him. Is he the most beautiful man?"

"Is he?" asked the host."

"If he's watching, absolutely!"

Nicole stayed one night at Club Marena, where Russell was also registered, according to news reports; then she returned to Los Angeles to be with her two children.

Danielle visited Russell once in Mexico during the summer and made plans to visit him again in October. Before that visit took place, according to *Us* magazine, Russell flew to Los Angeles and checked into his usual suite at the Hotel Bel-Air for a rendezvous with Nicole. The magazine reported that the couple enjoyed a two-hundred-and-forty-dollar room service lunch that apparently lasted four hours, after which Nicole "was whisked away as quickly as she arrived."

Danielle made her second visit to Mexico two weeks later. Russell had convinced her that his friendship with Nicole was totally platonic, so she seemed at ease with that, but she was not so comfortable with news reports over the summer that Meg Ryan had changed her mind and was urging Russell to resume their relationship.

Published stories alleged that Meg sent e-mails by the dozen to Russell urging him to get in contact with her. Whether that was true or not hardly mattered, for with headlines like "Lovesick Meg Ryan Stalking Russell Crowe" glaring out at Danielle from the newsstands, the idea of it made her furious. According to the *Star*, Danielle told a friend that "[Ryan] needs to get on with her life and let us get on with ours."

Danielle left Mexico after a few days, apparently convinced that her relationship with Russell was on solid ground. Within a day or so of Danielle's departure, Nicole flew to Mexico to be with Russell and, according to news reports, was spotted in a local bar kissing him on the lips and holding hands with him. One night a private lounge was reserved for the couple at a beach club called Papas & Beer, where a bartender told *Us* that it was a "very romantic evening for two."

Amid the musical chairs with the women in his life, Russell, who was at that point thirty-eight years of age, began to have concerns about growing old. When the on-set hairdresser failed to properly conceal Russell's gray hairs, he had the employee fired, according to news reports, and asked that the studio fly his personal hairdresser in from Sydney to do his hair at a cost of more than one hundred thousand dollars.

Despite the intrigues and setbacks of the previous months, Russell was in good spirits when Rick Lyman, a reporter for the *New York Times*, arrived on the set in Mexico for an interview. The actor yanked off his British naval tunic and pulled himself onto the rigging of HMS *Surprise*, the ship they were using in the film.

"You want to go up?" he asked, to the astonishment of a publicist, who gasped, "Oh, my heavens!"

The reporter, who was older and heavier, was a good sport about it and followed the actor up the rigging toward a wooden platform suspended about sixty-five feet above the deck. Russell navigated the final six feet, a tricky business that required more dexterity than the reporter possessed, causing him to stall several feet from his goal.

Lyman interpreted the experience as an example of Russell being a nice guy for a change, but those who knew the actor better would probably argue that it was just his way of letting the reporter know that he wasn't good enough to follow in his footsteps.

However, Lyman did walk away from the interview with one of the most revealing statements Russell had made in a long time. Asked if he saw any similarity between himself and the character he was playing, Russell answered, "At sea, he is extremely able, but on land, he is pretty hopeless—just like me, I guess."

Master and Commander: The Far Side of the World was a tough film to shoot, so when production wrapped at the end of September, Russell was emotionally and physically depleted. After working with band members to put the final touches on a new album scheduled for release by Artemis Records, he took stock of his schedule for 2003. He and the band were booked for a concert tour early in the year to promote the new album, after which he would be free to pursue new movie projects—and there were plenty of those on the burner.

Russell had committed to starring in three movies: *Cinderella Man*, the story of Depression-era boxer Jim Braddock; *Tripoli*, another Ridley Scott–directed epic, with Russell starring as William Eaton, an American who helped lead the overthrow of a corrupt Libyan ruler in the 1800s; and *The Long Green Mile*, an Australian World War II film that would provide Russell with his debut as a director, screenwriter, and producer.

Was it possible for Russell to release a new album and take his band on tour, star in two major motion pictures, and direct a film he had worked on for at least two years—all in the space of twelve months? Then there was the matter of what to do with Danielle and Nicole: how long could that balancing act possibly continue?

It was while those competing demands were circling inside his head like a Texas tornado that Russell received word of *Gladiator* costar Richard Harris's death in London on October 25. The actor had entered London Hospital in August to be treated for a chest infection, only to be told that he had Hodgkin's disease, a cancer that attacks the body's lymph nodes. The actor was thought to be responding well to chemotherapy when he suddenly died.

Russell flew from Mexico to London to attend the funeral. At London's Goring Hotel, where friends and family of the late actor had gathered for a wake, a very emotional Russell lifted a pint of Guinness in honor of his good friend and recited the lines from Patrick Kavanagh's "Sanctity," the same poem that had been edited out of his BAFTA acceptance speech.

A few days after the wake, Russell and his bodyguards went to an expensive Japanese restaurant before flying back to the United Sates. They had not been there long when Georgie Calder, the twenty-one-year-old daughter of British record producer Tony Calder, caught his eye from across the room.

According to Calder, he approached her table and introduced himself, then suddenly kissed her and licked her face. Revolted by his behavior, she pushed him away, only to have him ask her to join him at his hotel room. "He was utterly revolting," she told London's *Daily Mail*. "He was acting like he owned the place and everyone in it—including me." She described him as wearing a "crusty old shirt and trousers that he hadn't appeared to have changed for several days—and he smelt."

Finally realizing that he was not welcome at Calder's table, Russell retreated to his own table, where, according to witnesses, he proceeded to devour mounds of Japanese cuisine. It wasn't long before a familiar face caught his eye. It belonged to fellow New Zealander Eric Watson, the millionaire owner of the Warriors, a championship rugby team based in Russell's former hometown of Auckland.

Russell was pleasant at first when conversing with Watson, but then he started arguing with him, according to witnesses, calling his rugby players "coconuts or darkies." With that, one of the women in the restaurant started crying because of the racist comments, which prompted Watson to question Russell about why he was behaving so badly. Not receiving a satisfactory answer, he left his table to go to the men's room.

Watson had only been gone a short time when Russell got up from his table and followed him into the men's room. Minutes later one of Russell's bodyguards went to the men's room to check on his boss. When he opened the door, Russell was on the floor and Watson was standing over him, the actor's face badly bruised. If Russell had done his research before the fight, he would have known that Watson fancies himself a boxer and trains with the coach of New Zealand's heavyweight champion, David Tua. The bodyguard separated the two men, and they all went back out into the dining area.

A member of the restaurant staff called the police, but before they arrived, Russell got into an altercation with Watson's date, according to press reports, and started playing a game with his bodyguard, throwing plates across the room for the bodyguard to catch, as if he were a retriever running after his master's ball.

"[Russell] was out of control," a witness told the *Sun*. "To begin with it was funny. He was throwing plates and it was like something out of the movie *My Big Fat Greek Wedding*. But then the booze wore on and he turned aggressive and nasty. It was sad to see him in that state."

By the time the police arrived, everyone had settled down and the situation appeared to be under control. No one pressed charges, so the police left without making an arrest. Photographs taken of Russell leaving the restaurant show him with bruises and scratches around his right eye, scrapes on his forehead, and evidence of bruising on his chin.

Back in America, Russell tried to regroup, as bad publicity from the incident swirled around him. He obviously was near a breaking point. Encouraged by family and friends to return to Australia and take some time off, he looked at his schedule and saw no way to do so and still live up to his commitments.

Like a whittler shearing off the bark of a stick, Russell eliminated everything on his schedule for the next several months. The first casualty was the American tour with Thirty Odd Foot of Grunts. A notice of the tour cancellation was posted on the group's official website, gruntland.com, along with a letter from Russell stating that he was going to take some time off to be with his father (who was facing an operation to alleviate discomfort from carpal tunnel syndrome) and to spend more time with Danielle.

"I am in love with Danielle Spencer, but I don't get to spend nearly enough time with her," he wrote. "Danielle has been very patient with all the speculations of the past year or so which I thank her for. I feel a great need to wake up with her as many days of my life as I can."

Interviewed by a reporter from the *Daily Telegraph* before she took the stage at a Sydney hotel, Danielle said she was looking forward to having Russell home for Christmas. Asked if she would stick by him during his troubling times, she answered, "Yes, of course—I love him."

As Danielle was vowing to stand by her man, Russell, who had remained in New York to make a few purchases for his ranch, once again found himself the subject of unflattering headlines. "Crowe in a Chicken Tantrum," read the *New York Post* headline that topped a story about Russell's disagreement with a Manhattan hotel over a perceived shortage of chicken paillard. Before the chicken crisis, Russell reportedly "freaked out" when a fruit basket sent to his room contained fruit that had not been cut to his precise specifications.

Under a headline that read "Softy Russ Quits High Life for Loved Ones," Russell's hometown newspaper, the *Sydney Morning Herald*, reported that he was quitting show business to live with his parents and his "long-suffering girlfriend."

When Russell arrived in Sydney on November 25, news reporters noted that airport officials had arranged for the actor to depart through its executive terminal without being seen. Accompanying him, reported one newspaper, was more than half a ton of luggage, which was delivered to his harborside mansion by a catering truck.

One day after arriving in Sydney, Russell surprised everyone around him by proposing to Danielle after a romantic dinner at Darcy's, their favorite restaurant for more than a decade. He presented her with a diamond ring, believed to be worth more than one hundred thousand dollars, after which they celebrated with a bottle of Shaw & Smith sauvignon blanc wine. Later, they told friends that they planned a June wedding, though no date was set and skeptics were quick to start taking odds.

Did Russell's announced vacation and engagement mean that he was quitting show business? It went down that way in the Australian press, which reported rumors that he was calling it quits, but that was not true. It was just Russell's way of gaining leverage to realign his schedule.

Tripoli was postponed until 2004 so that Russell could try to jump-start *The Long Green Mile* and have time to appear in *Cinderella Man*, which was scheduled, finally, for November 2003. He was happy about that because it meant he would be reunited with Ron Howard and his partner Brian Grazer, with whom Russell had enjoyed such a good working relationship during *A Beautiful Mind*.

Amid the turmoil over the cancellation of the band's tour, Miramax decided not to release the documentary *Texas* for a theatrical run. Instead, it was released on DVD in February 2003, leaving the band twisting in the wind until its new album was released in April.

Swirling around Russell is a cacophony of voices that date back to early childhood. They cry out with uncertainty over his Maori ancestry, they moan in anguish over the frequent moves he made as a child, they hiss with disdain over his lack of formal education, and they murmur with confusion over the social ambivalence of his adolescence and early adulthood.

Had Russell not become a famous actor—and had he not received the celebrity protection afforded that profession—his rage might have made him a candidate for incarceration or a violent death. The Russell Crowes of the world have filled prisons and morgues to capacity. They carry their rage like a badge of honor, even in death.

Yet, despite overwhelming odds, Russell has overcome the voices to become one of the most talented actors of his generation. He may not be a genius, but he has a true genius for acting. The question is not whether he will deliver more Oscar-winning performances but whether he will self-destruct before he fulfills his destiny.

So you came here to see if I was crazy. To see if I'd screw everything up if I actually won. Maybe dance at the podium or strip naked and squawk like a chicken.... Would I embarrass you? Yes, I suppose it's possible.

John Nash in *A Beautiful Mind*

FILMOGRAPHY

PRISONERS OF THE SUN (1990)
Director: Stephen Wallace
Writer: Denis Whitburn, Brian A. Williams
Producers: Brian A. Williams, Richard Brennan, John Tarnoff,
   Charles Waterstreet, Denis Whitburn

Cast
Bryan Brown (Captain Cooper)
George Takei (Vice-Admiral Baron Takahashi)
Terry O'Quinn (Major Beckett)
John Bach (Major Roberts)
Toshi Shioya (Lieutenant Tanaka)
John Clarke (Sheedy)
Deborah Unger (Sister Littell)
John Polson (Private Jimmy Fenton)
Russell Crowe (Lieutenant Corbett)
Nicholas Eadie (Sergeant Keenan)

Summary:
Based on a true story, *Prisoners of the Sun* is about atrocities that the Japanese committed upon prisoners of war on the island of Ambon during World War II. More than a thousand Australian troops were held captive on the island, where they were subjected to torture and abuse before being put to death.

Bryan Brown plays the role of Captain Cooper, the prosecuting attorney at the postwar trial. He is bitter about the war crimes and pursues a conviction with dogged determination. His assistant is Lieutenant Corbett, played by Russell Crowe.

Almost all the action takes place inside a courtroom, so the film does tend to get sluggish at times as the principals resolve complicated legal issues, but for the most part it provides an honest examination of the costs of war, both political and moral.

THE CROSSING (1990)

Director: George Ogilvie
Writer: Ranald Allan
Producers: Al Clark, Jenny Day, Phil Gerlach, Sue Seeary

Cast

Russell Crowe (Johnny)
Robert Mammone (Sam)
Danielle Spencer (Meg)
Emily Lumbers (Jenny)
Rodney Bell (Shorty)
Ben Oxenbould (Heavyfoot)
Myles Collins (Stretch)
Marc Gray (Nort)
Megan Connolly (Kathleen)

Summary:

This Australian coming-of-age story begins with Russell Crowe's character, Johnny, making love to his girlfriend, Meg (Danielle Spencer). He was not her first choice for a boyfriend, but she got involved with him after her true love, Sam, moved to the city to pursue his dream of becoming an artist.

When Sam comes home to reclaim his girlfriend, he discovers that she is involved with his former best friend. The two men are very much different: Johnny is a hard-working farm boy who wants to marry Meg and become a farmer; by contrast, Sam is a dreamer who wants to make Meg's dream of escaping small-town life come true. Meg decides to stay with Johnny, but Sam is persistent. Her dilemma is solved by a tragic event that ends up changing everyone's life.

PROOF (1991)

Director: Jocelyn Moorhouse
Writer: Jocelyn Moorhouse
Producer: Lynda House

Cast

Hugo Weaving (Martin)
Geneviève Picot (Celia)
Russell Crowe (Andy)
Heather Mitchell (Martin's Mother)
Jeffrey Walker (Young Martin)
Daniel Pollock (Punk)
Frankie J. Holden (Brian)
Frank Gallacher (Vet)
Saskia Post (Waitress)
Belinda Davey (Doctor)

Summary:

Martin has been blind since birth. Now in his early thirties, he experiences life vicariously by taking photographs that he asks others to describe to him. Wanting to get closer to Martin is his housekeeper, Celia, an obsessive woman who is in love with him and feels frustrated by his rejections of her affection.

Quite by accident, Martin meets a young restaurant worker named Andy who volunteers to describe his photos to him. They become close friends, a development that makes Celia feel insecure. Pressured by the friendship, she undertakes a bold seduction that fails. She then successfully seduces Andy and uses that relationship as a wedge to drive between Martin and Andy

This is an excellent film, beautifully directed and acted, that deals with the enduring issues of loneliness, trust, and forgiveness.

SPOTSWOOD (a.k.a. The Efficiency Expert) (1991)

Director: Mark Joffe
Writers: Max Dann, Andrew Knight
Producers: Richard Brennan, Timothy White

Cast

Anthony Hopkins (Errol Wallace)
Ben Mendelsohn (Carey)
Alwyn Kurts (Mr. Ball)
Bruno Lawrence (Robert, Carey's Father)
John Walton (Jerry Finn)
Rebecca Rigg (Cheryl Ball)
Toni Collette (Wendy Robinson)
Russell Crowe (Kim Barry)
Angela Punch McGregor (Caroline Wallace)
Daniel Wyllie (Frank Fletcher)

Summary:

The story takes place in the 1960s, at a time when family-owned factories in Australia were finding it difficult to compete in an economy dominated by mammoth corporations.

Anthony Hopkins plays an efficiency expert named Errol Wallace who is sent to a moccasin factory to determine why it is losing money. To his astonishment, he discovers that the factory has been losing money for years. The factory's owner, Mr. Ball, has maintained full employment by selling off his assets.

Russell Crowe plays a low-level factory employee named Kim Barry. He is so eager to get ahead—and to curry favor with Wallace—that he steals documents for him to examine, so that he will know the truth about the factory.

After going over the records, the efficiency expert tells Mr. Ball what he already knows, namely, that if he doesn't lay off a substantial number of employees, he will be forced to go out of business. Mr. Ball does what he must, though with great reluctance. When Wallace sees how devastated the community is by the loss of jobs, he devises a plan that he hopes will get everyone back to work.

For all the talk about jobs and financial statements, this is a comedy populated with eccentric supporting characters who keep the story from lapsing into a corporate minidrama. And, of course, there is an obligatory love story in which Russell plays a despicable cad. This is not a great film, but it has its moments.

HAMMERS OVER THE ANVIL (1991)
Director: Ann Turner
Writers: Peter Hepworth, Alan Marshall (story), Ann Turner
Producers: Gus Howard, Ben Gannon, Peter Gawler, Barbara Gibbs,
   Peter Harvey-Wright

Cast
Charlotte Rampling (Grace McAlister)
Russell Crowe (East Driscoll)
Alexander Outhred (Alan Marshall)
Frankie J. Holden (Bushman)
Jake Frost (Joe Carmichael)
Alethea McGrath (Mrs. Bilson)
John Rafter Lee (McAlister)
Frank Gallacher (Mr. Thomas)
Amanda Douge (Nellie Bolster)

Summary:
This story begins with a horse trainer named East Driscoll taking a nude horseback ride in a river. Watching him is a young crippled boy named Alan Marshall (named after the actual author of the story), who is fascinated by Driscoll's strength and agility, two qualities that he does not possess.

Charlotte Rampling's character, Grace McAlister, is married to the richest man in the community. She is much younger than her husband and clearly has passions and needs that he is not addressing. She presents herself as an elegant, proper lady to the neighbors, but Driscoll knows a different side of her personality, for he spends time making love to her in the stable.

Everything changes when young Marshall walks in on them while they are having sex. He promises not to tell, but Grace McAlister eventually becomes fearful that she has endangered her marriage and she breaks off the romance. Heartbroken, Driscoll goes to a barn dance to talk to her, but she remains firm in her resolve not to see him again, and he goes riding off on his horse in a blind fury. Unfortunately, he is thrown from his horse and suffers brain damage, creating a test of character for Grace McAlister.

This is an adult film that tells a child's story with grace and compassion.

ROMPER STOMPER (1992)

Director: Geoffrey Wright
Writer: Geoffrey Wright
Producers: Daniel Scharf, Ian Pringle

Cast

Russell Crowe (Hando)
Daniel Pollock (Davey)
Jacqueline McKenzie (Gabe)
Alex Scott (Martin)
Leigh Russell (Sonny Jim)
Daniel Wyllie (Cackles)
James McKenna (Bubs)
Eric Mueck (Champ)
Frank Magree (Brett)

Summary:

Hando is the leader of a racist skinhead group that is upset over the immigration of Asians to Australia, primarily because it makes them feel displaced from their own roots. The group's members, who live in an abandoned warehouse, are jobless, homeless, loveless, and clueless about their future in a rapidly changing society.

Hando seems brighter than the other skinheads, but that's not saying much. He is obsessed with the city's changing racial demographics and vows to do something about it. The solution, he feels, can be found in the Nazi propaganda disseminated by a previous generation. He bears a Nazi swastika on his back and decorates his living quarters with symbols of the Nazi movement.

Hando's group of skinheads always seems on the verge of disintegration, but they survive by feeding off of each other's rage. That complex balance is altered when Gabe, the daughter of a wealthy film producer, enters the picture. From that point on, it is every man for himself.

This film was controversial when it was released in Australia, with some critics challenging whether racism was even an issue in that country. But it opened doors for Russell when it was released in America and provided him with his first taste of international fame.

LOVE IN LIMBO (1993)

Director: David Elfick
Writer: John Cundill
Producers: David Elfick, Nina Stevenson, John Winter

Cast

Craig Adams (Ken Riddle)
Rhondda Findleton (Gwen Riddle)
Martin Sacks (Max Wiseman)
Aden Young (Barry McJannet)
Russell Crowe (Arthur Baskin)
Maya Stange (Ivy Riddle)
Samantha Murray (Maisie)
Bill Young (Uncle Herbert)
Leith Taylor (Mrs. Rutherford)

Summary:

This coming-of-age comedy is about three young men (Ken, Arthur, and Barry) who travel to the Australian mining town of Kalgoorlie to lose their virginity in a brothel. Russell was excited about the role because it enabled him to portray a hapless nerd.

Love in Limbo is next to impossible to find outside Australia, but it is a very entertaining film. For a variety of reasons, it is one of Russell Crowe's favorite early efforts.

THE SILVER BRUMBY (a.k.a. THE SILVER STALLION) (1993)

Director: John Tatoulis
Writer: Elyne Mitchell (novel), Jon Stephens (screenplay)
Producers: Colin J. South, John Tatoulis

Cast

Caroline Goodall (Elyne Mitchell)
Russell Crowe (The Man)
Amiel Daemion (Indi Mitchell)
Johnny Raaen (Jock)
Buddy Tyson (Darcy)
Graeme Fullgrabe (Auctioneer)
Gary Amos (Rider)

Summary

Based on the novel by Elyne Mitchell, this children's story is about the adventures of a wild stallion that must cope not only with the natural dangers of living in the bush but with human fascination about its life.

The stallion, called a "brumby" in Aussie lingo, appears on Mitchell's ranch as she writes the story of its life for her young daughter, Indi. When Indi learns that her mother's story is true, she becomes upset because a wrangler (Russell Crowe) who lives nearby is determined to capture the wild horse to use for breeding stock.

This is not so much a story of good versus evil as it is a story of man versus nature. Faced with domination by man, the wild stallion makes a choice that transforms it into myth. This is an excellent story suitable for viewing by young children.

THE SUM OF US (1994)

Directors: Geoff Burton, Kevin Dowling
Writer: David Stevens
Producers: Kevin Dowling, Errol Sullivan, Hal McElroy, Hal Kessler

Cast

Jack Thompson (Harry Mitchell)
Russell Crowe (Jeff Mitchell)
John Polson (Greg)
Deborah Kennedy (Joyce Johnson)
Joss Moroney (Young Jeff)
Mitch Matthews (Gran)
Julie Herbert (Mary)
Des James (Football Coach)

Summary:

Harry Mitchell is a working class widower who, in addition to coping with the normal stresses of life, has had to adjust to living in the household with his homosexual son, Jeff. They get along well enough as they each pursue life partners, but when problems arise between them, it is not because Harry is disapproving of his son's gay lifestyle but because he tries too hard to support his son's decisions.

If you are not offended by the subject matter, you will probably find this film both funny and touching, especially in the fresh way it looks at dysfunctional family relationships. Jack Thompson and Russell Crowe (who has a make-out scene with another man) both deliver strong performances.

FOR THE MOMENT (1994)

Director: Aaron Kim Johnston
Writer: Aaron Kim Johnston
Producers: Aaron Kim Johnston, Joseph MacDonald, Ches Yetman

Cast

Russell Crowe (Lachlan)
Christianne Hirt (Lill)
Wanda Cannon (Betsy)
Scott Kraft (Zeek)
Peter Outerbridge (Johnny)
Sara McMillan (Kate)
Bruce Boa (Mr. Anderson)
Katelynd Johnston (Marion)
Tyler Woods (Charlie)

Summary:

Lachlan is an Australian soldier who travels to Canada via the Panama Canal during World War II to receive training as a fighter pilot. There he discovers an interesting assortment of would-be pilots, some of them from America. However, as fascinating as some of the student pilots are, they are nothing compared to the locals who live in a nearby rural Manitoba community.

There is Betsy, who sells whisky to the soldiers—and services them sexually if they require it—while her farmer husband is away fighting in the war. There is Kate, a farm girl who has fallen in love with a flyer. And there is Lill, Kate's older sister, who spends her time working the farm while her husband is overseas fighting for his country.

Lachlan falls in love with Lill, who resists at first but then slowly succumbs to his charms. How they deal with that adulterous romance is at the core of a story that runs parallel to the adventures of the pilots on the air base.

THE QUICK AND THE DEAD (1995)

Director: Sam Raimi
Writer: Simon Moore
Producers: Chuck Binder, Joshua Donen, Toby Jaffe, Patrick Markey,
    Allen Shapiro, Sharon Stone, Robert G. Tapert

Cast

Sharon Stone (Ellen, "The Lady")
Gene Hackman (John Herod)
Russell Crowe (Cort)
Leonardo DiCaprio (Fee "The Kid" Herod)

Tobin Bell (Dog Kelly)
Roberts Blossom (Doc Wallace)
Kevin Conway (Eugene Dred)
Keith David (Sgt. Clay Cantrell)
Lance Henriksen (Ace Hanlon)

Summary:

When Ellen rides into a western town run by a ruthless outlaw named John Herod, there is little indication that she has come on a mission of vengeance. The town is filled with gunslingers who have come to enroll in an elimination tournament hosted by Herod. The winner takes home a nice purse if he or she gets past Herod in the final shootout.

Cort is a former outlaw who once rode with Herod. When he quit the gang to become a preacher, he made a bitter enemy of Herod. Cort did not come voluntarily to the competition; he was delivered bound in chains, protesting that his gunslinging days were over. Herod would have none of that and made certain that the preacher took his place with the others in the tournament.

Of all the gunslingers in town, only Ellen has an ulterior motive. She wants to face down Herod because of what he did to her father when she was a child. This film was designed to be a parody on gunfighter Westerns, but apparently no one told Russell Crowe or Sharon Stone, for they played their roles with squint-eyed seriousness, providing weak performances that helped make the film a box-office disaster.

NO WAY BACK (1995)

Director: Frank A. Cappello
Writer: Frank A. Cappello
Producers: Joel Soisson, Aki Komine

Cast

Russell Crowe (FBI agent Zack Grant)
Helen Slater (Mary, the airline stewardess)
Etsushi Toyokawa (Yuji Kobayashi)
Michael Lerner (Frank Serlano)
Kyusaku Shimada (Tetsuro)
Kristopher Logan (Mr. Contingency)
Kelly Hu (Seiko Kobayashi)
Andrew J. Ferchland (Eric Grant)

Summary:

When FBI agent Zack Grant is assigned a case involving a Japanese businessman who was beaten to death by American skinheads, he decides to use an attractive Asian rookie agent, Seiko, to infiltrate the organization for the purpose of planting an electronic listening device in the leader's living quarters.

The case goes sour when Seiko assassinates the skinhead leader, who just happens to be the son of a mafia boss, and then commits suicide by jumping from a window. Grant traces the dead agent back to a Japanese gangster named Yuji and is surprised to learn that he is Seiko's brother (the murdered Japanese businessman was their father).

Grant arrests Yuji, but before he can bring him in, the FBI agent's young son is kidnapped by the mafia boss, who threatens to kill the boy unless Grant hands Yuji over to him. The film was released theatrically in Japan but never made it into American theaters. Instead, it was aired on HBO and subsequently released in video format.

VIRTUOSITY (1995)

Director: Brett Leonard
Writer: Eric Bernt
Producers: Gimel Everett, Gary Lucchesi, Robert McMinn, Howard W. Koch Jr.

Cast

Denzel Washington (Lieutenant Parker Barnes)
Kelly Lynch (Dr. Madison Carter)
Russell Crowe (SID 6.7)
Stephen Spinella (Dr. Darrel Lindenmeyer)
William Forsythe (William Cochran)
Louise Fletcher (Commissioner Elizabeth Deane)
William Fichtner (Wallace)
Costas Mandylor (John Donovan)

Summary:

Lt. Parker Barnes is a former police officer who was convicted of murdering the man who killed his wife and daughter. Because of his skills as a policeman, he is used by prison officials in a series of training films that pit him against a computer-generated villain named SID 6.7.

When SID escapes from the computer and terrorizes the public, Barnes is released from prison to hunt him down. If he's successful, prison officials promise, he will be given a full pardon. One condition of his release, however, is that he must partner with a criminal psychologist named Dr. Madison Carter.

There aren't many surprises in this fast-paced techno-thriller, but there is plenty of brutal action and a delightfully maniacal performance by Russell Crowe, who sometimes seems just a little bit too comfortable in the role.

ROUGH MAGIC (1995)

Director: Clare Peploe
Writers: James Hadley Chase (novel), Robert Mundi, William
Brookfield, Clare Peploe (screenplay)
Producers: Yves Attal, Declan Baldwin, Michele E. Carnes, Andrew S. Karsch,
Mary Ann Marino, Alain Mayor, Laurie Parker, Jonathan T. Taplin

Cast

Bridget Fonda (Myra)
Russell Crowe (Alec Ross)
Jim Broadbent (Doc Ansell)
D. W. Moffett (Cliff Wyatt)
Kenneth Mars (Magician)
Paul Rodriguez (Diego)
Andy Romano (Clayton)
Richard Schiff (Wiggins)

Summary:

This is an odd little movie about a magician's assistant named Myra who flees to Mexico when she witnesses the murder of her boss by her boyfriend, a wealthy sleazebag named Cliff who has serious political ambitions.

Cliff calls in a marker and arranges for a newspaper stringer named Alec Ross to locate her and file reports on her whereabouts until Cliff can get to Mexico to take care of business. Unfortunately for Alec he falls in love with Myra, who takes him on a wild journey in search of a magical elixir.

Before you can say wacky plot, Alec and Myra find themselves at odds with the universe, a situation that is perfect for Cliff's unexpected arrival. Someone gets the girl, but exactly who becomes a nonissue once Myra lays an egg.

L.A. CONFIDENTIAL (1997)

Director: Curtis Hanson
Writers: James Ellroy (novel), Brian Helgeland,
Curtis Hanson (screenplay)
Producers: Curtis Hanson, Brian Helgeland, Arnon Milchan,
Michael G. Nathanson, David L. Wolper

Cast

Kevin Spacey (Sergeant Jack Vincennes)
Russell Crowe (Office Wendell "Bud" White)

Guy Pearce (Detective Lt. Edmund Jennings Exley)
James Cromwell (Captain Dudley Liam Smith)
Kim Basinger (Lynn Bracken)
Danny DeVito (Sid Hudgens)
David Strathairn (Pierce Morehouse Patchett)
Ron Rifkin (D.A. Ellis Loew)

Summary:

The Los Angeles police department provides a backdrop for this story of 1950s-era crime and corruption. Three cops, none of whom particularly like each other, find themselves working together on a quest for truth.

Bud White is a brutal cop who has a difficult time controlling the rage that festers inside him; he's on a mission to protect women, but he's willing to break the rules whenever it serves his needs. Ed Exley is the son of a decorated cop, an ambitious whiz kid who will do anything to get ahead. Jack Vincennes likes to dress well and hang out with celebrities, and the only way he can do that is by bending the rules.

White, Exley, and Vincennes are drawn together when they get caught up in the middle of a high-level government conspiracy to replace mobsters with crooked cops on the organized-crime beat. It's a powerful story, backed up with solid acting. Russell Crowe got so deeply into Bud White's character that it took him months to leech the fist-slamming cop out of his system (some say he never did).

HEAVEN'S BURNING (1997)

Director: Craig Lahiff
Writer: Louis Nowra
Producers: Al Clark, Craig Lahiff, Helen Leake, Georgina Pope

Cast

Russell Crowe (Colin)
Youki Kudoh (Midori)
Kenji Isomura (Yukio)
Ray Barrett (Cam)
Robert Mammone (Mahood)
Petru Gheorghiu (Boorjan)
Anthony Phelan (Bishop)
Matthew Dyktynski (Moffat)

Summary:

While on her honeymoon in Australia, Japanese bride Midori decides that her arranged marriage is not one she can live with. To escape, she fakes her own kidnapping and calls the man she loves, a Tokyo businessman, in hopes that he will run away with her and start a new life. It is a plan they had put together before she left Tokyo, but faced with the reality of it, the businessman decides to stay in Tokyo.

With the police looking for her, Midori goes into a bank to cash a check. Before she can do that, she gets involved in a bank robbery and is taken hostage by a gang of Afghan robbers. Driving the getaway car is Colin, a garage owner who agreed to be the driver as a means of making extra money.

Colin ends up shooting two of the robbers to protect Midori. The two of them then go out on the road, Bonnie-and-Clyde–style, while pursued by the police, angry Afghan family members, and Midori's crazed husband, who feels that she has dishonored him.

BREAKING UP (1997)

Director: Robert Greenwood
Writer: Michael Cristofer
Producers: Cas Donovan, Brad Gordon, Robert Greenwald, David Matalon, Arnon Milchan, George Moffly, Craig Thurman Suttle

Cast
Russell Crowe (Steve)
Salma Hayek (Monica)
Abraham Alvarez (the minister)

Summary:
This film begins with Steve and Monica talking about their relationship—and it pretty much continues that way nonstop for the duration. As a couple they have arrived at the point where they can't live with each other and can't live without each other. So, after a two-year relationship, they decide to break up.

Although Salma Hayek makes Monica interesting to watch (and delivers an outstanding performance) and Russell Crowe provides his character some interesting moments, the film never quite gets off the ground. It opened in only a handful of theaters, earning a depressing $4,500 before it was released on video.

MYSTERY, ALASKA (1999)

Director: Jay Roach
Writers: David E. Kelley, Sean O'Byrne
Producers: Karen Baldwin, Richard Cohen, David E. Kelley, Howard Baldwin, Jack L. Gilardi Jr.

Cast
Russell Crowe (Sheriff John Biebe)
Hank Azaria (Charles Danner)

Mary McCormack (Donna Biebe)
Burt Reynolds (Judge Walter Burns)
Colm Meaney (Mayor Scott R. Pitcher)
Lolita Davidovich (Mary Jane Pitcher)
Maury Chaykin (Bailey Pruitt)
Ron Eldard (Matt "Skank" Marden)
Ryan Northcott (Stevie Weeks)

Summary:

Mystery, Alaska is a small town (population: 633) that doesn't have much going for it except an amateur hockey team that is considered the best in its class. When Charles Danner, a former resident who left to become a big-city sportswriter, does a feature on the town's hockey team in *Sports Illustrated*, it leads to an offer for them to play an exhibition game with the championship New York Rangers.

At first it seems like a gigantic honor, but when more details emerge, it seems more like a curse that could give the town its most embarrassing moment. Caught in the middle of everything is Sheriff John Biebe, one of the team's star players, who is booted off just before the challenge arrives from the Rangers.

This film has plenty of excellent hockey action, but its main attraction is the off-beat characters who struggle to find meaning in their ice-bound lives.

THE INSIDER (1999)

Director: Michael Mann
Writers: Marie Brenner (magazine article), Eric Roth,
   Michael Mann (screenplay)
Producers: Michael Mann, Pieter Ian Brugge

Cast

Al Pacino (Lowell Bergman)
Russell Crowe (Jeffrey Wigand)
Christopher Plummer (Mike Wallace)
Diane Venora (Liane Wigand)
Philip Baker Hall (Don Hewitt)
Lindsay Crouse (Sharon Tiller)
Debi Mazar (Debbie De Luca)
Gina Gershon (Helen Caperelli)
Michael Moore (himself)
Colm Feore (Richard Scruggs)

Summary:

Based on a true story about how television's *60 Minutes* backed down from broadcasting an interview with tobacco company whistleblower Jeffrey Wigand because executives feared a multimillion-dollar lawsuit from tobacco companies, this film starts out at a full run and never lets up.

Wigand is not a particularly sympathetic character, but when his former employer starts playing rough with him—and with CBS News over the broadcast of his interview—it is difficult not to root for the man and for the public-relations destruction of the tobacco companies. It's the same situation with Lowell Bergman, the aggressive producer who set up the Wigand interview; he's not especially likable, but his cause is so strong that he sucks you into his world before you know what has happened.

This is one of the best films of the past decade, and Russell Crowe's performance is often spellbinding.

GLADIATOR (2000)
Director: Ridley Scott
Writers: David H. Franzoni, John Logan
Producers: Douglas Wick, David Franzoni, Branko Lustig

Cast
Russell Crowe (General Maximus Decimus Meridius)
Joaquin Phoenix (Emperor Commodus)
Connie Nielsen (Lucilla)
Oliver Reed (Antonius Proximo)
Richard Harris (Emperor Marcus Aurelius)
Derek Jacobi (Senator Gracchus)
Djimon Hounsou (Juba)
David Schofield (Falco)

Summary:
After a great victory over the barbaric tribes of Germania by Roman General Maximus Decimus Meridius, one that allows Emperor Marcus Aurelius to return to Rome in triumph, the general tells the emperor that he wants to go to Spain to be with his family. Instead of granting him leave, the emperor tells him that he wants to name him successor to his throne.

Before that can happen, the emperor's son, Commodus, murders his father and succeeds him as emperor. Because he perceives Maximus to be a threat, he orders him murdered, along with his wife and son. Maximus escapes his captors and flees to Spain, where he discovers that he is too late to protect his family.

Maximus is captured by slave traders and sold to Antonius Proximo, who trains him to become a gladiator. Not until they travel to Rome to fight in the Colosseum does Maximus reveal his true identity—and he does so face-to-face with Emperor Commodus on the field of battle in full view of the cheering crowd. To avenge the death of his wife and son—and to honor the loving relationship that he had with Marcus Aurelius—Maximus has no choice but to fight Commodus to the death.

PROOF OF LIFE (2000)

Director: Taylor Hackford
Writers: William Prochnau (magazine article), Tony Gilroy (screenplay)
Producers: Tony Gilron, Taylor Hackford, Charles Mulvehill, Steven Reuther

Cast

Meg Ryan (Alice Bowman)
Russell Crowe (Terry Thorne)
David Morse (Peter Bowman)
Pamela Reed (Janis Goodman)
David Caruso (Dino)
Anthony Heald (Ted Fellner)
Stanley Anderson (Jerry)
Gottfried John (Eric Kessler)

Summary:

Peter and Alice Bowman are in South America so that Peter, an oil company engineer, can build a much-needed dam for his employer. When rebels kidnap Peter and hold him for ransom, the oil company discovers that Peter is not covered by insurance, and it tells Alice that she is on her own as far as getting her husband back is concerned.

Alice turns to Terry Thorne for help. He is a professional hostage negotiator who has had experience dealing with hard-core rebels. Because he is falling in love with Alice, he offers to help her without charge.

To get her husband back, all she has to do is raise nearly a million dollars from her family and friends so that Terry can pay the rebels off when the time comes. When negotiations break down, Terry decides to go into the jungle with his own mini-army to rescue Peter from his kidnappers.

A BEAUTIFUL MIND (2001)

Director: Ron Howard
Writers: Sylvia Nasar (book), Akiva Goldsman (screenplay)
Producers: Brian Grazer, Ron Howard, Todd Hallowell, Karen Kehela, Kathleen McGill, Maureen Peyrot, Aldric La'Auli Porter, Louisa Velis

Cast

Russell Crowe (Dr. John Nash)
Jennifer Connelly (Alicia Nash)
Ed Harris (William Parcher)
Christopher Plummer (Dr. Rosen)
Paul Bettany (Charles Herman)
Judd Hirsch (Helinger)
Adam Goldberg (Richard Sol)
Josh Lucas (Martin Hansen)

Summary:

When John Nash enrolls in graduate school at Princeton University, it is obvious to everyone around him that he is both brilliant and socially inept. Nonetheless, he manages to marry a beautiful physics student.

As time passes, Nash develops complicated mathematical formulas that are ultimately used to revolutionize long-held economic theories. Unfortunately, his impressive intellectual achievements are threatened by the onset of paranoid schizophrenia.

As Nash descends into the depths of madness, his wife works tirelessly to obtain help for him. She stands by him when no one else will. After years of personal torment, he overcomes his illness and returns to work as a researcher and teacher. It is at that point that he is informed that he has been chosen to receive the Nobel Prize in economics.

MASTER AND COMMANDER (2003)

Director: Peter Weir
Writers: Patrick O'Brian (novel), Peter Weir, John Collee, Larry Ferguson
Producers: Peter Weir, Alan B. Curtiss, Samuel Goldwyn Jr.,
Duncan Henderson, John Bard Manulis

Cast

Russell Crowe (Capt. Jack Aubrey)
Paul Bettany (Dr. Stephen Maturin)
Billy Boyd (Barrett Bonden)

Summary:

Amid the backdrop of the Napoleonic Wars, Captain Jack Aubrey sets sail to the far side of the world on a Royal Navy frigate (the HMS *Surprise*) that is manned by a motley crew of hardened adventurers and inexperienced sailors barely out of their teens.

Ship surgeon Stephen Maturin, who prides himself on his cello-playing ability, strikes up a close friendship with Aubrey, who fancies himself a decent violinist. When the two men are not tending to their duties aboard the ship, or firing on enemy ships, they retreat to the captain's quarters, where they perform their favorite musical pieces.

After the frigate is surprised at sea by a French warship, the *Acheron*, it escapes and makes it way around Cape Horn to the Galapagos Islands, where the *Acheron* makes the first of several mysterious appearances that spook Aubrey's superstitious crew.

TEXAS (2003)

Producers: Russell Crowe, Brett Leonard
Cinematographers: Brendan Fletcher, Duane Manwiller

Cast

Russell Crowe and Thirty Odd Foot of Grunts

Summary:

This is a seventy-eight-minute documentary about Russell Crowe and Thirty Odd Foot of Grunts. It begins in 2000, when TOFOG decide to record an album in Austin, Texas. The camera follows them from Sydney to London, where they rehearse for eight days, then on to Austin, where in addition to recording an album, they give three sell-out performances at Stubb's Bar-B-Q.

DISCOGRAPHY

ALBUMS

2001
Bastard Life or Clarity
Thirty Odd Foot of Grunts

Artemis Records
Producers: Kerry Tolhurst and TOFOG
Songs:
"Things Have Got to Change"
"Memorial Day"
"Hold You"
"Sail Those Same Oceans"
"The Legend of Barry Kable"
"Somebody's Else's Princess"
"Wendy"
"The Night That Davey Hit the Train"
"Swept Away Bayou (Facing the Headlights Alone)"
"Judas Cart"

1998
Gaslight
Thirty Odd Foot of Grunts

[Australian release, label unknown]
Producer: TOFOG
Songs:
"Circus"
"Chocolate"
"Oblique Is My Love"
"What's Her Name?"
"The Legend of Barry Kable"
"She's Not Impressed"
"David"
"What You Want Me to Forget"

"Nowhere"
"Eternity"
"Wendy"

1997

What's Her Name?
Thirty Odd Foot of Grunts

[Australian release—label unknown]
Producer: Thirty Odd Foot of Grunts
Songs:
"What's Her Name?"
"Oblique Is My Love"
"All the White Circles"
"Big Jet Planes"

1985

What's the Difference?
Roman Antix

Ode Records

SINGLES

"The Photograph Kills"/"High Horse Honey"
  Thirty Odd Foot of Grunts
  Producer: Charles Fischer

"Inside Her Eyes"/"The Legend of Barry Kable"
  Thirty Odd Foot of Grunts
  Producer: Thirty Odd Foot of Grunts

"Never Let Ya Slide"
  Russ le Roq
  Producer: Russell Crowe

"Shattered Glass (You Broke My Heart)"
  Russ le Roq
  Producer: Russell Crowe

"Pier 13"/"So You Made It Now"
  Russ le Roq
  Producer: Russell Crowe

"St. Kilda"/"Fire"
  Russ le Roq
  Producer: Russell Crowe

"I Just Wanna Be Like Marlon Brando"/"It Hurts"
  Russ le Roq
  Producer: Russell Crowe

BIBLIOGRAPHY

Books

Bronson, Fred. *Billboard Book of Number One Hits.* New York: Billboard Publications, 1985.

Cader, Michael. *People Weekly Almanac.* New York: Cader Books, 1999.

Goldsman, Akiva. *A Beautiful Mind: The Shooting Script.* New York: Newmarket Press, 2002.

McQueen, A. E. "New Zealand: Physical and Social Geography." *The Far East and Australasia.* London: Europa Publications, 1974.

Pike, Jeffrey (editor). *Insight Guides: Australia.* London: Apa Publications, 2002.

Magazines and Newspapers

Adie, Kilmeny. "Crowe's Grunts." *Illawarra Mercury,* December 1998.

Anderson, John. "Rough Magic." *Los Angeles Times,* May 30, 1997.

Ansen, David. "The Battle for Summer." *Newsweek,* May 2000

Ausiello, Michael. "Jodie Foster's Plum Role." *TV Guide,* March 29, 2002.

Bates, James. "It Just Couldn't Get Arrested." *Los Angeles Times,* February 11, 1998.

Barrera, Sandra. "'Odd' Man Out: Russell Crowe Rocks the House of Blues." *Los Angeles News,* August 28, 2001.

Barrett, Mary. "A Lothario? I Don't Have Time…" *Mail,* February, 10, 2002.

Bartolomeo. "Nicole and Russell's Secret Romance?" *Us Weekly,* November 11, 2002.

Basinger, Kim. "Russell Muscles In." *Interview,* September 1997.

Baum, Caroline. "Something to Crowe About." *Vogue Men*, April 1993.

Carr, Jay. "'Proof': A Sly, Wicked Comedy." *Boston Globe*, June 12, 1992.

————— "Good Performances Rescue 'The Sum of Us.'" *Boston Globe*, September 11, 1994.

————— "Virtual Reality Without 'Virtuosity.'" *Boston Globe*, August 4, 1995.

————— "Stone Stands Tall in the Saddle." *Boston Globe*, February 10, 1995.

Chancellor, Jonathan. "Crowe Pays $9.5M to Join the Elite Cast of Bay Watch." *Sydney Morning Herald* (date not available).

Chenery, Susan. "Sincerely Yours." *HQ*, summer 1991.

Collins, Terry. "The Real Crowe." *Central Coast Express*, December 1998.

Corcoran, Michael. "Crowe Kicks Out Jams at Texas BBQ Joint." *USA Today*, August 7, 2000.

Corliss, Richard. "Better Than Tabloid Tattle." *Time*, December 11, 2000.

————— "The Empire Strikes Back." *Time*, May 8, 2000.

Craig, Alex. "Who Are You Looking At?" *HQ*, June 2000.

Davis, Ivor. "I'm a Loser in Love." *Sunday Magazine*, February 2002.

Derryberry, Jil. "Cameo: Russell Crowe." *Interview*, August 1995.

Diamond, Jamie. "Straight Out of Australia, to L.A." *New York Times*, March 26, 1995.

Dicker, Ron. "Kinder, Gentler Crowe Promotes Latest Film." *Hartford Courant*, January 4, 2002.

Dinning, Mark. "The Man with Two Brains." *Empire*, April 2002.

Duren, Jackie. "Russell Crowe: The Bad Boy." *Us Weekly*, December 27, 2001.

——————— "After Seven Years Apart, Russell Crowe Reunites with a Former Love." *Us Weekly,* March 25, 2002.

Dwyer, Michael. "Six Odd Foot of Grunt." *The Sunday Age,* February 18, 2001.

——————— "The Grunt Factor." *Rolling Stone Australia,* June 2001.

Ebert, Roger. "The Efficiency Expert." *Chicago Sun-Times,* November 6, 1992.

——————— "Proof." *Chicago Sun-Times,* May 15, 1992.

——————— "The Efficiency Expert." *Chicago Sun-Times,* November 6, 1992.

——————— "Virtuosity." *Chicago Sun-Times,* August 4, 1995.

——————— "Rough Magic." *Chicago Sun-Times,* (date not available).

——————— "The Quick and the Dead." *Chicago Sun-Times,* February 10, 1995.

——————— "L.A. Confidential." *Chicago Sun-Times,* (date not available.)

——————— "The Insider." *Chicago Sun-Times,* (date not available).

——————— "Gladiator." *Chicago Sun-Times,* May 5, 2000.

——————— "Proof of Life." *Chicago Sun-Times,* December 8, 2000.

Edelstein, Jeff. "Aussie Salute." *The Trentonian,* March 28, 2001.

Feinstein, Howard. "As Crowe Flies." *Detour,* October 1997.

Froelich, Paula and Chris Wilson. "Crowe in a Chicken Tantrum." *New York Post,* November 20, 2002.

Gardner, Jane. "Russell Crowe Interview." *Heat* magazine, January 13-19, 2000.

Gee, Mike. "The House of Spencer." *Sydney Morning Herald,* May 19, 2001.

Germain, David. "Films 'Gladiator,' 'Traffic' Top Golden Globe Nominations." *San Jose Mercury,* December 22, 2000.

Gilbert, Matthew. "Confidently Speaking Kim Basinger has Been Through a Rough Period of Celebrity." *Boston Globe,* September 14, 1997.

Goodman, Chris. "Odd Grunts from Rocker Russell." *Sunday Express*, March 10, 2002.

Greenwald, Robert. "Breaking Up." *Austin Chronicle*, October 20, 1997.

Grove, Martin A. "Howard & Grazer's 'Mind' Looks Like Film to Beat for Best Picture." *Hollywood Reporter*, December 12, 2001.

Guthmann, Edward. "Russell Crowe Thoroughly Convincing as a Genius with Schizophrenia." *San Francisco Chronicle*, December 21, 2001.

Harrington, Richard. "Romper Stomper." *Washington Post*, September 24, 1993.

Hartl, John. "'Silver Stallion' Heads from Festival to Videotape." *Seattle Times*, June 9, 1994.

——————————— "Crowe's Career in Movies is on the Wing." *Seattle Times*, June 27, 1993.

——————————— Fantasy and Reality Collide in Complex 'L.A. Confidential.'" *Seattle Times*, September 21, 1997.

Harvey, Dennis. "Russell Crowe." *Variety*, January 28/February 3, 2002.

Hayne, Julie. "The Truth about Russell and Me." *New Idea*, May 18, 2002.

Hensley, Dennis. "Anthony Rapp Talks About Co-Starring with Russell Crowe." *The Advocate*, January 22, 2002.

Hessery, Ruth. "Boys on Film." *Elle*, January 1992.

——————————— "The Crowe Flies." *Sydney Morning Herald*, December 1, 1995.

Heyman, J. D. "Could It Be Love?" *Us Weekly*, March 25, 2002.

Hiscock, John. "Russell Crowe on Kidman, Madness and Math." *Daily Mirror*, January 5, 2002.

Hinson, Hal. "Prisoners of the Sun." August 17, 1991.

Horowitz, Mark. "Ron Howard." *New York*, December 2001.

Howe, Desson. "The Quick and the Dead." *Washington Post*, February 10, 1995.

Hunter, Stephen. "Fragile Genius of 'A Beautiful Mind.'" *Washington Post,* December 21, 2001.

Jameson, Julietta. "The Songbird Who Tamed a Gladiator." *Daily Telegraph,* March 2, 2002.

Keller, Janet K. "30 Odd Foot of Grunts, Bastard Life or Clarity." *St. Petersburg Times,* date unknown.

Kempley, Rita. "Proof." *Washington Post,* June 6, 1992.

———————— "The Efficiency Expert." *Washington Post,* November 6, 1992.

———————— "The Sum of Us." *Washington Post,* March 31, 1995.

Kirkland, Bruce. "'Heaven's Burning' Fine B-Movie Romp." *Toronto Sun,* January 23, 1998.

Koch, Philip. "Russell Crowe." *Sunday Telegraph,* March 3, 2002.

Koha, Nui Te. "Crowe at the Crossroads." *Weekend Magazine,* February 17, 2001.

LaSalle, Mick. "'Quick' Is Slow on the Draw." *San Francisco Chronicle,* February 10, 1995.

———————— "Clearing the Air." *San Francisco Chronicle,* November 5, 1999.

———————— "Sex! Crime! Cops!" *San Francisco Chronicle,* September 19, 1997.

Lateo, Karen. "Hollywood May Think He's a Bad Lad, but Russell Crowe is the Best Big Brother a Girl Could Have." *Australian Woman's Day,* April 1, 2002.

Lawson, Terry. "Star of 'The Insider' Grew into His Role." *Detroit Free Press,* November 4, 1999.

———————— "Penalty Box Is the Place for 'Mystery, Alaska.'" *Detroit Free Press,* October 1, 1999.

Lesmond, Pamela. "Interview with Danielle Spencer." *Hello,* March 27, 2001.

Lim, Dennis. "The Rules of the Game." *Village Voice,* December 19–25, 2001.

Lovece, Frank. "Russell Crowe Has Enough Ego to Be a Bad Guy You'll Remember." *Newsday,* August 6, 1995.

Lovell, Glenn. "'The Insider' Director Mann Tosses Back Brickbats to '60 Minutes.'" *San Jose Mercury News,* November 5, 1999.

Lowe, Andy. "The Rise and Rise of Russell Crowe." *Total Film,* January 2001.

Lyman, Rick. "'A Beautiful Mind' Wins Four Golden Globes." *New York Times,* January 21, 2002.

——————— "'Beautiful Mind' Wins; Best Actress Goes to Halle Berry." *New York Times,* March 25, 2002.

——————— "On the Seas Again, Guided by a Star." *New York Times,* October 13, 2002.

McGurk, Margaret A. "No 'Mystery': Kelley's Film Fit for TV." *Cincinnati Enquirer,* October 1, 1999.

Maddox, Gary. "Even by Russell's Standards It's Been a Big Week." *Sydney Morning Herald,* March 2, 2002.

Mahler, Jonathan. "The Making of a Gladiator." *Talk,* 2000.

Margulies, Julianna. "Jennifer Connelly." *Interview,* February 2002.

Martin, Michele. "The Two-Timing Gladiator." *Mail,* July 2, 2000.

Matthews, Philip. "Russell Crowe Has a Superstitious Relationship to His Own Fame." *New Zealand Listener Magazine,* March 24–30, 2001.

Millea, Holly. "Love is a Battlefield." *Entertainment Weekly,* March 29, 2002.

Mollard, Angela. "The Ambition That Drove *Gladiator* Star Russell Crowe to Hollywood Success." *Daily Mirror,* June 17, 2000.

——————— "Crowe Takes Flight." *New Idea,* September 8, 2001.

——————— "Is This the Woman Who Can Tame Russell Crowe?" *Daily Mail,* March 27, 2002.

Moon, Tom. "Rocker Crowe: The Act Is There, the Songs Aren't." *Philadelphia Inquirer,* August 30, 2001.

Moore, Roger. "Crow-Foster Film Project on Shelf for Now." *Orlando Sentinel,* September 8, 2000.

Morris, Wesley. "'Proof' Mostly Motion." December 8, 2000.

——————— "Circus Maximus." *San Francisco Examiner,* May 5, 2000.

Mottram, James. "Russell Crowe—Lighting Up Hollywood?" March 3–9, 2000.

Nashawaty, Chris. "The Big Night." *Entertainment Weekly,* April 5, 2002.

——————— "Clash of the Titans." *Entertainment Weekly,* March 22, 2002.

Newman, Bruce. "A Manipulative 'Mind': Crowe, Howard Make Madness Too Calculating." *San Jose Mercury News,* December 21, 2001.

Paget, Dale. "FBI Probes Plot to Kidnap Russell Crowe." *The Age,* March 2001.

Palmer, Martyn. "24 Hours with Russell Crowe." *Glamour, UK,* March 2002.

Paviour, Andiee. "Crowe's Feat." *Who,* October 10, 1994.

Pinsker, Beth. "'L.A. Confidential' Actor: From Drag Queen to Cop." *Seattle Times,* September 23, 1997.

Pond, Steve. "Oscar Finds a New Home." *Premiere,* January 2002.

Powers, Ann. "Now Who's That Frontman?" *New York Times,* August 31, 2001.

Rea, Steven. "That's No Lady, That's a Gunslinger." *Philadelphia Inquirer,* February 10, 1995.

Rebello, Stephen. "Taylor Hackford." *Movieline,* November 2000.

Reich, Sperling. "The Inside Mann." *Reel.com* (www.reel.com/reel.asp?node=oscars2000/interviews/mann.)

Richter, Erin. "Her Funny Valentine." *Entertainment Weekly,* February 16, 2001.

Ringel, Eleanor. "'Breaking Up' Grade: B." *Atlanta Journal-Constitution,* October 17, 1997.

Rodriguez, Rene. "Plotless Romper Stomper a Study of Real-Life Monsters." *Miami Herald,* December 3, 1993.

——————— "'Gladiator' Set Offers More Gore." *Miami Herald,* November 24, 2000.

Rosen, Steven. "Proof of Life a Real Grabber." *Denver Post,* December 8, 2000.

———————— "Unique Man Captured by Howard, Crowe." *Denver Post,* December 25, 2001.

Rosenberg, Scott. "Tired 'Virtuosity' Rehashes Action Cliches." *San Francisco Examiner,* August 4, 1995.

Ryan, Desmond. "Love is Blind in the Black Comedy 'Proof.'" *Philadelphia Inquirer,* May 27, 1992.

———————— "In Sum, He Was Just Right." *Philadelphia Inquirer,* April 10, 1995.

———————— "Russell Crowe Is a Titan in Stunning Roman Epic." *Philadelphia Inquirer,* May 5, 2000.

Sampson, Desmond. "Russell Crowe." *Pavement,* April/May 2002.

Sams, Christine, Eddie Fitzmaurice, and Jim O'Rourke. "Crowe's Racist Insult Lead to Punch-Up." *Sydney Morning Herald,* September 17, 2002.

Savlov, Marc. "Gruntwork." *Austin Chronicle,* August 2000.

Schickel, Richard. "Three L.A. Cops, One Philip Marlowe." *Time,* September 15, 1997.

Schruers, Fred. "Stone Free." *Premiere,* May 1993.

Sessums, Kevin. "Stone Goddess." *Vanity Fair,* April 1993.

Shannon, Jeff. "Brutally Stark 'Romper Stomper' Captures Adrenaline Rush of Hatred." *Seattle Times,* July 2, 1993.

Shnayerson, Michael. "The Intriguing Miss Connelly." *Vanity Fair,* September 2002.

Shulgasser, Barbara. "'Magic' Is Rough on the Audience." *San Francisco Examiner,* May 30, 1997.

Silverman, Stephen M. "Judge Tosses Out Crowe Plotters' Case." *People.com,* June 24, 2002.

——————— "Accused Crowe Plotters' Trial Heats Up." *People.com*, June 20, 2002.

Stevenson, Jane. "Debut Disc Nothing to Crowe About." *Toronto Sun*, February 17, 2002.

Sullivan, Mike. "Hot Headed." *Sun*, November 2002.

Slee, Amruta. "An Australian Actor Tries Life as a Neo-Nazi Punk." *New York Times*, June 6, 1993.

Spillman, Susan. "Semi-Nude Sharon Stone, on the (Cutting Room) Floor." *USA Today*, February 15, 1995.

Spines, Christine. "One from the Heart." *Premiere*, September 2002.

Stack, Peter. "'Mystery, Alaska' Is Puckish Fun." *San Francisco Chronicle*, October 1, 1999.

Strauss, Bob. "The Inside Story on 'Insider.'" *Boston Globe*, November 7, 1999.

Sullivan, Jim. "Crowe-Nappers Afoot?" *Boston Globe*, March 8, 2001.

Sutton, Candace. "Russell's Role in Nightclub Brawl No Oscar Winner." *Sydney Morning Herald*, April 7, 2002.

Svetkey, Benjamin. "Countin' Crowes." *Entertainment Weekly*, January 4, 2002.

Taylor, Jason. "'Rough Magic' Director Peploe Finally Gets Her Wish." *Abra Cadabra*, June 11, 1997.

Taylor, Phil. "The Importance of Being Eric." *Sunday Star*, October 6, 2002.

Thomas, Bret. "Sugar and Spite." *Sydney Morning Herald*, March 10, 2002.

Thomas, Karen. "Catch These Young Rising Stars." *USA Today*, June 24, 1993.

Thomas, Kevin. "The Sum of Us." *Los Angeles Times*, March 8, 1995.

——————— "For the Moment." *Los Angeles Times*, April 19, 1996.

——————— "Virtuosity." *Los Angeles Times*, August 4, 1995.

Turan, Kenneth. "L.A. Confidential." *Los Angeles Times*, April 12, 1999.

———————— "Mystery, Alaska." *Los Angeles Times,* October 1, 1999.

———————— "Proof of Life." *Los Angeles Times,* December 8, 2000.

Turner, Megan. "Return of the Anti-Frontman." *The Courier,* January 1999.

Upchurch, Michael. "First-Time Director Provides 'Proof' of Her Talent." *Seattle Times,* April 17, 1992.

Valby, Karen. "Truth Be Told." *Entertainment Weekly,* 2002 Forecast Double Issue.

Vigoda, Arlene. "Ryan: Marriage Was Over Long Before Press Knew." *USA Today,* October 11, 2000.

Waldegrave, Niki. "Why Movie Hunk Russell Crowe's Glamorous Girlfriend Stayed with My Mum." *Sunday Mirror,* June 2002.

Walters, Barry. "All of Us Should See 'The Sum of Us.'" *San Francisco Examiner,* March 17, 1995.

Wild, David. "Coming On Strong." *Us Weekly,* May 22, 2000.

Wloszczyna, Susan. "A 'Titanic' Night to Remember." *USA Today,* March 24, 1998.

Wyatt, Gene. "Heart of a Warrior." *Nashville Tennessean,* May 5, 2000.

Young, Lisa. "'Class of 2000' Creates a Buzz." Country.com, March 5, 2001.

Zanardo, Lisa. "The Real McCoy." *Go!,* December 1998

(unknown) "Stomping on Controversy." *Preview,* December 1992.

———————— "Crowe's Feat: Australian Actor Russell Crowe Isn't a Bad Guy—All the Time." *W,* July 1995.

———————— "Crowe Leaves Set for Surgery." *San Jose Mercury News,* September 13, 2000.

———————— "Crowe Brawls in London." Associated Press, November 14, 2002.

——————————— "Russell Crowe in London Restaurant, Sun Says." Reuters, November 13, 2002.

——————————— "Softy Russ Quits High Life for Loved Ones." *Sydney Morning Herald,* November 19, 2002.

——————————— "Standing By Her Man." *Daily Telegraph,* November 19, 2002.

——————————— "When Kiwis Come to Blows: What Demons Drive Crowe?" *Daily Telegraph,* November 16, 2002.

——————————— "Director Ron Howard Defends Russell Crowe after Obscene Gesture." Associated Press, March 29, 2001.

——————————— "Love in the Air for Kidman, Crowe." *Sydney Morning Herald,* October 9, 2002.

——————————— "'Beautiful Mind' Critics Draw Ire of Filmmakers and Crowe." *Sydney Morning Herald,* March 19, 2002.

——————————— "Apology: Russell Eats Crow after All." *People.com.*

——————————— "Crowe Apologizes after BAFTA Clash." *Sydney Morning Herald,* March 5, 2002.

——————————— "Crowe Reportedly Upset over Poem." Associated Press, March 5, 2002.

——————————— "Crowe Said to Lose Temper in Britain." Associated Press, February 27, 2002.

——————————— "Crowe's Outburst May Cost Him Oscar." Associated Press, March 1, 2002.

——————————— "Crowe's 30 Odd Feet of Unsold Albums." *Sydney Morning Herald,* March 16, 2002.

——————————— "Two Cleared in Crowe Blackmail Case." Associated Press, June 24, 2002.

——————————— "Turbocharged: Her Roots May Be Australian, but for Country Star Jamie O'Neal All Roads Led to Nashville." *People,* April 23, 2001.

——————————— "Accused Crowe Plotters' Trial Delayed." Associated Press, June 17, 2002.

Radio and Television

Late Night with Conan O'Brien. August 7, 1995

Entertainment Tonight. Interview with Christopher Plummer (date not available).

Tonight Show with Jay Leno. Interview with Russell Crowe (date not available).

Tonight Show with Jay Leno. Interview with Ron Howard (2002, date not available)

Australian Network 10. Interview with Ian "Molly" Meldrum (August 24, 2000).

Larry King Live. Interview with Russell Crowe and Ron Howard (January 18, 2002).

ABC PrimeTime. Diane Sawyer Interview with Russell Crowe (January 17, 2002).

The Ray Martin Show. Interview with Nicole Kidman (November 5, 2001).

INDEX